THE EVERYTHING®

GLUTEN-FREE & DAIRY-FREE BAKING COOKBOOK

ALICE WIGGINS

200 RECIPES FOR DELICIOUS BAKED GOODS WITHOUT GLUTEN OR DAIRY

ADAMS MEDIA

NEW YORK   LONDON   TORONTO   SYDNEY   NEW DELHI

For my incredibly supportive family and friends.

Adams Media
An Imprint of Simon & Schuster, Inc.
100 Technology Center Drive
Stoughton, MA 02072

An Everything® Series Book.
Everything® and everything.com® are registered trademarks of Simon & Schuster, Inc.

First Adams Media trade paperback edition September 2021

ADAMS MEDIA and colophon are trademarks of Simon & Schuster.

For information about special discounts for bulk purchases, please contact Simon & Schuster Special Sales at 1-866-506-1949 or business@simonandschuster.com.

The Simon & Schuster Speakers Bureau can bring authors to your live event. For more information or to book an event contact the Simon & Schuster Speakers Bureau at 1-866-248-3049 or visit our website at www.simonspeakers.com.

Interior design by Colleen Cunningham
Photographs by James Stefiuk

Manufactured in China

10 9 8 7 6 5

Library of Congress Cataloging-in-Publication Data
Names: Wiggins, Alice, author.
Title: The everything® gluten-free & dairy-free baking cookbook / Alice Wiggins.
Other titles: The everything® gluten-free and diary-free baking cookbook
Description: First Adams Media trade paperback edition. | Stoughton, MA: Adams Media, 2021. | Series: Everything® | Includes index.
Identifiers: LCCN 2021018945 | ISBN 9781507216187 (pb) | ISBN 9781507216194 (ebook)
Subjects: LCSH: Gluten-free diet--Recipes. | Milk-free diet--Recipes. | LCGFT: Cookbooks.
Classification: LCC RM237.86 .W54 2021 | DDC 641.5/639311--dc23
LC record available at https://lccn.loc.gov/2021018945

ISBN 978-1-5072-1618-7
ISBN 978-1-5072-1619-4 (ebook)

Dear Reader,

When I first found out I couldn't eat gluten and dairy, I honestly thought that I'd never be able to enjoy my favorite foods again. The long list of ingredients I could no longer eat felt overwhelming, and I struggled to know where to start! But over the years, as I've become more and more used to life without gluten and dairy, I've learned that you can still make and enjoy amazing food that tastes **just as delicious** as the real thing.

I grew up in a family that loved to bake, which is definitely where my passion for baking began, and I'm so excited to share this collection of two hundred easy-to-make, tried and tested recipes, which combine **old family favorites** such as my nan's Cornish Pasties and my mum's classic Christmas Cake with plenty of **new recipes** I've been developing over the years. From comforting winter pies and fresh bread, to celebration cakes, cupcakes, brownies, vegan options, and more, there's plenty to choose from!

I really hope you find this book useful and that it proves that you can still eat delicious food, even without gluten or dairy.

Alice

Welcome to the Everything® Series!

These handy, accessible books give you all you need to tackle a difficult project, gain a new hobby, comprehend a fascinating topic, prepare for an exam, or even brush up on something you learned back in school but have since forgotten.

You can choose to read an Everything® book from cover to cover or just pick out the information you want from our four useful boxes: Questions, Facts, Alerts, and Essentials. We give you everything you need to know on the subject, but throw in a lot of fun stuff along the way too.

question	fact
Answers to common questions.	Important snippets of information.

alert	essential
Urgent warnings.	Quick handy tips.

We now have more than 600 Everything® books in print, spanning such wide-ranging categories as cooking, health, parenting, personal finance, wedding planning, word puzzles, and so much more. When you're done reading them all, you can finally say you know Everything®!

PUBLISHER Karen Cooper

MANAGING EDITOR Lisa Laing

COPY CHIEF Casey Ebert

PRODUCTION EDITOR Jo-Anne Duhamel

ACQUISITIONS EDITOR Rebecca Tarr Thomas

SENIOR DEVELOPMENT EDITOR Sarah Doughty

EVERYTHING® SERIES COVER DESIGNER Erin Alexander

Contents

CHAPTER 7: QUICK BREADS AND LOAF CAKES **129**

CHAPTER 8: CELEBRATION CAKES **147**

Introduction

Fluffy rolls, rich desserts, savory pizzas, soft breads—you might think eating a gluten- and dairy-free diet means saying goodbye to your favorite baked goods, but that simply isn't true! With *The Everything® Gluten-Free & Dairy-Free Baking Cookbook*, you can bake and enjoy delicious foods that not only will keep you feeling well but are sure to have friends and family asking for more.

With the two hundred easy recipes provided in this book, there is absolutely no need to miss out on the bakes you love due to an allergy, intolerance, or other health reasons. From loaf cakes to sweet and savory pies, fresh bread, desserts, party food, celebration cakes, and more, there is something for every occasion, and no one will ever guess that delicious cake is both gluten- and dairy-free! You will be sure to find new favorites you'll want to bake again and again, such as:

- Fluffy Pancakes
- Cinnamon Buns
- Garlic Pizza Bread
- Dinner Rolls
- Chicken Pot Pie
- Lemon Drizzle Cake
- Chocolate Chip Cookies
- No-Bake Chocolate and Salted Caramel Tart
- And so much more!

All the ingredients used in this book can be found in most grocery or health food stores. And with step-by-step instructions and handy tips and suggestions, baking gluten- and dairy-free food has never been easier!

You will also find important information for transitioning to a gluten-free and/or dairy-free diet and making successful recipes. Chapter 1 takes a look at which foods contain gluten and dairy, from the obvious to the more obscure, along with the best gluten- and dairy-free alternatives to keep stocked in your pantry. It also covers questions you may have about gluten- and dairy-free baking, such as which gluten-free flour is best for fluffy cakes, which dairy-free butter works best for buttercream, and which additional gums you should be using in your baking. Not sure whether you have an allergy, intolerance, or celiac disease? This chapter also includes common symptoms of digestive issues, information on being tested, and further tips such as avoiding cross contamination when it comes to storing and preparing your food.

Living a gluten-free and dairy-free lifestyle does not mean you should miss out. In fact, you can actually enhance your culinary skills, whipping up tasty dishes tailored to your and your family's preferences. It's time to get baking!

CHAPTER 1

The Gluten- and Dairy-Free Diet

In this chapter you will find plenty of information to help you adapt to a gluten-free and dairy-free lifestyle, including common reasons for going gluten-free and/or dairy-free; symptoms of allergies, intolerance, or Celiac disease; and information on getting a diagnosis for an intolerance or allergy. This chapter also provides useful tips for eating gluten-free and dairy-free at home, preventing cross contamination, and eating out, as well as a handy section on the best baking alternatives to assist you on your baking journey.

If you are concerned about possible symptoms or have any health-related questions, you should talk with a medical professional, as this book is here to help with living a gluten-free and dairy-free lifestyle, not diagnose it.

The Gluten-Free Diet

Gluten-free diets have become popular due to the rising awareness around celiac disease and gluten intolerances, but what *is* gluten?

Gluten is the general name for the protein found in grains such as wheat, barley, spelt, and rye, which many people are unable to tolerate. This could be due to celiac disease, gluten sensitivities, or other medical conditions. There is also an increasing number of people worldwide choosing a gluten-free diet for other reasons. Read on to learn more about gluten intolerances, sensitivities, and Celiac disease.

Celiac Disease

Celiac disease is a serious autoimmune condition that is thought to affect around one in every one hundred people worldwide. Your body's immune system attacks its own tissues when you eat gluten, and this can cause damage to the lining of the gut. Symptoms can include diarrhea, nausea, vomiting, constipation, mouth ulcers, tiredness, anemia, headaches, joint pain, and unexpected weight loss. It can also cause many long-term complications if undiagnosed.

> **fact**
>
> If someone in your family has been diagnosed with celiac disease it is important to also get tested, even if you don't have any symptoms. Studies show that if a close family member has celiac disease, there is a one in ten chance you could also have it.

Testing for celiac disease involves a blood test to check for antibodies that indicate an immune reaction to gluten, followed by a biopsy to confirm the diagnosis. Once diagnosed, the only treatment for celiac disease is to eat a one hundred percent gluten-free diet, as just a single crumb of gluten can cause huge health complications.

Gluten Sensitivity

Many people experience digestive and health problems as a result of eating gluten but do not have celiac disease. There is no test to diagnose a gluten sensitivity, but doctors will usually ask you to keep a food diary to track symptoms. Symptoms can be very similar to those with celiac disease, such as gas, bloating, abdominal pain, headaches, and fatigue. People with a gluten sensitivity are unlikely to develop any severe long-term effects, but eating gluten can lead to discomfort.

Irritable Bowel Syndrome

Irritable bowel syndrome, or IBS, is a condition that affects the digestive system and causes symptoms such as stomach cramps, bloating, diarrhea, and constipation that tend to come and go over time. IBS is thought to affect one in every ten people and can significantly impact a person's quality of life. Many people with IBS manage their symptoms through the low-FODMAP diet. FODMAPs are found in a range of foods that are thought to be common triggers for people with IBS, including wheat and milk. The low-FODMAP diet is very restrictive and not recommended as a lifestyle diet. It should only be followed with the help of a doctor, registered dietician, or other healthcare professional.

Which Foods Contain Gluten?

One of the biggest challenges for people in the early stages of cutting out gluten is knowing what they can and can't eat. The following is a list of some of the most popular foods that may contain gluten; however, it is important to always check the ingredients before eating any food, as gluten can sometimes be found in products you wouldn't expect, such as soups and salad dressings.

- Breads, crackers, and wraps
- Pasta/noodles
- Cereals
- Flour
- Baked goods (cakes, cookies, pastries, pizza)
- Prepackaged snacks (chips, snack bars)
- Piecrusts
- Soups
- Ready-made meals
- Sauces and dressings (soy sauce, marinades, salad dressings)
- Beer

This list is a small proportion of gluten-containing foods. Always check the ingredients label for everything you eat to ensure it is safe.

Which Foods Are Okay to Eat?

You'll be pleased to know that there are plenty of naturally gluten-free foods out there, such as:

- Fruits and vegetables
- Eggs
- Meat and fish
- Nuts and seeds
- Herbs and spices
- Healthy fats and oils
- Certain grains (quinoa, rice, corn, amaranth, tapioca, sorghum, millet)

Keep in mind that this is not an exhaustive list. As you continue through this book, you'll discover just how many choices you have.

The Dairy-Free Diet

Dairy refers to any food or drink made from the milk products of animals. It includes products such as cheese, butter, yogurt, and ice cream. Many people are unable to tolerate dairy due to a dairy allergy or intolerance, lactose intolerance, IBS, or other medical reason. There are also an increasing number of people worldwide choosing to eat a vegan diet, meaning they do not eat any products derived from animals, including dairy. Read on for more information about dairy intolerances and sensitivities.

Dairy Allergies

A dairy allergy is an immunological reaction to the proteins in milk and products containing milk. When a person with a dairy allergy consumes dairy, their body can trigger a response to try to fight off the dangerous substance. Doctors can diagnose dairy allergies with skin-prick tests and blood tests, which measure the amount of immunoglobulin E antibodies in your blood. Symptoms of dairy allergies can range from life-threatening anaphylaxis to less serious reactions, such as hives. Dairy allergies are commonly more prevalent in children under the age of three; however, many adults also suffer. A person with a dairy allergy can be triggered by just a drop of milk, so it is important they stick to a totally dairy-free diet.

Dairy or Lactose Intolerance

Many people have difficulty digesting milk products, which can lead to an unpleasant reaction. There is no test to diagnose a dairy or lactose intolerance, but doctors will usually ask you to keep a food diary to track symptoms. Symptoms can include bloating, diarrhea, flatulence, stomach cramps, and nausea. In some cases, this can be caused by a milk protein intolerance, meaning milk products should be removed from the person's diet; however, in many cases these symptoms can be due to the person's inability to digest lactose. People who are lactose intolerant cannot digest the sugar in dairy. This is usually caused by too little of the enzyme (lactase) produced in the small intestine. Some people with a lactose intolerance or sensitivity are able to tolerate a very small amount of lactose.

Which Foods Contain Dairy?

One of the first challenges of adapting to a dairy-free diet is ensuring you know which foods contain dairy.

> **alert**
>
> Always be vigilant for those "hidden" dairy ingredients. An example of this is that some white wines use milk to reduce the bitterness in the clarifying process. This will be labeled on the bottle but is not always obvious.

The following is a list of some of the most popular foods that may contain dairy.

- Cow's milk
- Goat's milk
- Buttermilk
- Butter
- Yogurt
- Ice cream
- Cheese
- Sour cream
- Cream
- Baked goods (cakes, biscuits)
- Sauces (such as some salad dressings and reduced-fat mayonnaise)
- Puddings

Gluten-Free and Dairy-Free Baking Ingredients

Finding the right baking alternatives doesn't have to be expensive or complicated. The following sections explore some of the best and most popular replacements to assist you on your gluten-free and dairy-free baking journey.

Gluten-Free Flour Options

Your choice of gluten-free flour can really impact the success, texture, and taste of your final baked goods. Some of the most widely available gluten-free flour options include:

ALL-PURPOSE FLOUR BLENDS

The most popular blends of gluten-free flour are all-purpose blends, which contain a mixture of different flours and starches, produced to give successful results when baking. There are many different brands of all-purpose flour, and it is important to note that different brands can produce very different results depending on the ingredients included within the blend.

RICE FLOUR

This versatile flour blend is made from finely grinding white or brown rice to a soft and neutral-colored flour. Rice flour can generally be substituted for wheat flour when it's used as a thickening agent in recipes such as sauces and gravies; however, it is best mixed with other flour blends in baked goods, as it can produce quite a dense result on its own.

ALMOND FLOUR

Almond flour is one of the most popular healthy alternatives to wheat flour, packed with nutrients and made from blanched ground almonds. It has a sweet yet nutty flavor and is commonly used in baked goods such as muffins and piecrusts.

OAT FLOUR

Oat flour is made from grinding oats; however, it is essential that the oats used are labeled gluten-free and free from cross contamination. Oat flour is best used in cookies and quick breads, but it may leave your baked goods a little too moist. Make your own oat flour by blending gluten-free rolled oats in a food processor to form a fine flour.

COCONUT FLOUR

One of the most popular types of gluten-free flour, other than almond, is coconut flour, which is packed with nutrients and made by drying and grinding coconut meat to produce a light and powdery texture. Coconut flour is highly absorbent, so it cannot be substituted for wheat flour, as this would result in a very dry recipe.

GRAM FLOUR

Gram flour (also known as besan) is made from ground chickpeas to produce a rich and golden flour that is great for absorbing moisture. Chickpea flour has a nutty taste and is traditionally used in Indian and Middle Eastern cuisine in recipes such as onion bhajis and falafel.

---

question

What Flour Blend(s) Should I Use?

Different gluten-free flour blends can produce very different results in gluten-free baking. To get the best results from the recipes in this book it is recommended to use a blend of rice flour, potato starch, tapioca starch, and xanthan gum.

Starches

Starches are used in gluten-free all-purpose flour blends to provide elasticity and texture to baked goods. The most common types of gluten-free starches include:

- Potato Starch
- Cornstarch
- Tapioca Starch

These ingredients help with the structure that gluten typically provides in baking by replicating its sticky properties. They are normally used in small quantities.

Gums

In gluten-free baking, gums are used to help bind baked goods together and provide elasticity. The most popular gum is xanthan gum, which is a flavorless, white powdered thickener used to strengthen gluten-free baked goods and prevent them from crumbling. It is important to check whether your flour blend already contains xanthan gum, as adding too much can result in a gummy texture.

Dairy-Free Milk

Over the last few years supermarkets have started to stock more and more dairy-free milk alternatives. Some of the most common dairy-free milk alternatives used in baking are detailed in the following sections.

SOY MILK

Made from extracting the liquid from soybeans, soy milk is one of the most widely available milk alternatives to cow's milk. It has a mild, creamy flavor, which is hard to detect in breads, cakes, muffins, and other baked goods, and it can be used cup for cup in place of cow's milk.

ALMOND MILK

Almond milk is one of the most recommended types of milk for gluten-free baking. It contains a mixture of finely ground almonds and water and has a mild nutty flavor. It's widely available in supermarkets and can be used cup for cup in place of cow's milk.

COCONUT MILK

There are two main types of coconut milk: coconut milk beverage (usually labeled as coconut milk) and canned coconut milk, and it is important to not confuse them. Coconut milk beverage is a dairy-free milk alternative sold in cartons and made from coconut and water. It is typically used in smoothies or in place of milk in tea or coffee. Canned coconut milk is thick, creamy, and bright white. It is usually found in a can and can be used in Thai and Indian dishes as well as whipped to make a dairy-free cream.

RICE MILK

Rice milk is made from rice and water and is less creamy and tastes more neutral than other dairy-free milk alternatives. Rice milk is also a very allergy-friendly milk alternative, as it is free from nuts and soy; however, it can often be unreliable in baking due to its high water content.

OAT MILK

Oat milk has gained a lot of popularity in recent years and is made from blending oats with water to create a creamy dairy-free milk alternative. It has a neutral flavor and can be used cup for cup in place of cow's milk. Note that not all oat milk brands are gluten-free, so be sure to pick a brand that uses gluten-free oats.

Cooking Fats and Oils

Cooking fats and oils are an essential part of many baking recipes. Some of the most commonly used dairy-free alternatives are detailed in the following sections. These alternatives are also used in the recipes in this book.

VEGAN BUTTERY SPREAD

Vegan buttery spreads are smooth, creamy, and buttery in taste. They are typically made from a combination of different vegetable oils and are a good replacement for dairy-free butter in both cooking and spreading on toast.

VEGAN BUTTERY STICKS

Vegan buttery sticks are blocks of butter formulated by companies to be better for baking. They tend to be very similar to buttery spreads and are also made with vegetable oils. They are, however, created with more stability, so they work well in recipes for foods such as piecrust, cookies, and dairy-free buttercream frosting.

VEGETABLE OIL

Vegetable oil is a generic type of oil with a neutral flavor and is used in a lot of everyday cooking. It works well for deep-frying, stir-frying, and baking and is widely available.

COCONUT OIL

Coconut oil has grown in popularity in recent years and has a solid consistency. It is sweet and smooth and can be used as a substitute for butter in some recipes. It is also great for general cooking, frying, sautéing, and roasting.

EXTRA-VIRGIN OLIVE OIL

Extra-virgin olive oil is widely available and is a staple of the Mediterranean diet because of its high quality. However, due to its high cost and lower smoke point compared to many other oils, it is usually best left for dressings and dips rather than cooking and baking.

COOKING SPRAY

There are many different varieties of cooking sprays, including olive oil, coconut oil, and vegetable oil. They are generally used for greasing pans, pots, and skillets to prevent baked goods from sticking.

Gluten Free and Dairy-Free Baking Equipment

In addition to ingredient substitutes, there are some equipment essentials you'll want on hand when baking gluten-free and dairy-free. The list that follows includes the most popular baking pans/dishes and equipment used in the recipes throughout this book:

Baking Pans and Dishes:
- 8" round springform cake pan
- 8" deep round springform cake pan
- 9" round springform cake pan
- 9" deep round springform cake pan
- 9" square springform cake pan
- 9" round springform pie/tart pan
- 6" × 4" baking dish
- 8" × 8" baking dish
- 9" × 9" baking dish
- 9" × 13" baking dish
- 9" × 13" Swiss roll tin
- 2-pound loaf pan
- 9" × 5" loaf pan

- 9" oblong pie dish
- Twelve-cup muffin tin
- Large baking sheet

Electric Equipment:
- Kitchen scales or measuring cups*
- Electric hand mixer
- Food processor
- Stand mixer (optional)

Popular Baking Terms

The recipe instructions in this book also include some popular baking terms:

- **Blind Bake:** Blind baking, or prebaking, is the process of partially baking a piecrust before filling it. This is done when the piecrust takes longer to bake than the filling, or to prevent a soggy bottom in certain recipes. Blind baking involves lining the piecrust with parchment paper and filling it with ceramic or metal pastry weights, sometimes called baking beans. After baking the crust for a set amount of time, the parchment paper and weights are removed and the filling is added.
- **Stiff Peaks:** Stiff peaks are created by whisking egg whites until they stand up straight when the electric mixer is lifted. You should be able to hold the bowl upside down over your head, and the mixture will stay inside the bowl.
- **Egg Wash:** An egg wash is simply a beaten egg that can be brushed on top of pastries

*This book uses both imperial and metric measurements. However, as baking is all about precision, using metric measurements can often provide a more accurate result and therefore a better overall dish. Also note that the eggs used in all the recipes in this book are standard large US eggs, which are the same as standard medium UK eggs.

and breads before baking to give them a golden brown, more polished finish.

- **Fold:** Folding is the process of combining a light ingredient (such as egg whites) with a heavier mixture, while keeping as much air in the mixture as possible. This is done by using a spoon to lift the two mixtures together instead of beating them.
- **Beat:** Beating is the process of rigorously mixing ingredients together using a whisk or wooden spoon to ensure the ingredients are fully combined. This will take longer to achieve with a wooden spoon or hand whisk than an electric mixer or stand mixer.
- **Grease:** Greasing is the process of coating the inside of a baking pan or dish with butter or oil to prevent the baked good from sticking once it's out of the oven.

As you begin baking the recipes in this book, flip back to this section any time you need a refresher on a certain term.

US-to-UK Ingredient Converter

The recipes in this book have been created with ingredients accessible for both American and British bakers. As some ingredients are known by different names, the following is a handy American-to-British ingredient converter for the most popular items used:

US-to-UK Ingredient Converter

US	UK
Gluten-Free All-Purpose Flour	Gluten-Free Plain Flour
Gluten-Free Self-Rising Flour	Gluten-Free Self-Raising Flour (If you can't find self-raising flour, you can make your own by adding 2 teaspoons of baking powder to every 1 cup (160g) of gluten-free all-purpose flour.)
Baking Soda	Bicarbonate of Soda
Superfine Sugar	Caster Sugar
Cornstarch	Corn Flour
Confectioners' (or Powdered) Sugar	Icing Sugar
Soy Milk	Soya Milk
Molasses	Black Treacle
Heavy Cream	Double Cream
Zucchini	Courgette
Fresh Cilantro	Fresh Coriander
Corn Syrup	Golden Syrup (This is not a direct replacement. Corn syrup is slightly thinner than golden syrup but generally can be substituted without having to change the quantities of the recipe.)

The Gluten-Free and Dairy-Free Diet at Home

Transitioning to a gluten-free and/or dairy-free lifestyle at home can be challenging, but it is achievable. The following are tips and tricks for preventing cross contamination in the kitchen, meal preparation, and storing food at home:

- **Use a separate toaster if you have celiac disease.** This will help avoid cross contamination from gluten-containing foods. If you cannot use a separate toaster, toaster bags are readily available and can work well when traveling.
- **Use dedicated chopping boards and utensils to prepare food.** This will help minimize the chance of any cross contamination. Be careful with wooden items such as chopping boards and spoons, as they can be especially difficult to clean.
- **Make sure to carefully read food labels.** Sometimes gluten or dairy can be found in unexpected products. Watch out for labels that say, "May Contain," as this means that there is a risk that the product could be contaminated with gluten or dairy. Be aware that the rules on "May Contain" labeling can vary depending on the country you live in.
- **Get clean.** Thoroughly clean surfaces and wash your hands before cooking or preparing any gluten-free and dairy-free food.
- **Keep separate foods.** If you share a home with anyone who eats gluten and/or dairy, use your own separate condiments such as butter and jams.
- **Store gluten-free and dairy-free ingredients in separate areas, preferably higher up.** This will help prevent cross contamination.
- **Make sure to tell everyone in your household about your allergy or intolerance.** This is especially essential if you have family or roommates. It is a good idea to have your own refrigerator area and cupboard shelf in these situations to prevent cross contamination.

With these safeguards in place, your home will be prepared for your gluten-free and/or dairy-free diet. You can also ask your healthcare professional for advice on ensuring your home is safe in case of an allergy, intolerance, or other medical condition.

Eating Out on the Gluten-Free and Dairy-Free Diet

As the awareness of allergies and intolerances has grown, more and more restaurants have started offering gluten-free and dairy-free options. It is important, however, to know what to look for when eating out gluten-free or dairy-free. This can vary depending on whether you have celiac disease, an allergy, or a mild intolerance. Here are some tips for eating out on a gluten-free and/or dairy-free diet:

- **Inform the restaurant of your dietary needs.** It is essential to let your server know, so they can take the necessary precautions, even if a dish is already labeled as gluten-free and/or dairy-free.
- **Contact the restaurant ahead of time.** If you are nervous about eating at a particular restaurant, call ahead to see if they can accommodate you. This is a great way to feel relaxed and reassured before you even arrive at the restaurant.

- **Ask the restaurant about cross contamination.** Will your food be prepared in a separate area? Is there a dedicated fryer? Have the staff had the appropriate training on food allergies?

It is up to you to do your due diligence when eating out to ensure you are being safe and a restaurant is able to comply with your needs.

Traveling on the Gluten-Free and Dairy-Free Diet

There is no reason why being gluten-free and/or dairy-free should prevent you from traveling. However, it is important to do a little extra planning and research beforehand. Here are some tips for traveling while on a gluten-free and/or dairy-free diet:

- **Research the area where you will be staying, including restaurants, grocery stores, and hotels.** You can find lots of useful information online from people who have visited the same area. Planning ahead of your visit will save time and allow you to enjoy yourself while you are away.

- **Use dietary-needs language cards.** These can be purchased online and include a translation of your specific allergies and intolerances in different languages. This can prevent any language barriers when traveling.
- **Have snacks on hand.** When you are traveling, gluten-free and dairy-free snacks are essential, whether it's for the plane, car, or however else you're getting to your destination. Ideas for snacks to pack include snack bars, cereal, nut butter, crackers, protein bars, nuts, seeds, and chips.
- **Take meals into your own hands.** If you are feeling nervous about going away, booking accommodations with a kitchen means you can cook for yourself if necessary and can alleviate a lot of stress.

Wherever you're headed, this planning can help make your travels safe and stress-free.

Let's Get Baking

Now that you have learned the basics, as well as baking ingredient alternatives and essential equipment, it's time to bake! In the following chapters you'll discover two hundred delicious recipes. Flip back to the previous information at any point for a refresher on elements of the gluten-free and/or dairy-free diet, gluten and dairy substitutes, baking tools and terms, and tips for being safe and healthy whether at home or on the go.

CHAPTER 2

Breakfasts, Muffins, and Scones

Fluffy Pancakes

MAKES 6

Per Serving (1 pancake):

Calories	229
Fat	4g
Sodium	435mg
Carbohydrates	48g
Fiber	1g
Sugar	8g
Protein	2g

These easy-to-make American-style pancakes are light and fluffy, made with just seven ingredients for a tasty breakfast or brunch. Serve with bacon and maple syrup, berry compote, fresh fruit, or dairy-free chocolate spread and strawberries.

1¾ cups plus 2 tablespoons (300g) gluten-free self-rising flour

2 teaspoons baking powder

¹⁄16 teaspoon salt

4 tablespoons granulated sugar

½ teaspoon vanilla extract

1½ cups plus 2 tablespoons (390ml) dairy-free milk

6 teaspoons vegetable oil, divided

1   In a large mixing bowl, combine flour, baking powder, salt, and sugar. Add vanilla and milk and whisk well until consistency is a thick, lump-free batter.

2   In a large nonstick frying pan, heat 1 teaspoon oil over medium heat. Add one-sixth of batter to pan and cook until bubbles start to form, about 3 minutes. Flip with a spatula and cook another 2 minutes until golden brown. Transfer to a large plate and repeat cooking with remaining 5 teaspoons oil and batter to make six pancakes.

Cranberry, Hazelnut, and Almond Granola

Making your own granola couldn't be easier, and this energy-boosting breakfast recipe is the ideal start to your day. Plus, your whole house will smell amazing with this granola baking in the oven! Serve with dairy-free milk or yogurt and fresh strawberries.

4 tablespoons coconut oil

5 tablespoons pure maple syrup

½ teaspoon ground cinnamon

2 cups plus 2 tablespoons (200g) gluten-free rolled oats

1 cup (100g) roughly chopped almonds

1 cup (100g) roughly chopped hazelnuts

¼ teaspoon salt

¾ cup (100g) dried cranberries

1 Preheat oven to 350°F (180°C) and line a baking sheet with parchment paper.

2 In a large saucepan over medium heat, melt oil, maple syrup, and cinnamon until combined, about 2 minutes. Stir in oats, almonds, hazelnuts, and salt. Mix well until everything is coated.

3 Spread mixture out on prepared baking sheet and bake 20–25 minutes until golden brown, stirring every 5 minutes to ensure mixture doesn't burn.

4 Remove from oven and stir in cranberries. Leave to completely cool on baking sheet, about 20 minutes, and store in a jar at room temperature for up to 2 weeks.

SERVES 8

Per Serving:

Calories	393
Fat	23g
Sodium	74mg
Carbohydrates	40g
Fiber	6g
Sugar	17g
Protein	9g

ADAPT THE FLAVORS

The best part of this recipe is how adaptable it is. Add your favorite nuts, spices, seeds, and dried fruit to change up the flavors and use up any leftover ingredients from the cupboard.

Classic Crepes

MAKES 6

Per Serving (1 crepe):

Calories	149
Fat	7g
Sodium	113mg
Carbohydrates	17g
Fiber	2g
Sugar	1g
Protein	6g

EAT ANY TIME OF THE DAY

This simple recipe is delicious for breakfast, but you can have these crepes any time of the day with lots of different fillings, sweet or savory, such as peaches and cream, spinach, bacon and mushroom, or smoked ham with dairy-free cheese.

Breakfast doesn't get much better than a batch of fresh crepes. This easy recipe is perfect for the weekend. Top with vegan chocolate hazelnut spread and berries or lemon and sugar.

¾ cup plus 3 tablespoons (150g) gluten-free all-purpose flour

3 large eggs

1¼ cups plus 3 tablespoons (350ml) unsweetened almond or other dairy-free milk

2 tablespoons (30g) vegan buttery spread, divided

1 In a large bowl, whisk flour and eggs. Slowly add milk and continue to whisk 1–2 minutes until smooth.

2 Place 1 tablespoon buttery spread in a small microwave-safe bowl and microwave on high until melted, 15–20 seconds. Add to flour mixture and whisk until combined.

3 In a medium frying pan, heat ½ teaspoon buttery spread over medium heat. Pour a ladle of batter into pan and swirl pan so a thin layer covers bottom of pan.

4 Fry 2 minutes until bubbles form. Flip with a spatula and fry 1 minute until cooked through. Transfer crepe to a large plate and keep warm. Repeat with remaining batter, adding ½ teaspoon buttery spread to pan before each batter addition to avoid sticking. Serve warm.

Banana and Blueberry Breakfast Muffins

MIDMORNING SNACK

Change up this recipe for a midmorning snack by replacing the blueberries with dairy-free milk chocolate chips. Simply fold them in along with the oats.

These Banana and Blueberry Breakfast Muffins are always a treat and can be whipped up in just half an hour. A tasty and easy recipe to make the night before for a quick "on the go" breakfast option.

2 medium-sized ripe bananas, peeled and mashed

¼ cup plus 2 tablespoons (75g) packed light brown sugar

1 teaspoon vanilla extract

1 large egg

¼ cup (60g) vegan buttery spread, melted

½ cup (85g) gluten-free all-purpose flour

¼ teaspoon xanthan gum (omit if flour blend already contains this)

1 teaspoon baking powder

1 teaspoon baking soda

½ teaspoon ground cinnamon

½ teaspoon salt

½ cup (45g) gluten-free rolled oats

½ cup (100g) frozen blueberries

1 Preheat oven to 350°F (180°C) and line a twelve-cup muffin tin with cupcake liners.

2 In a large bowl, add banana, sugar, vanilla, and egg. Mix well, then stir in buttery spread.

3 In a separate large bowl, mix flour, xanthan gum, baking powder, baking soda, cinnamon, and salt. Add wet ingredients to dry ingredients and mix well until fully combined.

4 Fold in oats and blueberries.

5 Divide batter between prepared muffin cups and bake 20–25 minutes until golden brown and a skewer inserted in center comes out clean.

6 Store in an airtight container at room temperature for up to 2 days.

Apricot, Pumpkin Seed, and Raisin Breakfast Bars

This is a quick and easy recipe that's perfect for making the evening before as a grab and go breakfast the next morning. Or simply pop one in your bag for a healthy midmorning snack that will boost your energy and keep you going until lunch.

¼ cup plus 2 tablespoons (80g) coconut oil

¼ cup plus 1 tablespoon (100g) clear honey

2 cups (180g) gluten-free rolled oats

½ cup (95g) whole dried apricot, cut into small chunks

¾ cup (110g) pumpkin seeds

¾ cup (110g) raisins

¼ teaspoon salt

1 Preheat oven to 350°F (180°C) and line a 9" square springform cake pan with parchment paper.

2 In a medium saucepan, heat oil and honey over medium heat until melted and combined, about 2 minutes. Stir in oats, apricot, pumpkin seeds, raisins, and salt until fully coated.

3 Press mixture into prepared pan. Bake 25–30 minutes until golden brown.

4 Let cool in pan 1 hour, then refrigerate 1 hour before cutting to prevent bars from breaking. Store in an airtight container at room temperature for up to 3 days.

MAKES 9

Per Serving (1 bar):

Calories	320
Fat	14g
Sodium	69mg
Carbohydrates	43g
Fiber	4g
Sugar	24g
Protein	7g

ADAPT THE RECIPE

The great thing about these breakfast bars is how adaptable they are. Add dried cranberries, sunflower seeds, or chopped nuts to change up the flavor.

Simple Waffles

MAKES 4

Per Serving (1 waffle):

Calories	198
Fat	9g
Sodium	416mg
Carbohydrates	28g
Fiber	0g
Sugar	10g
Protein	3g

Enjoy these delicious waffles as an indulgent weekend breakfast or tasty dessert! Make them in your waffle maker and serve with fresh fruit, syrup, or sauces of your choice.

1 large egg

¾ cup plus 3 tablespoons (225ml) unsweetened almond or other dairy-free milk

2 tablespoons (30ml) vegetable oil

¾ cup (125g) gluten-free self-rising flour

1 teaspoon baking powder

3 tablespoons granulated sugar

¼ teaspoon salt

1 Grease a waffle iron with vegetable oil and preheat to 350°F (180°C).

2 In a large bowl, add egg, milk, and oil and whisk until combined. Add flour, baking powder, sugar, and salt and mix until combined.

3 Pour about ¼ batter into heated waffle maker, making sure not to overfill, and cook 5 minutes or until golden brown. Transfer to a large plate. Repeat with remaining batter to make four waffles. Serve warm.

Chocolate and Raspberry Baked Oats

SERVES 2

Per Serving:

Calories	308
Fat	7g
Sodium	109mg
Carbohydrates	51g
Fiber	9g
Sugar	11g
Protein	12g

These baked oats are packed full of delicious energy-boosting ingredients and are a great way of taking porridge to the next level! Serve with extra maple syrup and berries.

1 medium-sized ripe banana, peeled and mashed

1 cup (90g) gluten-free rolled oats

1 tablespoon cocoa powder

¾ cup plus 1 tablespoon (200ml) unsweetened almond or other dairy-free milk

1 large egg, beaten

1 teaspoon pure maple syrup

2 tablespoons fresh raspberries

1 Preheat oven to 350°F (180°C).

2 In a large bowl, add banana, oats, cocoa powder, milk, egg, and maple syrup. Mix well.

3 Fold in raspberries and transfer to an ungreased 6" × 4" baking dish. Bake 35 minutes until golden brown and cooked through. Serve warm.

Baked Hash Browns

These easy-to-make crispy Baked Hash Browns are made with just a handful of ingredients and are a great accompaniment to a hot breakfast.

14 ounces (400g) peeled white potatoes

½ medium peeled white onion

¼ teaspoon salt

⅛ teaspoon ground black pepper

1 tablespoon vegetable oil, for brushing

1 In a large saucepan filled with water, add potatoes and bring to a boil. Turn heat to medium and cook 5 minutes until partially cooked. Drain and let cool completely, about 15 minutes, in pan.

2 Preheat oven to 375°F (190°C) and line a baking sheet with parchment paper.

3 Grate potato and onion onto a clean tea towel, then squeeze out excess liquid from towel. In a large mixing bowl, combine drained potato and onion with salt and pepper and mix well with a fork.

4 Place an egg ring or cookie cutter onto prepared baking sheet and brush inside with oil. Add 1 tablespoon of mixture into ring, pressing down to form a circular hash brown patty. Remove ring and brush top with oil. Repeat with remaining hash brown mixture.

5 Bake 15 minutes, flip with a spatula, and bake another 15 minutes. Serve warm.

SERVES 6

Per Serving:

Calories	73
Fat	0g
Sodium	101mg
Carbohydrates	17g
Fiber	2g
Sugar	1g
Protein	2g

Sweet Corn Fritters with Avocado Salsa

These tasty fritters are made with simple pantry ingredients for a quick and nutritious breakfast the whole family will enjoy.

3 large eggs

2 tablespoons unsweetened almond or other dairy-free milk

1¾ cups (300g) corn kernels

2 medium scallions (spring onions), finely chopped

½ cup (80g) gluten-free all-purpose flour

1 teaspoon Italian seasoning

¼ teaspoon salt, divided

¼ teaspoon ground black pepper, divided

1 tablespoon vegetable oil

1 medium-sized ripe avocado, peeled, pitted, and finely chopped

½ small red onion, peeled and finely chopped

4 cherry tomatoes, finely chopped

1 tablespoon extra-virgin olive oil

1 tablespoon lime juice

¼ cup finely chopped fresh cilantro

SERVES 4

Per Serving (2 fritters):

Calories	285
Fat	16g
Sodium	218mg
Carbohydrates	29g
Fiber	6g
Sugar	6g
Protein	9g

FUN FACT

In the United States, *cilantro* is the name for the plant's leaves and stem, and *coriander* is the name for the plant's dried seeds. However, in the United Kingdom, both the leaves and stems are called coriander, and the dried seeds are called coriander seeds.

1 In a large bowl, whisk eggs and milk until combined. Add corn, scallions, flour, Italian seasoning, ⅛ teaspoon salt, and ⅛ teaspoon pepper and mix well to form a batter.

2 In a large frying pan, heat vegetable oil over medium heat. Use a tablespoon to scoop batter into pan to form eight fritters. Cook 3 minutes, then flip with a spatula and cook 3 minutes more.

3 In a small bowl, combine avocado, onion, tomatoes, olive oil, lime juice, cilantro, and remaining ⅛ teaspoon each salt and pepper. Serve with warm fritters.

Eggy Breakfast Muffins

MAKES 12

Per Serving (1 muffin):

Calories	59
Fat	4g
Sodium	127mg
Carbohydrates	2g
Fiber	0g
Sugar	1g
Protein	5g

MEAL PREP

These egg muffins can be cooked, cooled, and stored in an airtight container in the refrigerator for a quick and easy on-the-go breakfast or lunch. Simply reheat the muffins in the microwave until piping hot.

This is an easy, healthy, and filling breakfast and can be switched up with any leftovers you may have in the refrigerator, such as mushrooms, tomatoes, and dairy-free cheese. These muffins are great for breakfast or lunch!

4 slices bacon, chopped into small pieces

1 medium red bell pepper, seeded and diced

1 small white onion, diced

6 large eggs

3 tablespoons unsweetened almond or other dairy-free milk

½ teaspoon paprika

¼ teaspoon garlic granules

1 teaspoon dried chives

⅛ teaspoon salt

⅛ teaspoon ground black pepper

1   Preheat oven to 350°F (180°C) and line a twelve-cup muffin tin with cupcake liners.

2   In a large saucepan over medium heat, fry bacon, bell pepper, and onion until soft and cooked, about 5 minutes. Remove from heat.

3   In a large bowl, whisk eggs, milk, paprika, garlic, chives, salt, and black pepper. Add fried bacon, bell pepper, and onions to bowl, then divide mixture between twelve prepared muffin cups.

4   Bake 25 minutes until cooked through and a skewer inserted in center comes out clean. Serve warm.

Chocolate and Banana–Stuffed French Toast

Golden and crispy gluten-free fried bread is stuffed with dairy-free chocolate spread and slices of banana. It's a real treat for a weekend breakfast!

2 large eggs

½ cup (120ml) unsweetened almond or other dairy-free milk

2 tablespoons granulated sugar

1 teaspoon ground cinnamon

8 slices gluten-free bread

4 tablespoons dairy-free chocolate hazelnut spread

2 medium-sized ripe bananas, peeled and sliced

1 teaspoon vegetable oil

1 tablespoon confectioners' sugar

1 In a large bowl, whisk eggs, milk, granulated sugar, and cinnamon.

2 Spread 4 slices bread with chocolate spread and top with banana. Top with remaining 4 slices bread to form four sandwiches. Dip sandwiches in egg mixture, ensuring that both bread slices are coated.

3 In a large nonstick frying pan, heat oil over medium heat. Transfer coated sandwiches to pan and cook 3 minutes or until golden brown on bottom. Flip with a spatula and cook on other side an additional 3 minutes. Sprinkle with confectioners' sugar and serve warm.

SERVES 4

Per Serving (1 sandwich):

Calories	435
Fat	16g
Sodium	346mg
Carbohydrates	68g
Fiber	3g
Sugar	28g
Protein	7g

Raspberry Muffins

These light, moist muffins are bursting with fresh raspberries—an easy-to-make and delicious sweet treat that everyone will love.

1¾ cups plus 2 tablespoons (300g) gluten-free all-purpose flour

¼ teaspoon xanthan gum (omit if flour blend already contains this)

¾ cup (150g) superfine sugar

2 teaspoons baking powder

¼ teaspoon salt

1 cup plus 1 tablespoon (250ml) unsweetened almond milk

2 large eggs

¼ cup plus 2 tablespoons (80g) vegan buttery spread, melted

1¼ cups (150g) fresh raspberries

1 Preheat oven to 350°F (180°C) and line a twelve-cup muffin tin with cupcake liners.

2 In a large bowl, add flour, xanthan gum, sugar, baking powder, and salt. Mix well. In a separate large bowl, whisk milk, eggs, and buttery spread. Mix wet ingredients into dry ingredients and fold in raspberries.

3 Pour mixture into muffin cups. Bake 25 minutes or until a skewer inserted in center comes out clean. Let cool for 20 minutes. Store in an airtight container at room temperature for up to 3 days.

MAKES 12

Per Serving (1 muffin):

Calories	189
Fat	7g
Sodium	207mg
Carbohydrates	31g
Fiber	3g
Sugar	14g
Protein	3g

TOP TIP

To prevent the raspberries from sinking when the muffins bake, roll them in gluten-free all-purpose flour before folding them into the batter.

Breakfast Cookies

MAKES 10

Per Serving (1 cookie):

Calories	179
Fat	5g
Sodium	117mg
Carbohydrates	30g
Fiber	3g
Sugar	13g
Protein	5g

These one-bowl Breakfast Cookies are quick to make and easy to customize with different ingredients. They are filled with gluten-free oats, mashed banana, apple, and peanut butter to give you a great energy boost in the morning.

2 medium-sized ripe bananas, peeled and mashed

¼ cup plus 1 tablespoon (75g) peanut butter

¼ cup (80g) clear honey

1 teaspoon vanilla extract

½ teaspoon ground cinnamon

½ teaspoon salt

2 cups (180g) gluten-free rolled oats

1 large apple, peeled and cut into cubes

1 Preheat oven to 350°F (180°C) and line a baking sheet with parchment paper.

2 In a large bowl, add banana, peanut butter, honey, vanilla, cinnamon, and salt. Mix well. Add oats and apple. Stir until fully combined.

3 Roll mixture into balls using 1 tablespoon of mixture per ball. Place balls on prepared baking sheet and press down into a cookie shape (cookies will not spread in oven). Bake 15–17 minutes until cookies start to turn golden brown and firm.

4 Leave cookies to cool on a wire rack 1 hour. Serve after cooling, or store in an airtight container at room temperature for up to 2 days.

Peanut Butter and Raisin Oat Cookies

These six-ingredient oat cookies are filled with creamy peanut butter and raisins. They are completely free of refined sugar too, so they are great for a healthy treat or an on-the-go breakfast.

¾ cup (65g) gluten-free rolled oats

1 teaspoon baking powder

¼ cup plus 3 tablespoons (100g) smooth peanut butter

¼ cup (60g) coconut sugar

1 large egg

¼ cup plus 1 tablespoon (50g) raisins

1 Preheat oven to 350°F (180°C) and line a baking sheet with parchment paper.

2 In a small bowl, add oats and baking powder. Mix to combine. In a medium bowl, whisk peanut butter, sugar, and egg. Add dry ingredients to wet ingredients and mix well. Stir in raisins.

3 Roll dough into six balls and place on prepared baking sheet, pressing each ball down into a cookie shape. Bake 10 minutes.

4 Remove from oven and leave on sheet to cool, about 30 minutes, before eating. Store in an airtight container at room temperature for up to 3 days.

MAKES 6

Per Serving (1 cookie):

Calories	214
Fat	10g
Sodium	96mg
Carbohydrates	27g
Fiber	2g
Sugar	15g
Protein	7g

A BASE FOR DIFFERENT FLAVORS

This basic refined sugar–free cookie recipe is a great base for lots of ingredients. Switch the raisins for dairy-free milk chocolate chips, dried cranberries, or dried apricots, and add nuts and seeds depending on what you have in your kitchen.

Raisin Scones

Per Serving (1 scone):

Calories	263
Fat	9g
Sodium	428mg
Carbohydrates	45g
Fiber	1g
Sugar	12g
Protein	3g

KNEADING SCONE DOUGH

When making scones it is important to not over-knead your dough, as this can prevent the scones from rising in the oven.

These Raisin Scones are a British classic and are great as part of a picnic, afternoon tea, or as a tasty snack. They are best eaten warm, sliced in half, and spread with jam and dairy-free cream.

1¼ cups plus 2 tablespoons (225g) gluten-free self-rising flour

½ teaspoon xanthan gum (add just ¼ teaspoon if flour blend already contains this)

¼ teaspoon salt

1 teaspoon baking powder

¼ cup (55g) cubed vegan buttery sticks

2 tablespoons (25g) sugar

½ cup (75g) raisins

½ cup plus 1 tablespoon (140ml) unsweetened almond or other dairy-free milk

1 large egg, beaten

1   Preheat oven to 400°F (200°C) and line a baking sheet with parchment paper.

2   In a large bowl, mix flour, xanthan gum, salt, and baking powder. Add buttery sticks, rubbing in with your fingers to form a bread crumb consistency. Stir in sugar and raisins.

3   Slowly add milk, mixing until you have a soft but firm dough. Lightly knead dough on a lightly floured surface and pat out to about 1½" thick. Use a cookie cutter to cut rounds and place on prepared baking sheet.

4   Brush rounds with egg and bake 15 minutes until scones have risen and are golden brown.

5   Serve warm or store in an airtight container at room temperature for up to 2 days and reheat before eating.

Cheese Scones

Enjoy these tasty and easy-to-bake Cheese Scones as part of a picnic, afternoon snack, or lunch. They are best eaten warm and spread with plenty of dairy-free butter.

1¼ cups plus 2 tablespoons (225g) gluten-free self-rising flour

½ teaspoon xanthan gum (add just ¼ teaspoon if flour blend already contains this)

¼ teaspoon salt

1 teaspoon baking powder

¼ cup (55g) cubed vegan buttery sticks

1½ cups (120g) grated dairy-free Cheddar cheese alternative

1 teaspoon gluten-free mustard

¼ cup plus 3 tablespoons (100ml) unsweetened almond or other dairy-free milk

1 large egg, beaten

1 Preheat oven to 400°F (200°C) and line a baking sheet with parchment paper.

2 In a large bowl, mix flour, xanthan gum, salt, and baking powder. Add buttery sticks, rubbing in with your fingers to form a bread crumb consistency. Add cheese and mustard and mix until evenly distributed.

3 Slowly add milk, mixing until dough is soft but firm (you may not need all the milk). Lightly knead dough on a lightly floured surface and pat out to about 1½" thick. Use a cookie cutter to cut rounds and place on prepared baking sheet.

4 Brush rounds with egg and bake 15 minutes until scones have risen and are golden brown.

5 Serve warm or store in an airtight container at room temperature for up to 2 days and reheat before eating.

MAKES 6

Per Serving (1 scone):

Calories	288
Fat	16g
Sodium	703mg
Carbohydrates	36g
Fiber	2g
Sugar	0g
Protein	2g

Blueberry Almond Crumble Muffins

MAKES 12

Per Serving (1 muffin):

Calories	284
Fat	12g
Sodium	283mg
Carbohydrates	42g
Fiber	1g
Sugar	24g
Protein	2g

MAKE YOUR OWN SUPERFINE SUGAR

Did you know that if you are struggling to get hold of superfine (caster) sugar you can make your own? Simply blitz granulated sugar in a food processor to form a finer sand consistency.

These bakery-style muffins are packed full of delicious blueberries and topped with a sweet almond crumble.

¼ cup plus 2 tablespoons (60g) gluten-free all-purpose flour

3 tablespoons (40g) cubed dairy-free vegan buttery sticks

¼ cup (50g) packed light brown sugar

2 tablespoons sliced almonds

½ cup plus 1 tablespoon (120g) vegan buttery sticks, softened

1 cup plus 1 tablespoon (220g) superfine sugar

2 large eggs

1 teaspoon vanilla extract

1¼ cups plus 2 tablespoons (220g) gluten-free self-rising flour

¼ teaspoon xanthan gum (omit if flour blend already contains this)

1 teaspoon baking powder

¼ teaspoon salt

¼ cup plus 3 tablespoons (100ml) unsweetened almond or other dairy-free milk

¾ cup (150g) fresh blueberries

1 Preheat oven to 375°F (190°C) and line a twelve-cup muffin tin with cupcake liners.

2 In a medium bowl, add flour and cubed buttery sticks, using your fingers to form a bread crumb consistency. Stir in brown sugar and almonds. Set aside.

3 In a large bowl, beat softened buttery sticks and superfine sugar until creamy. Add eggs and vanilla and beat until combined.

4 In a medium bowl, combine flour, xanthan gum, baking powder, and salt. Add flour mixture to sugar mixture and mix well.

5 Stir in milk, then carefully fold in blueberries.

6 Divide mixture between twelve muffin cups and sprinkle with almond crumble mixture. Bake 25–30 minutes or until a skewer inserted in center comes out clean.

7 Cool muffins in tin 5 minutes, then remove and cool on a wire rack at least 20 minutes before serving. Store in an airtight container at room temperature for up to 3 days.

Chocolate Chip Muffins

These bakery-style Chocolate Chip Muffins are soft and moist on the inside, with a golden top. They are quick and easy to make, and are perfect as dessert or a midafternoon treat.

1¼ cups (200g) gluten-free all-purpose flour

¼ teaspoon xanthan gum (omit if flour blend already contains this)

½ teaspoon salt

1 teaspoon baking powder

½ teaspoon baking soda

¼ cup plus 2 tablespoons (80g) vegan buttery sticks

¼ cup plus 2 tablespoons (80g) superfine sugar

¼ cup (50g) packed light brown sugar

1 teaspoon vanilla extract

1 large egg

¾ cup plus 1 tablespoon (200ml) unsweetened almond or other dairy-free milk

1 cup (180g) dairy-free milk chocolate chips

1 Preheat oven to 350°F (180°C) and line a twelve-cup muffin tin with cupcake liners.

2 In a large bowl, mix flour, xanthan gum, salt, baking powder, and baking soda. In a medium bowl, beat buttery sticks, superfine sugar, and brown sugar until creamy. Add vanilla and egg and mix until combined.

3 Add wet ingredients to dry ingredients and combine. Slowly add milk, whisking until combined. Fold in chocolate chips.

4 Divide mixture between ten muffin cups and bake 25 minutes or until a skewer inserted in center comes out clean.

5 Transfer muffins to a wire rack to cool completely, about 20 minutes. Store in an airtight container at room temperature for up to 2 days.

Lemon and Poppy Seed Muffins

Zesty and moist, these bakery-style Lemon and Poppy Seed Muffins are topped with a citrus iced glaze. They are delicious for breakfast or on a coffee break.

1½ cups plus 1 tablespoon (250g) gluten-free self-rising flour

¼ teaspoon xanthan gum (omit if flour blend already contains this)

¾ cup plus 2 tablespoons (175g) superfine sugar

2 tablespoons poppy seeds

1 teaspoon baking powder

¼ teaspoon salt

Zest of 1 medium lemon

¼ cup plus 3 tablespoons (100g) vegan buttery spread, melted and cooled

¾ cup plus 2 tablespoons (200g) dairy-free plain yogurt

¼ cup (60ml) unsweetened almond or other dairy-free milk

2 large eggs

Juice of 2 medium lemons, divided

¾ cup plus 1 tablespoon (120g) confectioners' sugar

MAKES 12

Per Serving (1 muffin):

Calories	255
Fat	8g
Sodium	253mg
Carbohydrates	43g
Fiber	1g
Sugar	25g
Protein	2g

1 Preheat oven to 350°F (180°C) and line a twelve-cup muffin tin with cupcake liners.

2 In a large bowl, add flour, xanthan gum, superfine sugar, poppy seeds, baking powder, salt, and lemon zest. Mix well.

3 In a medium bowl, add melted buttery spread, yogurt, milk, eggs, and juice from 1 lemon. Whisk well. Add wet ingredients to dry ingredients and combine.

4 Divide mixture between twelve muffin cups. Bake 25 minutes or until a skewer inserted in center comes out clean. Transfer muffins to a wire rack to cool completely, about 20 minutes.

5 In a medium bowl, mix confectioners' sugar with remaining lemon juice. Drizzle over muffins. Store muffins in an airtight container at room temperature for up to 3 days.

Cherry Bakewell Muffins

This recipe combines delicious almond and cherry flavors inside a tasty muffin. If you are a fan of Cherry Bakewells, you will love these moreish muffins.

1¼ cups plus 2 tablespoons (130g) ground almonds

1¼ cups (200g) gluten-free self-rising flour

½ cup (100g) superfine sugar

1 teaspoon baking powder

¼ teaspoon xanthan gum (omit if flour blend already contains this)

2 large eggs

1 cup plus 1 tablespoon (250ml) unsweetened almond or other dairy-free milk

3 tablespoons plus 1 teaspoon (50ml) vegetable oil

¾ cup (150g) glacé cherries, divided

½ cup (120g) grated marzipan

½ cup plus 3 tablespoons (100g) confectioners' sugar

1 tablespoon water

½ cup (50g) flaked almonds

1 Preheat oven to 350°F (180°C) and line a twelve-cup muffin tin with cupcake liners.

2 In a large bowl, mix ground almonds, flour, superfine sugar, baking powder, and xanthan gum. In a medium bowl, whisk eggs, milk, and oil. Gradually pour wet ingredients into dry ingredients, mixing well.

3 Add cherries (saving ⅓ for topping) and marzipan and mix to combine. Divide mixture between twelve muffin cups and bake 20 minutes until golden brown and a skewer inserted in center comes out clean.

4 Transfer muffins to a wire rack to cool completely, about 20 minutes. In a small bowl, mix confectioners' sugar with water and drizzle over cooled muffins. Top with remaining cherries and flaked almonds. Store in an airtight container at room temperature for up to 2 days.

Orange and Cranberry Muffins

Packed full of tangy cranberries and drizzled in a sweet orange glaze, these soft and fluffy muffins will have your home smelling incredible.

¼ cup plus 3 tablespoons (100g) vegan buttery sticks

¼ cup plus 3 tablespoons (85g) superfine sugar

¼ cup (50g) packed light brown sugar

2 large eggs

1 teaspoon vanilla extract

¼ cup plus 2 tablespoons (100g) dairy-free plain yogurt

Zest of 1 large orange

1¼ cup (200g) gluten-free all-purpose flour

¼ teaspoon xanthan gum (omit if flour blend already contains this)

1 teaspoon baking soda

1 teaspoon baking powder

1 teaspoon ground cinnamon

¼ teaspoon salt

4 tablespoons orange juice, divided

1 tablespoon unsweetened almond or other dairy-free milk

1 cup frozen cranberries

¾ cup (110g) confectioners' sugar

MAKES 10

Per Serving (1 muffin):

Calories	255
Fat	9g
Sodium	326mg
Carbohydrates	41g
Fiber	3g
Sugar	26g
Protein	3g

1 Preheat oven to 375°F (190°C) and line a twelve-cup muffin tin with ten cupcake liners.

2 In a large bowl, beat buttery sticks, superfine sugar, and brown sugar together until creamy. Add eggs, vanilla, yogurt, and orange zest and beat until combined.

3 In a separate large bowl, combine flour, xanthan gum, baking soda, baking powder, cinnamon, and salt. Fold dry ingredients into wet ingredients. Mix in 2 tablespoons orange juice and milk and fold in cranberries.

4 Divide mixture between ten muffin cups. Bake 25 minutes or until a skewer inserted in center comes out clean. Leave muffins in tin to cool.

5 In a small bowl, make a glaze by mixing confectioners' sugar with remaining 2 tablespoons orange juice. Drizzle over muffins. Store in an airtight container at room temperature for up to 3 days.

Banana and Chocolate Swirl Muffins

These moist banana muffins topped with swirls of dairy-free vegan chocolate hazelnut spread are a delicious treat. They are best served warm and fresh from the oven.

2 medium-sized ripe bananas, peeled and mashed

1 large egg

¼ cup (55g) granulated sugar

¼ cup (50g) packed light brown sugar

¼ cup plus 2 tablespoons (80g) vegan buttery spread, melted

1¼ cups (200g) gluten-free all-purpose flour

1 teaspoon baking powder

1 teaspoon baking soda

¼ teaspoon xanthan gum (omit if flour blend already contains this)

¼ teaspoon salt

4 tablespoons dairy-free vegan chocolate hazelnut spread

1 Preheat oven to 350°F (180°C) and line a twelve-cup muffin tin with cupcake liners.

2 In a large bowl, whisk banana and egg. Add granulated sugar, brown sugar, and buttery spread. Beat until fully combined.

3 In a separate large bowl, stir together flour, baking powder, baking soda, xanthan gum, and salt. Add to banana mixture and mix well.

4 Divide mixture between twelve muffin cups and top each with 1 teaspoon chocolate hazelnut spread. Use a wooden skewer or thin knife to swirl spread.

5 Bake 20–25 minutes or until a skewer inserted in center comes out clean. Remove muffins from tin and cool slightly on a wire rack 5 minutes before serving.

6 Store in an airtight container at room temperature for up to 2 days.

MAKES 12

Per Serving (1 muffin):

Calories	182
Fat	8g
Sodium	256mg
Carbohydrates	26g
Fiber	2g
Sugar	15g
Protein	2g

BAKING WITH BANANAS

Never throw away overripe bananas! When it comes to baking with bananas, the riper the better, as the riper the banana, the sweeter the flavor. If you are tight on time, you can always freeze them in chunks to use for baking another day.

Baked Cinnamon Sugar Doughnuts

MAKES 12

Per Serving (1 doughnut):

Calories	171
Fat	6g
Sodium	221mg
Carbohydrates	28g
Fiber	0g
Sugar	18g
Protein	2g

DOUGHNUT TIN REPLACEMENT

This recipe requires a doughnut tin, which is easy to find for sale online. A cupcake tin also works well.

These quick doughnuts are baked in the oven instead of fried, but they still have the amazing texture of a fried doughnut—with a sweet cinnamon sugar coating.

¾ cup plus 3 tablespoons (150g) gluten-free self-rising flour

¼ teaspoon xanthan gum (omit if flour blend already contains this)

½ teaspoon baking powder

½ teaspoon salt

½ cup plus 1 tablespoon (110g) superfine sugar

½ cup (120ml) unsweetened almond or other dairy-free milk

2 large eggs

1½ tablespoons vegetable oil

1 teaspoon vanilla extract

½ cup (110g) granulated sugar

1 teaspoon ground cinnamon

¼ cup (55g) vegan buttery spread, melted

1 Preheat oven to 350°F (180°C) and grease a doughnut tin with oil or cooking spray.

2 In a large bowl, add flour, xanthan gum, baking powder, salt, and superfine sugar and mix well. In a medium bowl, whisk milk, eggs, oil, and vanilla. Add wet ingredients to dry ingredients and mix well.

3 Pour batter into prepared tin to fill each cavity to about three-quarters full. Bake 10–12 minutes until golden brown.

4 Remove from oven, let cool in tin 5 minutes, then remove from tin and leave to completely cool on a wire rack, about 30 minutes.

5 In a small bowl, make cinnamon sugar coating by mixing granulated sugar and cinnamon. Brush cooled doughnuts with melted buttery spread and dip into cinnamon sugar coating. Store in an airtight container at room temperature for up to 48 hours.

CHAPTER 3

Yeast Breads

Simple White Bread

This simple oven-baked bread is soft, delicious, and perfect for slicing for sandwiches. Serve warm and fresh from the oven.

SERVES 10

Per Serving:

Calories	228
Fat	6g
Sodium	262mg
Carbohydrates	37g
Fiber	5g
Sugar	3g
Protein	6g

1¼ cups plus 2 tablespoons (325ml) unsweetened almond or dairy-free milk

2 teaspoons instant yeast

2 tablespoons granulated sugar, divided

2½ cups plus 2 tablespoons (425g) gluten-free bread (or strong) flour blend

1½ teaspoons xanthan gum (omit if flour blend already contains this)

1 teaspoon baking powder

½ teaspoon salt

2 large eggs, lightly beaten

2 teaspoons apple cider vinegar

¼ cup (55g) vegan buttery spread, melted and cooled

1 Grease a 9" × 5" loaf pan with vegetable oil or cooking spray.

2 In a small microwave-safe bowl, heat milk in microwave on high to about 110°F (43°C). (This feels like warm bathwater to touch.) Add yeast and 1 tablespoon sugar, mix well, and set aside in a warm place for 10 minutes until frothy.

3 In a large bowl, combine flour, xanthan gum, baking powder, salt, and remaining 1 tablespoon sugar. Form a well in center of mixture and add eggs, vinegar, buttery spread, and yeast mixture. Transfer to a stand mixer fitted with a paddle attachment or use a wooden spoon to stir until mixture forms a thick, sticky dough.

4 Transfer mixture to prepared pan, cover with oiled plastic wrap, and set aside in a warm place for 30–45 minutes until dough has risen to about 150 percent of original size.

5 Preheat oven to 375°F (190°C).

6 Bake 50–60 minutes until bread is golden brown and sounds hollow when you tap it. Cool slightly in pan 10 minutes, then remove bread and serve warm or at room temperature.

Crumpets

You can't beat a homemade Crumpet, and these are fluffy, tasty, and well worth the effort. Serve toasted and spread with dairy-free butter for breakfast or a midmorning snack.

MAKES 12

Per Serving (1 crumpet):

Calories	92
Fat	1g
Sodium	216mg
Carbohydrates	19g
Fiber	1g
Sugar	1g
Protein	1g

HOMEMADE SELF-RISING FLOUR

If you can't find self-rising flour, you can make your own by adding 2 teaspoons of baking powder to every 1 cup (160g) of gluten-free all-purpose flour.

1¼ cups plus 3 tablespoons (350ml) unsweetened almond or other dairy-free milk

1 tablespoon instant yeast

2 teaspoons granulated sugar

1½ cups plus 3 tablespoons (275g) gluten-free self-rising flour

1 teaspoon xanthan gum (omit if flour blend already contains this)

½ teaspoon baking soda

¼ teaspoon salt

2 tablespoons lukewarm water

1 tablespoon vegetable oil, divided

1 In a medium microwave-safe bowl, heat milk in microwave on high to about 110°F (43°C). (This feels like warm bathwater to touch.) Add yeast and sugar, mix well, and leave in a warm place for 10 minutes until frothy.

2 In a large bowl, mix flour, xanthan gum, baking soda, and salt. Pour in frothy yeast mixture and mix well until lump-free. Cover with oiled plastic wrap and leave in a warm place for 90 minutes.

3 After 90 minutes, batter should have thickened slightly and will be frothy. Add water and stir thoroughly. Mixture should be runny enough to pour into frying pan and not too thick.

4 In a large frying pan, heat ½ tablespoon vegetable oil over medium heat. Grease crumpet rings or cookie cutters with remaining ½ tablespoon oil and place in pan. Pour about 2½ tablespoons crumpet mixture into each ring (crumpets won't cook completely if rings are overfilled). Leave 5–7 minutes without touching or moving rings until little bubbles form on surface.

5 Remove rings and flip crumpets over with a spatula. Bottom of crumpets should be golden brown and crispy. Cook an additional 1–2 minutes until golden brown on other side.

6 Serve warm or store in an airtight container at room temperature for up to 2 days and toast before eating.

Cinnamon and Raisin Bread

This sweet cinnamon and raisin loaf is delicious served fresh out the oven with dairy-free butter or jam.

1 cup plus 2 tablespoons (275ml) unsweetened almond or other dairy-free milk

2¼ teaspoons instant yeast

2 tablespoons granulated sugar, divided

2½ cups (400g) gluten-free bread (or strong) flour blend

2 teaspoons xanthan gum (add just 1 teaspoon if flour blend already contains this)

1 teaspoon baking powder

¼ teaspoon salt

2 teaspoons ground cinnamon

1 cup (150g) raisins

1 large egg, lightly beaten

1 teaspoon apple cider vinegar

3 tablespoons plus 1 teaspoon (50ml) vegetable oil

SERVES 10	
Per Serving:	
Calories	261
Fat	6g
Sodium	153mg
Carbohydrates	47g
Fiber	6g
Sugar	11g
Protein	6g

1 Grease a 2-pound loaf pan with vegetable oil or cooking spray.

2 In a medium microwave-safe bowl, heat milk in microwave on high to about 110°F (43°C). (This feels like warm bathwater to touch.) Add instant yeast and 1 tablespoon sugar, mix well, and leave in a warm place for 10 minutes until frothy.

3 In a large bowl, mix remaining 1 tablespoon sugar, flour, xanthan gum, baking powder, salt, cinnamon, and raisins. Add egg, vinegar, oil, and frothy yeast mixture. Transfer to a stand mixer fitted with a paddle attachment or use a wooden spoon to mix well until a thick and sticky dough forms.

4 Transfer dough to prepared pan and smooth top with a knife. Cover with oiled plastic wrap and leave in a warm place for about 1 hour or until loaf is about 150 percent of original size.

5 Preheat oven to 400°F (200°C) and bake loaf 40–45 minutes until golden brown and cooked through. Serve warm.

Cinnamon Buns

MAKES 10

Per Serving (1 bun):

Calories	342
Fat	9g
Sodium	268mg
Carbohydrates	61g
Fiber	5g
Sugar	28g
Protein	5g

These fluffy and delicious buns are filled with cinnamon sugar and topped with an iced drizzle. This recipe does take a little bit more time to make than some of the other recipes in this book, but it's so worth it!

BUNS

¾ cup (175ml) unsweetened almond or other dairy-free milk

2¼ teaspoons instant yeast

¼ cup plus 3 tablespoons (85g) granulated sugar, divided

1 large egg, lightly beaten

¼ cup (55g) vegan buttery spread, melted

2½ cups (400g) gluten-free bread (or strong) flour blend

1½ teaspoons xanthan gum (omit if flour blend already contains this)

2 teaspoons baking powder

¼ teaspoon salt

FILLING

3 tablespoons (45g) vegan buttery spread, melted and divided

¼ cup plus 3 tablespoons (90g) packed light brown sugar

2 teaspoons ground cinnamon

TOPPING

¾ cup (110g) confectioners' sugar

1 tablespoon boiling water

BUNS

1 In a large microwave-safe bowl, heat milk in microwave on high to about 110°F (43°C). (This feels like warm bathwater to touch.) Add yeast and 2 teaspoons granulated sugar. Mix well and leave in a warm place for 10 minutes until frothy.

2 Add egg, melted buttery spread, and remaining granulated sugar to frothy mixture. Mix until combined.

3 Stir in flour, xanthan gum, baking powder, and salt and mix well to form a sticky but elastic dough that pulls away from side of bowl (if dough is too sticky, add extra flour). Form into a rough ball and place in a separate large, well-oiled bowl. Cover with oiled plastic wrap and leave in a warm place for 1 hour.

4 Transfer dough to a lightly floured surface and roll out into a rectangle about ¼" thick.

FILLING

1 Brush dough rectangle with 2 tablespoons melted buttery spread. In a small bowl, mix brown sugar and cinnamon and spread evenly over buttery spread.

2 Carefully roll up dough lengthwise to form a log. Cut into ten equal rolls and place on a baking sheet lined with parchment paper. Leave in a warm place for 30 minutes.

3 Preheat oven to 350°F (180°C). Brush Buns with remaining 1 tablespoon melted buttery spread and bake 25 minutes until golden brown. Remove from oven and let cool on baking sheet.

TOPPING

In a small bowl, combine confectioners' sugar and boiling water. Drizzle over Buns. Serve immediately or store in an airtight container at room temperature for up to 2 days. Heat in microwave on high for 20 seconds before eating.

Sticky Maple and Pecan Buns

MAKES 10

Per Serving (1 bun):

Calories	495
Fat	23g
Sodium	308mg
Carbohydrates	66g
Fiber	7g
Sugar	31g
Protein	6g

These sweet and sticky maple pecan buns are the perfect treat, full of buttery cinnamon sugar and topped with a sticky caramel sauce and toasted pecans.

BUNS

¾ cup (175ml) unsweetened almond or other dairy-free milk

2¼ teaspoons instant yeast

¼ cup plus 3 tablespoons (85g) granulated sugar, divided

1 large egg, lightly beaten

¼ cup (55g) vegan buttery spread, melted

2½ cups (400g) gluten-free bread (or strong) flour blend

1½ teaspoons xanthan gum (omit if flour blend already contains this)

2 teaspoons baking powder

¼ teaspoon salt

FILLING

¼ cup plus 2 tablespoons (75g) packed light brown sugar

2 teaspoons ground cinnamon

¾ cup (75g) pecans

3 tablespoons (40g) vegan buttery spread, melted

TOPPING

3 tablespoons plus 2 teaspoons (50g) vegan buttery spread

½ cup (125ml) pure maple syrup

¼ cup (50g) packed light brown sugar

¾ cup (75g) pecans

BUNS

1 In a large microwave-safe bowl, heat milk in microwave on high to about 110°F (43°C). (This feels like warm bathwater to touch.) Add yeast and 2 teaspoons sugar, mix well, and leave in a warm place for 10 minutes until frothy.

2 Add egg, melted buttery spread, and remaining sugar to frothy mixture. Mix until combined.

3 Stir in flour, xanthan gum, baking powder, and salt and mix well to form a sticky but elastic dough that pulls away from side of bowl (if dough is too sticky, add extra flour). Form into a rough ball and place in a large, well-oiled bowl. Cover with oiled plastic wrap and leave in a warm place for 1 hour.

FILLING

1 In a food processor, pulse brown sugar, cinnamon, and pecans until combined. Set aside for 1 hour. Transfer dough to a lightly floured surface and roll out to a rectangle about ¼" thick. Brush with melted buttery spread and sprinkle evenly with Filling.
2 Carefully roll up dough lengthwise into a log. Cut into ten equal rolls.

TOPPING

In a small saucepan, heat buttery spread, maple syrup, and brown sugar over medium heat until melted and smooth, about 2–3 minutes.

ASSEMBLY

1 Pour Topping into a 9" baking dish so bottom of dish is coated and sprinkle with pecans. Place Buns on top of Topping in dish with a ¾" gap between each Bun. Cover with oiled plastic wrap and leave in a warm place for 30 minutes.
2 Preheat oven to 350°F (180°C). Bake Buns 25 minutes until golden brown.
3 Remove from oven and let cool in pan 10 minutes. Serve immediately or store in an airtight container at room temperature for up to 2 days. Heat in microwave on high for 20 seconds before eating.

Bagels

TOP TIP

Different brands of gluten-free flour can work in different ways. If the dough is too sticky when mixing, you may need to add a little more flour. Alternatively, if the dough is too firm, you may need to add a little more water. The ideal texture is a sticky but firm dough that can be molded into balls.

These soft and chewy homemade Bagels can be easily customized with your favorite toppings and fillings, such as cinnamon and raisins or sesame seeds.

BAGELS

1¼ cups plus 3 tablespoons (350ml) water

2 teaspoons instant yeast

2 teaspoons granulated sugar

3 cups plus 2 tablespoons (500g) gluten-free bread (or strong) flour blend

1½ teaspoons xanthan gum (omit if flour blend already contains this)

2 teaspoons baking powder

1 teaspoon salt

1 teaspoon apple cider vinegar

¼ cup plus 2 tablespoons (85g) vegan buttery spread, melted and cooled

1 large egg, beaten

WATER BATH

12 cups water

2 tablespoons honey

BAGELS

1   In a medium microwave-safe bowl, heat water in microwave on high to about 110°F (43°C). (This feels like warm bathwater to touch.) Add yeast and sugar, mix well, and leave in a warm place for 10 minutes until frothy.

2   In a large bowl, combine flour, xanthan gum, baking powder, and salt. Make a well in center and add vinegar, melted buttery spread, and frothy yeast mixture. Transfer to a stand mixer fitted with a paddle attachment or use a wooden spoon to mix well until a thick, sticky dough forms. Cover bowl with oiled plastic wrap and leave in a warm place for 30 minutes.

3   Turn out dough onto a lightly floured surface, knead until smooth, and divide into eight equal pieces. Roll each piece into a ball and use your fingers to gently press through center to form a hole. Evenly space balls on a baking sheet lined with parchment paper, cover with oiled plastic wrap, and leave in a warm place for 15 minutes.

WATER BATH

1 Preheat oven to 400°F (200°C). In a medium saucepan, add water and honey and bring to a boil over high heat, then reduce to medium heat.

2 Carefully drop bagels into water bath one at a time. Boil 30 seconds, flip with a pair of tongs, and boil another 30 seconds. Remove with a slotted spoon and return to baking sheet.

3 Brush Bagels with egg and bake 25 minutes until tops are golden and Bagels are cooked through. Remove from oven and let cool on baking sheet for 10 minutes before slicing and serving warm. Store in an airtight container at room temperature up to 2 days and reheat before eating.

Rosemary Focaccia

This simple Italian classic topped with fresh rosemary is delicious served on its own, dipped in extra-virgin olive oil, or served as a side dish to your favorite meal.

1¼ cups plus 3 tablespoons (350ml) water

2¼ teaspoons instant yeast

1 tablespoon granulated sugar

2 cups plus 3 tablespoons (350g) gluten-free bread (or strong) flour blend

1 teaspoon xanthan gum (omit if flour blend already contains this)

1½ teaspoons baking powder

½ teaspoon sea salt, divided

3 tablespoons extra-virgin olive oil, divided

¼ teaspoon ground black pepper

1 tablespoon finely chopped fresh rosemary

SERVES 12

Per Serving:

Calories	135
Fat	3g
Sodium	137mg
Carbohydrates	24g
Fiber	4g
Sugar	1g
Protein	3g

1 In a small microwave-safe bowl, heat water in microwave on high to about 110°F (43°C). (This feels like warm bathwater to touch.) Add yeast and sugar, mix well, and set aside in a warm place for 10 minutes until frothy.

2 In a large bowl, combine flour, xanthan gum, baking powder, and ¼ teaspoon salt. Make a well in center and add yeast mixture and 2 table-spoons oil. Mix well until combined (dough will be more like a batter at this point). Cover bowl with oiled plastic wrap and set aside in a warm place for 1 hour.

3 Preheat oven to 400°F (200°C) and line a rimmed baking sheet with parchment paper and drizzle paper with remaining 1 tablespoon oil.

4 Transfer dough to prepared baking sheet and use your fingers to gently press out to a rectangular shape, about 1" thick. Press dimples into dough. Sprinkle with remaining ¼ teaspoon salt, pepper, and rosemary.

5 Bake for 20–25 minutes until golden brown. Serve warm.

Garlic and Herb Naan-Style Bread

SERVES 6

Per Serving (1 naan):

Calories	251
Fat	11g
Sodium	311mg
Carbohydrates	35g
Fiber	5g
Sugar	4g
Protein	5g

This easy-to-make naan-style bread is perfect served with your favorite Indian dish. Brushed with a dairy-free garlic and herb butter, it will quickly become a staple recipe in your household!

NAAN

½ cup (120ml) water

1 teaspoon instant yeast

2 teaspoons granulated sugar

1½ cups plus 3 tablespoons (275g) gluten-free all-purpose flour

1 teaspoon xanthan gum (omit if flour blend already contains this)

½ teaspoon baking powder

½ teaspoon salt

2 tablespoons (30g) vegan buttery spread, melted

½ cup (125ml) dairy-free plain yogurt

3 teaspoons vegetable oil, for frying

TOPPING

2 tablespoons vegan buttery spread, melted

1 teaspoon Italian seasoning

¼ teaspoon garlic granules

NAAN

1 In a medium microwave-safe bowl, heat water in microwave on high to about 110°F (43°C). (This feels like warm bathwater to touch.) Add yeast and sugar, mix well, and leave in a warm place for 10 minutes until frothy.

2 In a large bowl, mix flour, xanthan gum, baking powder, and salt. Make a well in center and pour in melted buttery spread, yogurt, and frothy yeast mixture.

3 Using your hands, mix well to form a soft dough that comes together in a sticky ball (if dough is too wet add a little extra flour ¼ teaspoon at a time). Cover bowl with oiled plastic wrap and leave in a warm place 1 hour.

4 Turn out dough onto a lightly floured surface and sprinkle a little flour on top. Divide into six pieces and roll out each piece with a floured rolling pin to form a teardrop shape.

5 In a large frying pan, heat 1 teaspoon vegetable oil over medium heat and fry naan two pieces at a time, 3 minutes on each side. Transfer fried naan to a large plate.

TOPPING

In a small bowl, mix melted buttery spread with Italian seasoning and garlic granules. Brush top of bread with Topping. Serve warm.

Herby Flat Breads

These naturally vegan Herby Flat Breads are the perfect accompaniment to any Middle Eastern meal. Serve warm and straight from the pan.

½ cup (120ml) water

1 teaspoon instant yeast

2 teaspoons granulated sugar

1½ cups plus 3 tablespoons (275g) gluten-free all-purpose flour

1 teaspoon xanthan gum (omit if flour blend already contains this)

½ teaspoon baking powder

½ teaspoon salt

2 tablespoons (30g) vegan buttery spread, melted

½ cup (125ml) dairy-free plain yogurt

3 tablespoons finely chopped fresh parsley

⅛ teaspoon ground black pepper

3 teaspoons vegetable oil, for frying

SERVES 6

Per Serving (1 flat bread):

Calories	218
Fat	7g
Sodium	277mg
Carbohydrates	35g
Fiber	5g
Sugar	4g
Protein	5g

1 In a medium microwave-safe bowl, heat water in microwave on high to about 110°F (43°C). (This feels like warm bathwater to touch.) Add yeast and sugar, mix well, and leave in a warm place for 10 minutes until frothy.

2 In a large bowl, mix together flour, xanthan gum, baking powder, and salt. Make a well in center and pour in melted buttery spread, yogurt, and frothy yeast mixture. Add parsley and pepper.

3 Using your hands, mix well to form a soft dough that comes together in a sticky ball (if dough is too wet add a little extra flour ¼ teaspoon at a time). Cover bowl with oiled plastic wrap and leave in a warm place for 1 hour.

4 Turn out dough onto a lightly floured surface and sprinkle a little flour on top. Divide into six pieces and roll each piece out with a floured rolling pin to form a teardrop shape.

5 In a large frying pan, heat 1 teaspoon vegetable oil over medium heat and fry flat bread two pieces at a time, 3 minutes on each side. Transfer fried flat breads to a large plate. Serve warm.

Fried Doughnut Rings

MAKES 12

Per Serving (1 doughnut ring):

Calories	275
Fat	12g
Sodium	241mg
Carbohydrates	39g
Fiber	4g
Sugar	12g
Protein	4g

Is there anything better than the taste and smell of fresh, warm doughnuts fried and coated in a layer of sugar? These are a real treat!

¾ cup (180ml) unsweetened almond or other dairy-free milk

2 teaspoons instant yeast

½ cup plus 6 teaspoons (145g) granulated sugar, divided

2½ cups (400g) gluten-free bread (or strong) flour blend

½ teaspoon xanthan gum (omit if flour blend already contains this)

2 teaspoons baking powder

½ teaspoon salt

¼ cup (55g) vegan buttery spread, melted

1 large egg, lightly beaten

Vegetable oil, for frying

1 In a medium microwave-safe bowl, heat milk in microwave on high to about 110°F (43°C). (This feels like warm bathwater to touch.) Add yeast and 2 teaspoons sugar, mix well, and leave in a warm place for 10 minutes until frothy.

2 In a large bowl, combine ¼ cup plus 4 teaspoons sugar, flour, xanthan gum, baking powder, and salt. Make a well in center and add melted buttery spread, egg, and frothy yeast mixture. Transfer to a stand mixer fitted with a paddle attachment or use a wooden spoon to mix well until a thick and sticky dough forms. Cover bowl with oiled plastic wrap and leave in a warm place for about 1 hour or until dough is doubled in size.

3 Turn out dough onto a lightly floured surface and roll out to about ½" thick. Using a cookie cutter or the bottom of a round drinking glass, cut ring shapes out of dough and cut smaller rings out of centers. Carefully place rings on a baking sheet lined with parchment paper, cover with oiled plastic wrap, and leave in a warm place for 1 hour.

4 In a medium saucepan, pour oil to about two-thirds full. Heat over high heat until oil reaches 320°F (160°C) and carefully place doughnut rings two at a time in oil. Fry on one side 2–3 minutes until golden brown, flip with a slotted spoon, and fry an additional 2–3 minutes until other side is golden brown and middle is cooked through.

5 Carefully remove fried doughnuts from oil with a slotted spoon onto a large piece of paper towel. While doughnuts are still warm, coat in remaining ¼ cup sugar. Serve warm.

Fried Jam Doughnuts

These fresh Fried Jam Doughnuts are filled with delicious raspberry jam—a treat everyone will love.

¾ cup (180ml) unsweetened almond or other dairy-free milk

2 teaspoons instant yeast

½ cup plus 6 teaspoons (145g) granulated sugar, divided

2½ cups (400g) gluten-free bread (or strong) flour blend

½ teaspoon xanthan gum (omit if flour blend already contains this)

2 teaspoons baking powder

½ teaspoon salt

¼ cup (55g) vegan buttery spread, melted

1 large egg, lightly beaten

Vegetable oil, for frying

12 tablespoons raspberry Jam

MAKES 12

Per Serving (1 doughnut):

Calories	327
Fat	11g
Sodium	248mg
Carbohydrates	52g
Fiber	4g
Sugar	22g
Protein	4g

1 In a medium microwave-safe bowl, heat milk in microwave on high to about 110°F (43°C). (This feels like warm bathwater to touch.) Add yeast and 2 teaspoons sugar, mix well, and leave in a warm place for 10 minutes until frothy.

2 In a large bowl, combine ¼ cup plus 4 teaspoons sugar, flour, xanthan gum, baking powder, and salt. Make a well in center and add melted buttery spread, egg, and frothy yeast mixture. Transfer to a stand mixer fitted with a paddle attachment or use a wooden spoon to mix well until a thick and sticky dough forms. Cover bowl with oiled plastic wrap and leave in a warm place for about 1 hour or until dough is doubled in size.

3 Turn out dough onto a lightly floured surface and roll out to about ½" thick. Using a cookie cutter or bottom of a round drinking glass cut circular shapes out of dough and carefully place shapes onto a lined baking sheet. Cover with oiled plastic wrap and leave in a warm place for 1 hour.

4 In a medium saucepan, pour oil to about two-thirds full. Heat over high heat to 320°F (160°C), then carefully place doughnuts two at a time into oil. Fry on one side 3–4 minutes until golden brown, flip with a slotted spoon, and fry an additional 3–4 minutes until golden brown on other side and middle is cooked through. Carefully remove doughnuts from oil with a slotted spoon onto a large piece of paper towel.

5 While doughnuts are still warm, coat in remaining ¼ cup sugar. Using a piping nozzle, pipe jam into center of doughnuts. Serve warm.

Hot Cross Buns

Per Serving (1 bun):

Calories	405
Fat	10g
Sodium	310mg
Carbohydrates	71g
Fiber	8g
Sugar	20g
Protein	9g

These perfectly spiced Hot Cross Buns are packed with cinnamon and raisins and make a delicious breakfast or snack. Top them with dairy-free butter for extra decadence.

BUNS

¾ cup plus 1 tablespoon (200ml) unsweetened almond or other dairy-free milk

Zest of 1 medium orange

2 tablespoons plus 2 teaspoons (35g) vegan buttery spread

1 large egg

1 tablespoon extra-virgin olive oil

¼ cup plus 1 tablespoon (60g) sugar

2 cups plus 3 tablespoons (350g) gluten-free bread (or strong) flour blend

1 teaspoon xanthan gum (omit if flour blend already contains this)

2 teaspoons instant yeast

½ teaspoon salt

1 teaspoon ground cinnamon

½ cup plus 3 tablespoons (100g) raisins

TOPPING

1 large egg, beaten

1 tablespoon gluten-free all-purpose flour

1 tablespoon water

BUNS

1 In a medium saucepan, heat milk, orange zest, and buttery spread over medium heat until buttery spread is melted and bubbles appear around edge of saucepan, about 4–5 minutes. Remove from heat.

2 In a small bowl, beat egg and oil. In a medium bowl, mix sugar, flour, xanthan gum, yeast, salt, cinnamon, and raisins. Pour milk mixture and egg mixture into dry ingredients and mix well to form a thick dough.

3 Line a baking sheet with parchment paper and grease paper with oil or cooking spray. Divide dough into six balls and place balls onto prepared baking sheet. Cover with oiled plastic wrap. Leave in warm place for 1 hour.

TOPPING

1 Preheat oven to 350°F (180°C) and brush Buns with egg. In a small bowl, mix flour with water to form a paste. Spoon paste into a piping bag and pipe a cross shape over top of each Bun.

2 Bake 25 minutes or until golden brown and cooked through. Serve warm and straight from oven.

Dinner Rolls

These soft, fluffy, easy-to-make Dinner Rolls are a perfect addition to any meal! You'll never need to buy rolls again. Serve warm and straight from the oven.

1 cup plus 2 tablespoons (275ml) unsweetened almond or other dairy-free milk

2 teaspoons instant yeast

2 teaspoons plus 2 tablespoons granulated sugar, divided

2¾ cups plus 1 tablespoon (450g) gluten-free bread (or strong) flour blend

1½ teaspoons xanthan gum (omit if flour blend already contains this)

½ teaspoon salt

2 large eggs, lightly beaten

1 teaspoon apple cider vinegar

3 tablespoons plus 2 teaspoons (50g) vegan buttery sticks, melted, plus 1 tablespoon for brushing

1 In a medium microwave-safe bowl, heat milk in microwave on high to about 110°F (43°C). (This feels like warm bathwater to touch.) Add yeast and 2 teaspoons sugar, mix well, and leave in a warm place for 10 minutes until frothy.

2 In a large bowl, combine flour, xanthan gum, remaining 2 tablespoons sugar, and salt. Make a well in center and add eggs, vinegar, 3 tablespoons plus 2 teaspoons melted buttery sticks, and frothy yeast mixture. Transfer to a stand mixture fitted with a paddle attachment or use a wooden spoon to mix well to form a thick, sticky dough.

3 Grease two 7" cake pans with vegetable oil or cooking spray. Using an ice cream scoop, scoop five balls of dough into each cake pan, making sure to space them apart. Cover with oiled plastic wrap and leave in a warm place for 1 hour.

4 Preheat oven to 400°F (200°C). Brush rolls with remaining 1 tablespoon melted buttery sticks and bake 25 minutes or until golden brown and cooked through. Serve fresh from oven.

MAKES 10

Per Serving (1 roll):

Calories	247
Fat	7g
Sodium	217mg
Carbohydrates	39g
Fiber	5g
Sugar	3g
Protein	6g

SCOOPING STICKY DOUGH

Running the ice cream scoop under cold water prior to scooping out each ball of dough will help with sticking.

English Breakfast Muffins

These traditional English Breakfast Muffins taste just like the real thing! They are dusted in cornmeal and taste perfect served with dairy-free butter or jam.

¾ cup plus 1 tablespoon (200ml) unsweetened almond or other dairy-free milk

2 teaspoons instant yeast

2 teaspoons granulated sugar

1½ cups plus 1 tablespoon (250g) gluten-free bread (or strong) flour blend

1 teaspoon xanthan gum (omit if flour blend already contains this)

1 teaspoon baking powder

¼ teaspoon salt

2 tablespoons (30g) buttery spread, melted and cooled

2 large eggs, lightly beaten

3 teaspoons vegetable oil

4 teaspoons cornmeal

1 In a medium microwave-safe bowl, heat milk in microwave on high to about 110°F (43°C). (This feels like warm bathwater to touch.) Add yeast and sugar, mix well, and leave in a warm place for 10 minutes until frothy.

2 In a large bowl, combine flour, xanthan gum, baking powder, and salt and mix well. Add buttery spread, eggs, and frothy yeast mixture and beat well until fully combined and a thick, sticky batter is formed. Cover with oiled plastic wrap and leave in a warm place for 1 hour.

3 In a large frying pan, heat 1 teaspoon oil over medium-low heat. Grease egg rings with oil and place rings in pan. Sprinkle ½ teaspoon cornmeal into each ring and spoon batter into rings to about three-quarters full (muffins won't cook through if rings are overfilled). Cook 8 minutes until golden brown. Sprinkle tops of muffins with more cornmeal, flip with a spatula, and cook another 6–8 minutes until golden brown on the other side and cooked through.

4 Use tongs to remove rings and cook muffins 1 minute. Serve warm or store in an airtight container at room temperature for up to 2 days and reheat before eating.

CHAPTER 4

Savory Pies and Pizzas

Savory Pastry Crust

SERVES 8

Per Serving:

Calories	279
Fat	19g
Sodium	249mg
Carbohydrates	25g
Fiber	4g
Sugar	1g
Protein	4g

This pastry recipe is flaky and buttery and is a great base to lots of savory pies and tarts. You'll be surprised at how easy it is to make and how versatile it is!

1¾ cups plus 2 tablespoons (300g) gluten-free all-purpose flour

1½ teaspoons xanthan gum (omit if flour blend already contains this)

¼ teaspoon salt

¾ cup plus 1 tablespoon (175g) cubed and cold dairy-free vegan buttery sticks

1 large egg

3–4 tablespoons water

1 In a large bowl, add flour, xanthan gum, and salt. Mix well.
2 Add buttery sticks, using a fork to cut into flour until mixture resembles bread crumbs. Stir in egg.
3 Add cold water 1 tablespoon at a time and mix well until mixture starts to form a smooth dough.
4 Turn out dough onto a lightly floured surface and knead until smooth. Wrap dough in plastic wrap and refrigerate for at least 1 hour before using.

Garlic Pizza Bread

MAKES 2

Per Serving (1 pizza bread):

Calories	886
Fat	41g
Sodium	898mg
Carbohydrates	123g
Fiber	20g
Sugar	9g
Protein	17g

This recipe makes a delicious pizza base that is topped with dairy-free garlic butter. Serve as an accompaniment to your favorite dinner or on its own as an appetizer.

Easy Pizza Base dough (see recipe in this chapter)

1 teaspoon extra-virgin olive oil

¼ cup (60g) vegan buttery spread, melted

½ teaspoon garlic granules

1 teaspoon Italian seasoning

1 Preheat oven to 410°F (210°C) at least half an hour prior to cooking pizza. Divide dough into two pieces. Set one piece aside for later (dough can be stored in refrigerator for up to 48 hours) and use a floured rolling pin to roll out other half into a thin crust on a large piece of parchment paper sprinkled with flour. Brush edges of crust with oil.
2 Bake crust on parchment paper about 8 minutes.
3 While crust is baking, in a small bowl, mix melted buttery spread with garlic granules and Italian seasoning.
4 Remove crust from oven and spoon on garlic butter. Bake crust another 8 minutes and serve warm.

Cheese, Tomato, and Basil Quiche

This quiche combines simple yet tasty flavors and is perfect as a summertime dinner in the garden, served with a green salad and new potatoes.

1 batch Savory Pastry Crust (see recipe in this chapter)

1 cup small halved plum tomatoes

1 tablespoon extra-virgin olive oil

¼ teaspoon salt, divided

¼ teaspoon ground black pepper, divided

2 tablespoons torn basil leaves, divided

3 large eggs

½ cup plus 2 tablespoons (150ml) unsweetened almond or other dairy-free milk

1¼ cups (100g) grated dairy-free Cheddar cheese alternative

1 Preheat oven to 350°F (180°C) and grease a 9" round springform quiche dish with vegetable oil.

2 Roll out pastry on a lightly floured surface to slightly larger than quiche dish. Carefully line dish with rolled-out pastry and trim excess pastry from edges. Prick base with a fork.

3 Place parchment paper or foil tightly against crust and fill with pastry weights or baking beans. Blind bake crust 10 minutes. Remove paper and weights and bake another 5 minutes. Remove from oven and set aside.

4 Place tomatoes on a baking sheet, drizzle with oil, and top with half salt, half pepper, and half basil leaves. Bake 10 minutes. Remove from oven and leave oven on.

5 In a medium bowl, beat eggs and whisk in milk and remaining salt and pepper. Evenly spread tomato mixture and cheese over pastry base. Pour milk and egg mixture over top and bake 20–25 minutes on middle rack until golden brown.

6 Remove from oven and let cool in dish completely, about 1 hour. Serve topped with remaining 1 tablespoon basil leaves. Cover and store any leftovers in refrigerator for up to 2 days.

Easy Pizza Base

MAKES 2

Per Serving (1 pizza base):

Calories	712
Fat	19g
Sodium	2,178mg
Carbohydrates	132g
Fiber	22g
Sugar	15g
Protein	18g

You'll never need to buy a ready-made pizza crust again! Top the pizza with dairy-free cheese and your favorite toppings.

PIZZA BASE

1 cup plus 1 tablespoon (250ml) water

2¼ teaspoons instant yeast

2 teaspoons granulated sugar

2 cups plus 3 tablespoons (350g) gluten-free all-purpose flour

1½ teaspoons xanthan gum (omit if flour blend already contains this)

½ teaspoon salt

1 tablespoon plus 1 teaspoon (20g) vegan buttery spread, melted

1 teaspoon extra-virgin olive oil

PIZZA SAUCE

1 teaspoon extra-virgin olive oil

2 cloves garlic, peeled and finely chopped

1 cup (225g) tomato passata

1 teaspoon dried oregano

1 teaspoon Italian seasoning

⅛ teaspoon salt

⅛ teaspoon ground black pepper

PIZZA BASE

1 In a medium microwave-safe bowl, heat water in microwave on high to 110°F (43°C). (This feels like warm bathwater to touch.) Stir in yeast and sugar and leave in a warm place for 10 minutes until frothy.

2 In a large bowl, combine flour, xanthan gum, and salt. Make a well in center and pour in buttery spread and frothy yeast mixture. Mix well until a soft and sticky dough forms.

3 Transfer dough to a large oiled bowl, cover with oiled plastic wrap, and leave in a warm place for 1 hour. Chill in refrigerator 30 minutes.

4 Preheat oven to 410°F (210°C) at least half an hour prior to cooking pizza. Place dough on a lightly floured surface and sprinkle extra flour on top. Knead dough until smooth and divide into two pieces. Set one piece of dough aside for later (dough can be stored in refrigerator up to 48 hours) and use a floured rolling pin to roll out remaining half into a thin crust on a large piece of parchment paper sprinkled with flour. Brush edges of crust with oil.

5 Bake crust on parchment paper 8 minutes.

PIZZA SAUCE

1 In a small saucepan, heat oil over medium heat 1 minute. Add garlic and fry about 2 minutes until fragrant. Add tomato passata, oregano, Italian seasoning, salt, and pepper. Simmer 5 minutes.

2 Top cooked Pizza Base with Pizza Sauce. Bake another 8 minutes and serve warm.

Smoky Bacon and Leek Quiche

A delicious summertime treat that can be served for lunch, dinner, or as part of a picnic. This quiche recipe is easily adaptable, depending on what ingredients you have in the refrigerator.

1 batch Savory Pastry Crust (see recipe in this chapter)

2 medium leeks, sliced

1 cup (150g) smoked bacon lardons

1 tablespoon plus 1 teaspoon (20g) vegan buttery spread

3 large eggs

½ cup plus 2 tablespoons (150ml) unsweetened almond or other dairy-free milk

¼ cup fresh basil leaves, divided

⅛ teaspoon salt

⅛ teaspoon ground black pepper

1 cup small halved plum tomatoes

SERVES 6

Per Serving:

Calories	529
Fat	37g
Sodium	676mg
Carbohydrates	39g
Fiber	6g
Sugar	4g
Protein	13g

TOP TIP

Make sure the quiche is fully cooled before cutting and eating; this will ensure it is set.

1 Preheat oven to 350°F (180°C) and grease a 9" round springform quiche dish with vegetable oil.

2 Remove pastry from refrigerator and roll out on a lightly floured surface to slightly larger than quiche dish. Carefully line dish with rolled-out pastry and trim excess pastry from edges. Prick base with a fork.

3 Place parchment paper or foil tightly against crust and fill with pastry weights or baking beans. Blind bake for 10 minutes. Remove paper and weights and bake another 5 minutes. Remove from oven and set aside. Leave oven on.

4 While pastry bakes, in a medium pan, sauté leeks and bacon lardons in buttery spread over low heat until soft, about 5 minutes, stirring regularly to make sure they cook evenly.

5 In a medium bowl, beat eggs and whisk in milk, half basil leaves, salt, and pepper. Spread leek, bacon mixture, and tomatoes over pastry base evenly. Pour milk and egg mixture over top.

6 Bake 20–25 minutes in center of oven until golden brown.

7 Remove from oven and let cool in dish completely, about 1 hour. Top with remaining basil leaves and serve, or cover and store in refrigerator for up to 2 days.

Vegetarian Pesto and Roasted Vegetable Tart

An easy and tasty rustic-looking open tart, this recipe is filled with tomato pesto, roasted vegetables, and a dairy-free feta cheese alternative. It's a savory dish that you can serve for lunch or dinner.

ZUCCHINI VERSUS COURGETTE

Zucchini and courgette are actually the exact same ingredient: "Zucchini" is generally the name used in the US, and "courgette" is the name used in the UK.

1 batch Savory Pastry Crust (see recipe in this chapter)
3 tablespoons dairy-free sundried tomato pesto
5 cherry tomatoes, halved
1 medium zucchini, trimmed and thinly sliced
1 large yellow bell pepper, seeded and thinly sliced
½ cup (75g) cubed dairy-free feta cheese alternative
1 large egg, beaten

1 Preheat oven to 375°F (190°C) and line a baking sheet with parchment paper.
2 Roll out pastry dough on a lightly floured surface into an oval shape. Transfer oval to prepared baking sheet.
3 With a sharp knife, lightly score a line about 1" from edge of oval. Spread pesto inside line, then top with tomato, zucchini, and bell pepper. Sprinkle feta cubes on top of vegetables.
4 Fold edges of pastry to slightly cover filling, leaving a large open space in center. Brush pastry with egg and bake 40–45 minutes until golden brown and cooked through. Serve warm.

Leek and Mushroom Pie

SERVES 4

Per Serving:

Calories	749
Fat	48g
Sodium	740mg
Carbohydrates	72g
Fiber	12g
Sugar	9g
Protein	16g

A creamy vegetarian pie full of leeks and mushrooms, this dish is delicious served on a cold evening with potatoes and vegetables—the ultimate comfort food.

1 teaspoon extra-virgin olive oil

1 medium white onion, peeled and diced

2 cloves garlic, peeled and crushed

3 medium leeks, sliced

1 pound (450g) sliced white button mushrooms

⅛ teaspoon salt

⅛ teaspoon ground black pepper

1 teaspoon Italian seasoning

1 teaspoon fresh thyme leaves

2 tablespoons (30g) vegan buttery spread

3 tablespoons (30g) gluten-free all-purpose flour

1½ cups plus 3 tablespoons (400ml) unsweetened almond or other dairy-free milk

¼ teaspoon ground nutmeg

1 batch Savory Pastry Crust (see recipe in this chapter)

1 large egg, beaten

1 In a large frying pan, heat oil over high heat. Add onion and garlic and fry until translucent, about 10 minutes. Add leeks and fry another 2 minutes, then add mushrooms, salt, pepper, Italian seasoning, and thyme and cook another 5 minutes.

2 In a small saucepan, heat buttery spread and flour over medium heat. Whisk until combined, then slowly add milk, whisking until a smooth mixture forms. Continue to mix until mixture starts to thicken. Stir in nutmeg and pour milk mixture over leek and mushroom mixture and set aside.

3 Preheat oven to 350°F (180°C) and grease a 9" oblong pie dish with vegetable oil.

4 Remove pastry from refrigerator. Cut off one-third of pastry (for topping) and set aside. Roll out remaining pastry on a lightly floured surface to slightly larger than pie dish. Carefully line dish with rolled-out pastry and trim excess pastry from edges. Prick base with a fork. Spoon filling into pie shell, then roll out remaining dough for top. Brush pie rim with a little water, then drape pastry lid over top. Seal edges and crimp with a fork. Cut three slits in top of pie for steam to escape and brush with egg.

5 Bake 45 minutes. Set aside 10 minutes before serving warm.

Sausage, Sage, and Onion Braid

A delicious crowd-pleasing dish filled with the flavors of sage, onion, and sausages. This sausage braid is great as part of a picnic or a buffet spread or as a tasty lunch or dinner. It may look complicated, but it's actually really quick and easy to make!

1 teaspoon vegan buttery spread

½ medium white onion, peeled and diced

6 pork sausages, cases removed

1 teaspoon dried sage

⅛ teaspoon salt

⅛ teaspoon ground black pepper

1 batch Savory Pastry Crust (see recipe in this chapter)

1 large egg, beaten

1 Preheat oven to 350°F (180°C).

2 In a small saucepan, melt buttery spread, then add onion and fry until translucent, about 5 minutes.

3 In a large bowl, mix onion mixture, sausages, sage, salt, and pepper.

4 Remove pastry from refrigerator and roll out on a lightly floured surface into a rectangle shape about ¼" thick. Add sausage and onion mix in a strip to middle of pastry and cut rectangular pieces from each corner of pastry. This will leave a piece of pastry on either end of the braid to tuck over sausage mixture. Cut horizontal strips across edges of pastry and create a braid with alternate strips of pastry from either side of mixture.

5 Once braided, place on a baking sheet lined with parchment paper and brush with egg. Cook 50 minutes until pastry is golden brown and filling is cooked through. Serve warm.

SERVES 6

Per Serving:

Calories	483
Fat	34g
Sodium	584mg
Carbohydrates	35g
Fiber	6g
Sugar	2g
Protein	10g

MAKE IT VEGETARIAN

It's easy to make this a vegetarian dish; just use vegetarian sausages instead of meat ones! If you want to make this for a holiday dinner, add some fresh cranberries to the sausage mix to make it really festive.

Hearty Beef Pie

Per Serving:

Calories	787
Fat	47g
Sodium	1,160mg
Carbohydrates	59g
Fiber	10g
Sugar	5g
Protein	35g

STOCK CUBES

Not all stock cubes are naturally gluten- and dairy-free, so make sure to double-check ingredients before purchasing.

This traditional beef pie is filled with a delicious, rich, thick gravy and tender pieces of beef. Enjoy this as a delicious family dinner on a cold winter evening with creamy mashed potatoes and seasonal vegetables. Comfort food doesn't get much better than this!

1 tablespoon extra-virgin olive oil

1 pound (450g) diced beef chuck

1 medium white onion, peeled and diced

1 large carrot, peeled and diced

2 cloves garlic, peeled and crushed

2 tablespoons gluten-free all-purpose flour

$\frac{1}{8}$ teaspoon salt

$\frac{1}{8}$ teaspoon ground black pepper

2 gluten-free beef stock cubes

1$\frac{1}{2}$ cups plus 3 tablespoons (400ml) boiling water

1 tablespoon fresh parsley leaves

1 tablespoon fresh thyme leaves

1 batch Savory Pastry Crust (see recipe in this chapter)

1 large egg, beaten

1 In a large frying pan, heat oil over high heat and add beef. Cook until browned, about 5 minutes. Remove beef and turn heat down to medium-high. Add onion, carrot, and garlic and fry until onion is translucent, about 10 minutes.

2 Add beef back to pan and stir in flour, salt, and pepper. Dissolve stock cubes in boiling water and pour into pan along with parsley and thyme. Bring to a boil over high heat, then simmer over medium-low heat about 50 minutes, stirring occasionally until you have a thick gravy-like sauce.

3 Preheat oven to 350°F (180°C) and grease a 9" oblong pie dish with vegetable oil.

4 Remove pastry from refrigerator, cut off one-third of pastry (for topping), and set aside. Roll out rest of pastry on a lightly floured surface to slightly larger than pie dish. Carefully line dish with rolled-out pastry and trim excess pastry from edges. Prick base with a fork.

5 Spoon filling into pie shell, then roll out remaining dough for top. Brush pie rim with a little water, then drape over top of pie mixture. Seal edges and crimp with a fork. Cut three slits in top of pie for steam to escape and brush with egg.

6 Bake 45 minutes, set aside 10 minutes before serving warm.

Ham, Leek, and Potato Pie

Use up any leftover ham with this comforting and creamy pie encased in flaky short-crust pastry. A warming winter dish everyone will love.

1 large russet potato, peeled and cubed

3 tablespoons vegan buttery spread

1 medium white onion, peeled and diced

2 cloves garlic, peeled and finely chopped

2 leeks, finely chopped

2 tablespoons gluten-free all-purpose flour

1¼ cups (300ml) gluten-free chicken stock

½ cup (120ml) dairy-free heavy cream

1 tablespoon gluten-free mustard

7 ounces (200g) shredded cooked ham

⅛ teaspoon salt

⅛ teaspoon ground black pepper

1 teaspoon Italian seasoning

1 batch Savory Pastry Crust (see recipe in this chapter)

1 large egg, beaten

SERVES 4

Per Serving:

Calories	979
Fat	62g
Sodium	1,523mg
Carbohydrates	81g
Fiber	11g
Sugar	7g
Protein	25g

CHECKING LABELS

Not all brands of mustard and chicken stock are both gluten-free and dairy-free. Always check the ingredients label before purchasing.

1 In a medium saucepan, add potatoes to boiling water and boil 10 minutes until they begin to soften. Drain and set aside.

2 In a large frying pan, heat buttery spread over medium heat. Add onion and garlic and fry until translucent, about 10 minutes. Add leeks and fry about 3 minutes more.

3 Stir in flour, then add stock, continuing to stir until mixture has thickened. Once thickened, remove from heat and stir in cream and mustard followed by ham and potato. Season with salt, pepper, and Italian seasoning. Set aside.

4 Preheat oven to 350°F (180°C) and grease a 9" oblong pie dish with vegetable oil.

5 Remove pastry from refrigerator. Cut off one-third of pastry (for topping) and set aside. Roll out rest of pastry on a lightly floured surface to slightly larger than pie dish. Carefully line dish with rolled-out pastry and trim excess pastry from edges. Prick base with a fork.

6 Spoon filling into pie shell, then roll out remaining dough for top. Brush pie rim with a little water, then drape pastry lid over top. Seal edges and crimp using a fork. Cut three slits in top of pie for steam to escape and brush with egg.

7 Bake 45 minutes. Set aside 10 minutes before serving warm.

Lasagna

SERVES 6

Per Serving:

Calories	452
Fat	21g
Sodium	783mg
Carbohydrates	48g
Fiber	6g
Sugar	8g
Protein	20g

MAKE IT MEAT-FREE

This recipe can easily be made meat-free by using a vegetarian ground beef alternative such as Beyond Beef. Alternatively, roast a mix of vegetables such as onion, sweet potatoes, bell peppers, butternut squash, and zucchini and use this as the "meat" layer.

This classic Lasagna combines an easy Bolognese sauce layered with gluten-free lasagna sheets and a homemade dairy-free white sauce.

1 medium white onion, peeled and diced

2 cloves garlic, peeled and finely chopped

1 pound (500g) ground beef

1 large red bell pepper, seeded and diced

1¾ cups (400g) canned chopped tomatoes

1¾ cups (400g) tomato passata

1 gluten-free vegetable stock cube

1 teaspoon dried oregano

2 teaspoons Italian seasoning

1 teaspoon white wine vinegar

¼ teaspoon salt, divided

¼ teaspoon ground black pepper, divided

3 tablespoons vegan buttery spread

2 tablespoons gluten-free all-purpose flour

1½ cups plus 3 tablespoons (400ml) unsweetened almond or other dairy-free milk

1 teaspoon gluten-free mustard

1/16 teaspoon ground nutmeg

12 gluten-free dry lasagna sheets

1¾ cups (150g) grated dairy-free Cheddar cheese alternative

1 Preheat oven to 350°F (180°C).

2 In a large frying pan, sauté onion, garlic, and beef until beef is brown, about 10 minutes. Drain any fat from beef, then add bell pepper, tomatoes, tomato passata, stock cube, oregano, Italian seasoning, vinegar, ⅛ teaspoon salt, and ⅛ teaspoon black pepper. Mix well and simmer for 20 minutes.

3 Meanwhile, in a small saucepan, melt buttery spread over medium-low heat, then whisk in flour until thick. Slowly pour in milk, whisking continuously, about 10 minutes, until sauce has thickened. Stir in mustard, nutmeg, and remaining ⅛ teaspoon salt and ⅛ teaspoon pepper. Set aside.

4 In a large pot of boiling water, cook lasagna sheets over high heat about 5 minutes. Drain well and set aside.

5 Spread one-third of tomato sauce into a deep 9" × 13" baking dish, cover with 4 lasagna sheets, and drizzle over one-third of white sauce. Repeat to make a second and third layer, topping third layer with cheese.

6 Bake 35–40 minutes until golden brown and cooked through. Serve straight from the oven.

Chicken Pot Pie

This classic Chicken Pot Pie has buttery pastry, dairy-free creamy sauce, and a mix of chicken, potatoes, and vegetables. It's a one-pot meal that is comforting and satisfying. Just add some warm, crusty gluten-free bread, and you have a really tasty, filling dish.

2 large russet potatoes, peeled and diced

1 large carrot, peeled and diced

¼ cup (60g) vegan buttery spread

1 medium white onion, peeled and diced

¼ cup (40g) gluten-free all-purpose flour

⅛ teaspoon salt

⅛ teaspoon ground black pepper

½ teaspoon dried thyme

¼ teaspoon garlic granules

1¼ cups plus 3 tablespoons (350ml) gluten-free chicken stock

½ cup (125ml) unsweetened almond or other dairy-free milk

3 cups (400g) cooked shredded chicken breast

½ cup (100g) frozen peas

1 batch Savory Pastry Crust (see recipe in this chapter)

1 large egg, beaten

SERVES 4

Per Serving:

Calories	1,008
Fat	56g
Sodium	1,106mg
Carbohydrates	85g
Fiber	13g
Sugar	9g
Protein	46g

ADAPT THE RECIPE

Adapt the recipe depending on what leftovers you have in the refrigerator. This also works really well with leftover turkey or any mixed vegetables you may have in the freezer.

1 In a large saucepan of boiling water, add potatoes and carrot. Boil 10 minutes, drain, and set aside.

2 In a large frying pan, heat buttery spread over medium heat, then add onion. Fry until translucent, about 10 minutes. Stir in flour, salt, pepper, thyme, and garlic granules and mix until combined. Gradually add stock and milk, continuing to stir until mixture comes to a boil. Keep stirring until mixture starts to thicken, then add chicken, peas, potatoes, and carrot. Remove from heat.

3 Preheat oven to 350°F (180°C) and remove pastry from refrigerator. Cut off one-third of pastry (for topping) and set aside. Roll out remaining pastry on a lightly floured surface to slightly larger than a 9" oblong pie dish. Carefully line dish with rolled-out pastry and trim excess pastry from edges. Prick base with a fork. Spoon filling into pie shell, then roll out remaining dough for top. Brush pie rim with a little water, then drape pastry lid over top. Seal edges and crimp with a fork. Cut three slits in top of pie for steam to escape and brush with egg.

4 Bake 45 minutes. Set aside 10 minutes before serving warm.

Cornish Pasties

These traditional British Cornish Pasties combine pastry pockets filled with beef, potato, rutabaga, and onion. If you're from the United Kingdom, you might know a rutabaga as a swede.

1 large russet potato, peeled and cubed

1 medium white onion, peeled and diced

1 small rutabaga, peeled and cubed

8 ounces (250g) beef stew meat, cut into small chunks

½ teaspoon salt

½ teaspoon ground black pepper

1 batch Savory Pastry Crust (see recipe in this chapter)

3 teaspoons gluten-free gravy mix

3 teaspoons vegan buttery spread

1 large egg, beaten

SERVES 3	
Per Serving (1 pasty):	
Calories	996
Fat	59g
Sodium	1,209mg
Carbohydrates	88g
Fiber	14g
Sugar	8g
Protein	33g

1   In a large bowl, combine potato, onion, rutabaga, and beef. Season with salt and pepper, mix well, and set aside.

2   Preheat oven to 350°F (180°C) and line a baking sheet with parchment paper.

3   Divide pastry into three pieces. Roll out one piece on a lightly floured surface, using a floured rolling pin to form an 8" circle.

4   Layer one-third of meat and potato mixture onto one side of pastry circle, leaving a 1" border around the outside. Sprinkle filling with 1 teaspoon gravy mix and top with 1 teaspoon buttery spread.

5   Brush border of dough with egg and carefully fold unfilled half of pastry over filled half. Use your fingers to crimp edges together to create a seal. Place on prepared baking sheet and brush top of pasty with egg.

6   Use remaining dough, filling, and egg to make two more pasties. Bake 45–50 minutes until golden brown and cooked through. Serve warm.

Easy Sausage Rolls

MAKES 12

Per Serving (1 roll):

Calories	242
Fat	17g
Sodium	293mg
Carbohydrates	17g
Fiber	3g
Sugar	1g
Protein	5g

These quick sausage rolls use homemade pastry and are perfect for lunch, dinner, or as part of a picnic. Just use vegetarian sausages if you prefer a meat-free version, but be sure they are gluten-free.

2 tablespoons gluten-free mustard

6 gluten-free pork sausages, cases removed

1 batch Savory Pastry Crust (see recipe in this chapter)

1 large egg, beaten

1 tablespoon white sesame seeds

1 Preheat oven to 350°F (180°C) and line a baking sheet with parchment paper. In a large bowl, add mustard and sausages, mixing well until fully combined.

2 Remove pastry from refrigerator and roll out on a lightly floured surface to form a large rectangle about ¼" thick. Cut rectangle in half lengthwise.

3 Halve sausage mixture and lay each half along long edge of one pastry strip. Tightly roll meat up in pastry to form two long, thin sausage roll shapes. Cut each roll into six pieces and place on prepared baking sheet. Brush with egg and sprinkle with sesame seeds.

4 Bake 35 minutes or until golden brown and cooked through. Serve warm and fresh from oven, or let cool 1 hour and store covered in refrigerator for up to 2 days.

CHAPTER 5

Snacks and Party Foods

Chocolate Mini Rolls

MAKES 10

Per Serving (1 roll):

Calories	319
Fat	20g
Sodium	98mg
Carbohydrates	36g
Fiber	3g
Sugar	31g
Protein	5g

Enjoy this tasty childhood classic: A chocolate swiss roll swirled together with buttercream and coated with more chocolate.

CAKE

3 large eggs, whites and yolks separated

¼ cup plus 2 tablespoons (75g) superfine sugar, divided

¼ cup (30g) cocoa powder

1 tablespoon plus 1 teaspoon (20g) vegan buttery spread, melted

1 teaspoon vanilla extract

2 tablespoons boiling water

FILLING

¼ cup plus 1 tablespoon (75g) vegan buttery sticks

1 cup (150g) confectioners' sugar

1 teaspoon unsweetened almond or other dairy-free milk

TOPPING

1½ cups (275g) dairy-free milk chocolate, melted

¼ cup (50g) dairy-free white chocolate, melted

CAKE

1 Preheat oven to 350°F (180°C) and line a 9" × 13" Swiss roll tin with parchment paper.

2 In a large bowl, whisk egg yolks and ¼ cup superfine sugar with an electric mixer on medium speed until thick. Add cocoa powder, melted buttery spread, vanilla, and water, and whisk until combined. In a medium bowl, whisk egg whites to stiff peaks, add remaining 2 tablespoons superfine sugar, and continue whisking.

3 Fold egg whites into cocoa mixture, then transfer to prepared tin, smoothing out with a knife so mixture fills pan evenly.

4 Bake 15–18 minutes until springy and cooked through. Remove from oven and place a damp towel over top until cool, about 30 minutes.

FILLING

1 In a medium bowl, beat buttery sticks with an electric mixer on medium speed until soft. Gradually add confectioners' sugar, continuing to beat up to 5 minutes until combined and creamy. Add milk and continue beating.

2 Once cake is cool, carefully remove from tin and place on a work surface with short edge facing you. Peel off parchment paper. Spread with Filling, then roll up tightly, stopping when you get to middle. Repeat with other edge until both rolls meet in middle. Cut down center, then cut each roll into five pieces. Chill in refrigerator 30 minutes.

TOPPING

Coat rolls in melted chocolate and place back in refrigerator to set, about 1 hour. Drizzle white chocolate over rolls to decorate and chill an additional 30 minutes. Store in an airtight container in the refrigerator for up to 3 days.

Baked Arancini Balls

These classic Italian risotto balls are coated with bread crumbs and baked in the oven instead of deep-fried for a healthier alternative.

MAKES 12

Per Serving (1 ball):

Calories	193
Fat	4g
Sodium	502mg
Carbohydrates	34g
Fiber	2g
Sugar	1g
Protein	5g

RISOTTO

1 tablespoon vegan buttery spread

1 medium white onion, peeled and finely chopped

2 cloves garlic, peeled and finely chopped

1 teaspoon fresh thyme leaves

⅛ teaspoon salt

⅛ teaspoon ground black pepper

1½ cups (250g) dry risotto rice

½ cup (125ml) dry white wine

4 cups plus 3 tablespoons (1 liter) gluten-free vegetable stock

¾ cup (60g) grated dairy-free Cheddar cheese alternative

Juice of half medium lemon

COATING

2 large eggs, beaten

¼ cup (45g) gluten-free all-purpose flour

1 cup (100g) gluten-free bread crumbs

RISOTTO

1 In a large frying pan, heat buttery spread over medium-high heat until melted. Add onion and garlic and fry until translucent, about 10 minutes. Add thyme, salt, and pepper and stir until coated.

2 Add risotto, then pour in wine. Mix well and cook 2 minutes until liquid starts to reduce. Add quarter of stock and simmer 20–25 minutes, adding another quarter of stock each time rice soaks up previous stock until rice is fully cooked. Stir in cheese and lemon juice, set aside.

COATING

1 Preheat oven to 350°F (180°C) and line a baking sheet with parchment paper.

2 Prepare three small bowls for coating, one with beaten egg, one with flour, and one with bread crumbs. Scoop 1 tablespoon of risotto mixture and roll into a ball. Coat in flour, followed by egg, and finally bread crumbs. Place on prepared baking sheet and lightly spray with cooking oil. Repeat with remaining Risotto.

3 Bake 25–30 minutes until balls are golden brown. Serve straight from the oven.

Baked Vegetable Samosas

This clever twist on samosas uses rice paper filled with a spiced potato mixture, brushed with vegetable oil, and baked in the oven for crunch.

2 large russet potatoes, peeled and chopped into small chunks

1 large carrot, peeled and chopped into small chunks

½ cup frozen peas

1 teaspoon vegetable oil plus 1 tablespoon for brushing

½ medium white onion, peeled and finely chopped

2 cloves garlic, peeled and finely chopped

1 teaspoon medium curry powder

½ teaspoon ground garam masala

1 teaspoon ground coriander

¼ teaspoon ground ginger

8 rice paper wrappers

MAKES 8

Per Serving (1 samosa):

Calories	103
Fat	2g
Sodium	57mg
Carbohydrates	20g
Fiber	2g
Sugar	2g
Protein	2g

1 In a large saucepan with enough water to cover, add potatoes and carrots. Bring to a boil and cook until tender, about 10–15 minutes. Set aside. In a small microwave-safe bowl, cook peas in microwave on high, about 3–4 minutes. Set aside.

2 In a large frying pan, heat 1 teaspoon oil over medium-high heat. Add onion and garlic and fry until translucent, about 10 minutes. Add curry powder, garam masala, coriander, and ginger and stir until onion mixture is fully coated. Stir in potatoes, carrots, and peas and crush slightly with a potato masher. Set aside.

3 Preheat oven to 350°F (180°C) and line a baking sheet with parchment paper.

4 In a wide bowl of warm water, carefully place a sheet of rice paper and submerge about 10 seconds to soften. Immediately remove from water and place on a flat work surface.

5 Spoon about ⅛ filling into bottom left quarter of semicircle. Fold rice paper over top, then side to create a triangle shape. Fold edges under and place on prepared baking sheet. Repeat with remaining ingredients to make eight filled samosas. Brush with remaining 1 tablespoon oil.

6 Bake 25 minutes, turning halfway through cooking. Serve immediately.

Cheese and Chive Potato Skins

Turn baked potatoes into something special with these loaded potato skins filled with dairy-free cheese and cream cheese, red pepper, scallions, and fresh chives.

ADAPT THE RECIPE

For a meaty version, this recipe is delicious with bacon chopped into small pieces, fried, and added to the potato mixture.

3 large russet potatoes

1 tablespoon extra-virgin olive oil

1 tablespoon vegan buttery spread

½ teaspoon salt

½ teaspoon ground black pepper

3 scallions (spring onions), finely chopped

1 large red bell pepper, seeded and diced

1½ cups (120g) grated dairy-free Cheddar cheese alternative, divided

¼ cup finely chopped fresh chives, divided

¼ cup (60g) dairy-free cream cheese alternative

1 Preheat oven to 350°F (180°C).

2 Rub potatoes with oil and bake 75 minutes on an ungreased baking sheet.

3 Remove potatoes from oven and set aside 5 minutes until cool enough to handle. Leave oven on.

4 Cut each cooled potato in half. Scoop out most of potato flesh, leaving a small amount around edges to keep their shape. Place hollowed-out potato skins on ungreased baking sheet.

5 In a large bowl, add potato flesh and mash with a fork or potato masher. Stir in buttery spread, salt, black pepper, scallion, bell pepper, ¾ cup Cheddar, and 2 tablespoons chives.

6 Spoon mashed potato mixture into skins and top with remaining ¾ cup Cheddar. Bake 20 minutes.

7 Serve warm, topped with cream cheese and remaining 2 tablespoons chives.

Scotch Eggs

MAKES 6

Per Serving (1 egg):

Calories	259
Fat	16g
Sodium	349mg
Carbohydrates	20g
Fiber	2g
Sugar	1g
Protein	7g

TOP TIP

Don't have the oil too hot for frying. It should be a medium heat, just hot enough to gently brown the bread crumbs.

Enjoy these tasty Scotch Eggs as part of a picnic, lunch, or any occasion! These delicious eggs are wrapped in sausage meat and coated in crispy gluten-free bread crumbs.

6 large eggs

6 gluten-free pork sausages, cases removed

1 tablespoon gluten-free whole-grain mustard

2 tablespoons fresh basil leaves

2 large beaten eggs, divided in half

⅛ teaspoon ground black pepper

¼ cup plus 1 tablespoon (50g) gluten-free all-purpose flour

1 cup (100g) gluten-free bread crumbs

3 tablespoons vegetable oil, for frying

1 In a medium saucepan with enough water to cover, add 6 eggs and bring to a boil over high heat. Once boiling, simmer 6 minutes over medium heat.

2 Remove eggs from water and let cool completely, about 1 hour. Once cooled, carefully remove shells, and set eggs aside.

3 In a food processor, process sausages, mustard, basil, and 1 beaten egg until evenly mixed. Season with pepper. Divide sausage mixture into six pieces and place each onto a separate piece of plastic wrap. Flatten.

4 Place a boiled egg onto each flattened piece of sausage meat and use plastic wrap to gently roll sausage meat around egg until completely encased. Place wrapped eggs in refrigerator 30 minutes.

5 Preheat oven to 350°F (180°C).

6 Prepare three small bowls, one with 1 beaten egg, one with flour, and one with bread crumbs. Remove wrapped eggs from refrigerator and roll each in flour, followed by beaten egg, and finally bread crumbs.

7 In a large pan, fry coated balls over medium heat in about ⅓" of oil, turning them occasionally until golden brown. This will take about 2 minutes each side.

8 Once browned, place on a baking sheet lined with parchment paper and bake 10 minutes. Chill to serve and store in refrigerator for up to 2 days.

Baked Vegetable Spring Rolls with Peanut Dipping Sauce

You can't beat homemade crispy spring rolls, and you won't believe how delicious this baked recipe is, dipped in a homemade peanut sauce.

SPRING ROLLS

½ cup (90g) cooked rice noodles

1 teaspoon sesame oil

⅛ teaspoon salt

12 rice paper wrappers

2 medium carrots, peeled and finely sliced

1 medium red bell pepper, seeded and finely sliced

1 cup (100g) bean sprouts

¼ cup finely chopped fresh cilantro

2 tablespoons vegetable oil, for brushing

PEANUT SAUCE

¼ cup plus 2 tablespoons (80g) smooth peanut butter

1 teaspoon rice wine vinegar

1 tablespoon gluten-free soy sauce

1 tablespoon pure maple syrup

1 tablespoon sesame oil

2 tablespoons water

MAKES 12

Per Serving (1 roll plus ½ tablespoon peanut sauce):

Calories	120
Fat	6g
Sodium	169mg
Carbohydrates	15g
Fiber	1g
Sugar	3g
Protein	3g

SPRING ROLLS

1 Preheat oven to 350°F (180°C) and line a baking sheet with parchment paper.

2 In a medium bowl, toss noodles with sesame oil and salt and set aside. In a wide bowl of warm water, carefully place a sheet of rice paper and submerge 10 seconds to soften. Immediately remove from water and place on a flat work surface.

3 Fill roll by adding one and a half of noodles, carrots, peppers, bean sprouts, and cilantro horizontally along bottom one-third of rice paper wrapper, leaving about 1" of open rice paper around edges.

4 Fold lower edge of rice paper up and over filling. Fold both short sides over filling, and roll up like a burrito. Repeat with remaining ingredients to make twelve spring rolls.

5 Place spring rolls onto prepared baking sheet and brush with vegetable oil. Bake 25 minutes until crispy, turning halfway through cooking.

PEANUT SAUCE

In a medium bowl, mix peanut butter, vinegar, soy sauce, maple syrup, sesame oil, and water. Serve alongside warm Spring Rolls.

Onion Bhajis

These quick and easy Onion Bhajis are a great side dish for any Indian meal. They are made by mixing together gram flour with spices to form a batter, then frying in oil until golden and crispy.

MAKES 8	
Per Serving (1 bhaji):	
Calories	98
Fat	5g
Sodium	14mg
Carbohydrates	10g
Fiber	2g
Sugar	3g
Protein	3g

½ cup plus 2 tablespoons (100g) gram flour

½ teaspoon ground turmeric

1 teaspoon paprika

½ teaspoon ground cumin

½ teaspoon chili powder

1 teaspoon ground coriander

½ cup (100ml) cold water

2 medium white onions, peeled and finely sliced

Vegetable oil, for frying

1 In a large bowl, add flour, turmeric, paprika, cumin, chili powder, and coriander. Mix well, then add water to form a thick paste.

2 Add onion into batter and stir until coated.

3 In a large saucepan, heat 2" oil over high heat until it reaches 338°F (170°C). Spoon 1 tablespoon of onion mixture into oil and fry about 4 minutes until golden and crisp. Remove with a slotted spoon and place on a piece of paper towel. Continue frying rest of battered onions 1 tablespoon at a time. Serve warm.

Baked Falafel

Naturally gluten-free and vegan, these falafel balls are filled with chickpeas, herbs, and spices and are perfect served with hummus and gluten-free pita bread for a healthy and filling lunch.

MAKES 10	
Per Serving (1 falafel):	
Calories	57
Fat	2g
Sodium	91mg
Carbohydrates	7g
Fiber	2g
Sugar	1g
Protein	2g

1 can (14-ounce or 400g) chickpeas, drained

1 clove garlic, peeled and crushed

1 teaspoon extra-virgin olive oil plus 1 tablespoon for drizzling

1 teaspoon ground cumin

2 tablespoons fresh cilantro

⅛ teaspoon salt

⅛ teaspoon ground black pepper

2 tablespoons gluten-free all-purpose flour

1 Preheat oven to 350°F (180°C) and line a baking sheet with parchment paper.

2 In a food processor, pulse all ingredients until smooth and combined. Roll into ten equal-sized balls and place on prepared baking sheet.

3 Drizzle with oil and bake 25 minutes until cooked through. Cool 10 minutes, then eat warm or store in an airtight container in refrigerator for up to 5 days.

Baked "Fried" Chicken

Enjoy the crispy taste of fried chicken without having to use oil! This oven-baked chicken is tender and delicious, coated in gluten-free bread crumbs and a delicious mix of herbs and spices.

1 cup (240ml) soy milk

1 tablespoon lemon juice

8 (3-ounce) boneless, skin-on chicken thighs

¾ cup (120g) gluten-free all-purpose flour

1 cup (150g) gluten-free bread crumbs

¼ teaspoon salt

1 teaspoon onion powder

1 teaspoon garlic powder

1 teaspoon dried oregano

1 teaspoon dried basil

1 teaspoon paprika

1 In a large bowl, mix milk and lemon juice to form a dairy-free butter-milk alternative. Leave to sit for 10 minutes. Add chicken and coat in mixture. Cover and place in refrigerator to soak, about 1 hour.

2 In a medium bowl, add flour. In a separate medium bowl, add bread crumbs, salt, onion powder, garlic powder, oregano, basil, and paprika. Mix well.

3 Preheat oven to 400°F (200°C) and line a baking sheet with parchment paper.

4 Remove chicken from refrigerator. Coat in flour, then dip back into leftover buttermilk mixture. Dip in bread crumbs mixture, ensuring it is fully coated.

5 Place coated chicken on prepared baking sheet and bake 45 minutes until chicken is cooked through and internal temperature is 165°F, turning halfway through cooking. Serve warm.

SERVES 4

Per Serving (2 chicken thighs):

Calories	410
Fat	17g
Sodium	439mg
Carbohydrates	30g
Fiber	3g
Sugar	2g
Protein	31g

TOP TIP

This recipe can also be used to make chicken drumsticks or chicken goujons. Simply adjust the baking time depending on the size of the chicken to ensure it's cooked through.

Blinis with Smoked Salmon

Impress your guests with a delicious platter of fresh blinis served with dairy-free cream cheese, smoked salmon, and fresh chives. These make for a great appetizer or party canapé.

SERVES 4

Per Serving:

Calories	353
Fat	21g
Sodium	982mg
Carbohydrates	35g
Fiber	4g
Sugar	2g
Protein	11g

1 cup plus 1 tablespoon (175g) gluten-free all-purpose flour

½ teaspoon baking powder

¼ teaspoon salt

¼ teaspoon ground black pepper

1 large egg

1 tablespoon extra-virgin olive oil

¾ cup plus 1 tablespoon (200ml) unsweetened almond or soy milk

2 tablespoons vegan buttery spread

½ cup (120g) dairy-free cream cheese

3 tablespoons lemon juice

2 teaspoons chopped fresh chives

3½ ounces (100g) thinly sliced smoked salmon

1 In a large bowl, combine flour, baking powder, salt, and pepper. Make a well in center of flour mixture. Add egg and oil to well and whisk together.

2 Gradually whisk in milk to form a smooth batter.

3 In a large frying pan, melt buttery spread over medium heat. Spoon batter into pan 1 tablespoon at a time and fry 2 minutes. Flip with a slotted spoon and fry another 1 minute. Transfer blinis to a warm platter.

4 Serve warm with cream cheese, lemon juice, chives, and smoked salmon.

Mac and Cheese

This is the ultimate creamy Mac and Cheese recipe, topped with a crunchy bread crumb topping. This comforting dinner will fast become a family favorite!

MAC AND CHEESE

9 ounces (250g) gluten-free macaroni shells

¼ cup (55g) vegan buttery spread

¼ cup plus 1 tablespoon (50g) gluten-free all-purpose flour

2 tablespoons nutritional yeast

2 cups plus 1 tablespoon (500ml) unsweetened almond or other dairy-free milk

1 tablespoon gluten-free mustard

½ teaspoon garlic granules

1¾ cups (150g) grated dairy-free Cheddar cheese alternative

⅛ teaspoon salt

⅛ teaspoon ground black pepper

CRUNCHY TOPPING

1 tablespoon extra-virgin olive oil

½ cup (50g) gluten-free bread crumbs

1 tablespoon nutritional yeast

⅛ teaspoon salt

⅛ teaspoon ground black pepper

¼ teaspoon smoked paprika

1 teaspoon fresh thyme leaves

MAC AND CHEESE

1 Preheat oven to 350°F (180°C).

2 In a large saucepan, add water to ¾ full and bring to a boil. Add macaroni. Cook according to package instructions, then drain and set aside.

3 In a large frying pan, heat buttery spread over medium heat. Add flour and nutritional yeast, and whisk until thick. Slowly add milk and continue to whisk until mixture starts to thicken slightly. Stir in mustard, garlic granules, cheese, salt, and pepper and mix until a thick sauce forms.

4 Pour cooked shells into sauce and mix until coated. Pour into a 9" × 13" baking dish.

CRUNCHY TOPPING

1 In a medium bowl, mix oil, bread crumbs, nutritional yeast, salt, pepper, paprika, and thyme. Sprinkle over shells.

2 Bake 25 minutes until topping is golden brown. Serve warm.

Yorkshire Puddings

You won't believe that these four-ingredient Yorkshire Puddings are both gluten- and dairy-free! Yorkshire Puddings are a British classic similar to an American popover. Serve with roast beef, potatoes, and vegetables—and lots of gravy.

4 tablespoons vegetable oil

2 large eggs

½ cup plus 1 tablespoon (70g) cornstarch

½ cup (120ml) unsweetened almond or other dairy-free milk

1 Preheat oven to 400°F (200°C).

2 Pour 1 tablespoon oil into each hole of a four hole Yorkshire Pudding tin. Heat tin in oven 20 minutes.

3 While oil heats, in a large bowl, add eggs and cornstarch and whisk until combined. Slowly add milk and continue to whisk until a thin batter forms. Set aside.

4 Carefully remove tin from oven and pour batter evenly into each hole. Bake 25 minutes until golden and well risen. Do not open oven door during baking. Serve straight from oven.

SERVES 4

Per Serving (1 pudding):

Calories	229
Fat	16g
Sodium	59mg
Carbohydrates	16g
Fiber	0g
Sugar	0g
Protein	3g

TOP TIP

If you can't find a Yorkshire Pudding tin, this recipe also works really well in a muffin tin.

Party Rings

MAKES 20

Per Serving (1 ring):

Calories	163
Fat	5g
Sodium	50mg
Carbohydrates	28g
Fiber	1g
Sugar	21g
Protein	1g

This is a fun and nostalgic treat enjoyed by children and adults alike. A simple vanilla-flavored cookie is frosted with funky-colored feathered icing to create a fun and tasty dessert.

1¼ cups plus 2 tablespoons (225g) gluten-free all-purpose flour

¼ teaspoon xanthan gum (omit if flour blend already contains this)

½ cup plus 1 tablespoon (125g) cubed vegan buttery sticks

½ cup plus 2 tablespoons (125g) superfine sugar

1 large egg, lightly beaten

1 teaspoon vanilla extract

2 cups plus 1 tablespoon (300g) confectioners' sugar

4 colors gel food coloring

1 In a food processor, pulse flour, xanthan gum, and buttery sticks until mixture resembles bread crumbs, then add superfine sugar, egg, and vanilla and pulse until combined.

2 Turn out dough onto a lightly floured surface and knead to form a disc. Wrap in plastic wrap and refrigerate for 30 minutes.

3 Preheat oven to 350°F (180°C) and line two baking sheets with parchment paper. Roll out pastry on a lightly floured surface into a disc shape with a floured rolling pin to about ¼" thick. With a cookie cutter, cut circular shapes out of dough, then cut a smaller circle in middle of each shape to form rings, rerolling leftover dough when required.

4 Place rings onto prepared baking sheets and bake 10 minutes until pale golden. Leave on sheets to cool completely, about 1 hour.

5 Divide confectioners' sugar between four small bowls and add 1 tablespoon water to each bowl to create a smooth (but not too runny) icing. Add a few drops of different food coloring to each bowl and mix well.

6 Carefully dip each cooled ring into a bowl. Place on a wire rack and immediately drizzle ring with an alternate color in a horizontal line. Using a toothpick or a skewer, drag lines vertically to create a feathered effect. Repeat with remaining rings. Let set about 1 hour, then store in an airtight container at room temperature for up to 3 days.

CHAPTER 6
Classic Cakes and Cupcakes

Mini Doughnut–Topped Cupcakes

Take your cupcakes to the next level by topping them with dairy-free buttercream and mini sugar doughnuts! These cupcakes really do look (and taste!) the part.

MAKES 12

Per Serving (1 doughnut-topped cupcake):

Calories	483
Fat	25g
Sodium	411mg
Carbohydrates	63g
Fiber	0g
Sugar	46g
Protein	3g

CUPCAKES

¾ cup plus 1 tablespoon (175g) vegan buttery sticks

¾ cup plus 2 tablespoons (175g) superfine sugar

3 large eggs

1 teaspoon vanilla extract

1 cup plus 1 tablespoon (175g) gluten-free self-rising flour

¼ teaspoon xanthan gum (omit if flour blend already contains this)

½ teaspoon baking powder

MINI DOUGHNUTS

¼ cup plus 3 tablespoons (75g) gluten-free self-rising flour

¼ teaspoon baking powder

¼ teaspoon salt

¼ cup (55g) superfine sugar

1 large egg

¼ cup (60ml) unsweetened almond or other dairy-free milk

1 tablespoon vegetable oil

½ teaspoon vanilla extract

2 tablespoons vegan buttery spread, melted

2 tablespoons granulated sugar

BUTTERCREAM

½ cup plus 3 tablespoons (150g) vegan buttery sticks

2 cups plus 1 tablespoon (300g) confectioners' sugar

1 teaspoon vanilla extract

CUPCAKES

1 Preheat oven to 350°F (180°C) and line a twelve-cup muffin tin with cupcake liners.

2 In a large bowl, whisk together buttery sticks and superfine sugar until creamy. Add eggs and vanilla and whisk until combined. Fold in flour, xanthan gum, and baking powder.

3 Divide mixture between muffin cups and bake 20 minutes until golden brown and a skewer inserted in center comes out clean. Let cool completely, about 1 hour.

MINI DOUGHNUTS

1 While cupcakes cool, grease a mini doughnut tray with vegetable oil.
2 In a large bowl, add flour, baking powder, salt, and superfine sugar and mix well. In a medium bowl, whisk egg, milk, oil, and vanilla. Add wet ingredients to dry ingredients and mix well.
3 Pour batter into prepared tray to about three-quarters full and bake 8–10 minutes until golden brown.
4 Remove from oven, let cool in tray 5 minutes, then remove from tray and leave to completely cool, about 30 minutes, on a wire rack.
5 Once cool, brush with melted buttery spread and coat in granulated sugar.

BUTTERCREAM

In a medium bowl, beat buttery sticks on medium speed with an electric mixer until soft. Gradually add confectioners' sugar, continuing to beat up to 5 minutes until combined and creamy. Add vanilla and beat until smooth and creamy.

ASSEMBLY

Pipe Buttercream onto Cupcakes and press a Mini Doughnut onto each Cupcake. Store in an airtight container at room temperature for up to 2 days.

Lemon Meringue Cupcakes

All the flavors of a lemon meringue pie in a cupcake! The tasty vanilla cake is filled with oozy lemon curd and topped with a fluffy meringue topping.

Per Serving (1 cupcake):

Calories	404
Fat	20g
Sodium	325mg
Carbohydrates	55g
Fiber	0g
Sugar	41g
Protein	4g

CUPCAKES

¾ cup (160g) vegan buttery sticks

¾ cup plus 1 tablespoon (160g) superfine sugar

3 large eggs

1 tablespoon grated lemon zest

1 teaspoon vanilla extract

1 cup (160g) gluten-free self-rising flour

¼ teaspoon xanthan gum (omit if flour blend already contains this)

1 teaspoon baking powder

LEMON CURD FILLING

1 large egg

¼ cup (55g) vegan buttery spread

1 tablespoon grated lemon zest

¼ cup (60ml) lemon juice

½ cup (100g) superfine sugar

MERINGUE TOPPING

3 large egg whites

¾ cup (150g) superfine sugar

1 teaspoon vanilla extract

CUPCAKES

1 Preheat oven to 350°F (180°C) and line a twelve-cup muffin tin with 10 cupcake liners.

2 In a large bowl, add buttery sticks and sugar and beat with an electric mixer until light and fluffy. Add eggs one at a time, beating in between each addition. Stir in lemon zest and vanilla. In a medium bowl, combine flour, xanthan gum, and baking powder and add to batter. Beat until combined.

3 Divide mixture between ten muffin cups. Bake for 20–25 minutes or until a skewer inserted in center comes out clean. Cool in tin for 5 minutes, then remove from tin and transfer to a wire rack to cool completely, about 30 minutes.

continued on next page

continued

LEMON CURD FILLING

1 In a medium saucepan over medium-low heat, combine egg, buttery spread, lemon zest, lemon juice, and sugar. Cook, stirring for 2–3 minutes until buttery spread melts.

2 Increase heat to medium and cook, stirring constantly, 3–4 minutes, until mixture starts to boil and thicken. Remove from heat, transfer to a medium bowl, and refrigerate 2 hours.

MERINGUE TOPPING

In a medium bowl, beat egg whites with an electric mixer to form stiff peaks, starting with mixer on slow, then increasing speed. Add sugar 1 teaspoon at a time and keep beating until glossy and thick. Add vanilla and whisk. Transfer to a piping bag.

ASSEMBLY

1 Use a serrated knife to cut a small hole in top of each Cupcake. Fill each hole with a teaspoon of Lemon Curd Filling. Pipe meringue over top of each Cupcake.

2 Use a chef's blowtorch to brown tops of Meringue Topping. If you don't have a torch, place Cupcakes on a baking sheet and bake at 425°F (220°C) 5 minutes to brown. Store in an airtight container at room temperature for up to 3 days.

Chocolate Cupcakes

These classic Chocolate Cupcakes are made from simple everyday kitchen ingredients, combining a rich and fudgy chocolate cake with a chocolate buttercream. The cupcake recipe is a great base for topping with your favorite frosting and decorations.

CUPCAKES

1 cup (200g) superfine sugar

1 cup (160g) gluten-free all-purpose flour

1½ teaspoons baking powder

¼ teaspoon xanthan gum (omit if flour blend already contains this)

¼ cup plus 3 tablespoons (50g) cocoa powder

½ teaspoon salt

½ cup (120ml) unsweetened almond or other dairy-free milk

2 large eggs

1 teaspoon vanilla extract

¼ cup (60g) vegan buttery spread, melted

¼ cup plus 3 tablespoons (100ml) hot coffee

BUTTERCREAM

¾ cup plus 2 tablespoons (200g) vegan buttery sticks

2¼ cups plus 2 tablespoons (350g) confectioners' sugar

¼ cup plus 3 tablespoons (50g) cocoa powder

MAKES 12

Per Serving (1 cupcake):

Calories	403
Fat	19g
Sodium	342mg
Carbohydrates	60g
Fiber	4g
Sugar	46g
Protein	4g

CUPCAKES

1 Preheat oven to 350°F (180°C) and line a twelve-cup muffin tin with cupcake liners.

2 In a large bowl, add superfine sugar, flour, baking powder, xanthan gum, cocoa powder, and salt.

3 In a medium bowl, whisk milk, eggs, vanilla, and melted buttery spread. Add wet ingredients to dry ingredients, then add coffee and mix well.

4 Divide mixture between twelve muffin cups. Bake 20 minutes or until a skewer inserted in center comes out clean. Let cool about 1 hour.

BUTTERCREAM

1 In a medium bowl, beat buttery sticks with an electric mixer on medium speed until soft. Gradually add confectioners' sugar and cocoa powder, continuing to beat up to 5 minutes until combined and creamy.

2 Pipe Buttercream onto Cupcakes and store in an airtight container at room temperature for up to 3 days.

Raspberry and White Chocolate Cupcakes

MAKES 12

Per Serving (1 cupcake):

Calories	584
Fat	32g
Sodium	368mg
Carbohydrates	72g
Fiber	1g
Sugar	56g
Protein	3g

These cupcakes feature a vanilla cake with fresh raspberries and are topped with a dairy-free white chocolate buttercream. They are perfect for a valentine treat or any other day of the year!

CUPCAKES

1 cup (220g) vegan buttery sticks

1 cup plus 1 tablespoon (220g) superfine sugar

4 large eggs

1 teaspoon vanilla extract

1¼ cups plus 2 tablespoons (220g) gluten-free self-rising flour

¼ teaspoon xanthan gum (omit if flour blend already contains this)

¾ cup (120g) fresh raspberries

BUTTERCREAM AND DECORATION

¾ cup plus 2 tablespoons (200g) vegan buttery sticks

2¾ cups (400g) confectioners' sugar

½ cup plus 1 tablespoon (100g) dairy-free white chocolate, melted

12 fresh raspberries

CUPCAKES

1 Preheat oven to 350°F (180°C) and line a twelve-cup muffin tin with cupcake liners.

2 In a large bowl, add buttery spread and superfine sugar and beat until light and fluffy. Add eggs one at a time, continuing to mix. Add vanilla and beat.

3 Stir in flour and xanthan gum and mix until combined. Fold in raspberries and divide mixture between twelve muffin cups.

4 Bake 25 minutes or until a skewer inserted in center comes out clean. Let cool for 1 hour.

BUTTERCREAM AND DECORATION

In a medium bowl, beat buttery sticks with an electric mixer on medium speed until soft. Gradually add confectioners' sugar, continuing to beat up to 5 minutes until combined and creamy. Add melted chocolate and beat.

ASSEMBLY

Pipe Buttercream onto Cupcakes and top each Cupcake with a raspberry. Store in an airtight container at room temperature for up to 3 days.

Cappuccino Cupcakes

These Cappuccino Cupcakes are perfect for coffee lovers. They combine a fluffy coffee-flavored cake with a coffee buttercream and grated chocolate topping.

MAKES 12

CUPCAKES

1 cup (220g) vegan buttery sticks

1 cup plus 1 tablespoon (220g) superfine sugar

4 large eggs

2 teaspoons instant coffee mix

3 tablespoons boiling water

1¼ cups plus 2 tablespoons (220g) gluten-free self-rising flour

¼ cup (30g) cocoa powder

1 teaspoon baking powder

¼ teaspoon xanthan gum (omit if flour blend already contains this)

BUTTERCREAM

¾ cup plus 2 tablespoons (200g) vegan buttery sticks

2¾ cups (400g) confectioners' sugar

2 teaspoons instant coffee mix

1 tablespoon boiling water

1 tablespoon grated dairy-free dark chocolate

Per Serving (1 cupcake):

Calories	545
Fat	30g
Sodium	401mg
Carbohydrates	68g
Fiber	1g
Sugar	51g
Protein	3g

TOP TIP

Be careful when adding the coffee to the buttercream. Let the coffee cool a little so it doesn't cause the mixture to curdle. Add a small amount at a time and continue to whisk with every drop added.

CUPCAKES

1 Preheat oven to 350°F (180°C) and line a twelve-cup muffin tin with cupcake liners.

2 In a large bowl, add buttery sticks and superfine sugar. Beat with an electric mixer on medium speed until creamy, then add eggs one at a time, continuing to whisk.

3 Mix coffee with boiling water and add to mixture along with flour, cocoa powder, baking powder, and xanthan gum. Mix well.

4 Divide mixture between twelve muffin cups. Bake 20–25 minutes or until a skewer inserted in center comes out clean. Let cool for 1 hour.

BUTTERCREAM

1 In a large bowl, beat buttery sticks with an electric mixer on medium speed until soft. Gradually add confectioners' sugar, continuing to beat up to 5 minutes until combined and creamy. Mix coffee with boiling water, let cool for 10 minutes, then add to Buttercream. Whisk to combine.

2 Pipe Buttercream onto Cupcakes. Top with grated chocolate. Store in an airtight container at room temperature for up to 3 days.

Mint Chocolate Chip Cupcakes

These cupcakes are definitely for fans of all things mint-chocolate-chip flavored!

CUPCAKES

1 cup (220g) vegan buttery sticks

1 cup plus 1 tablespoon (220g) superfine sugar

4 large eggs

1 teaspoon peppermint extract

1 teaspoon vanilla extract

1¼ cups (200g) gluten-free self-rising flour

¼ teaspoon xanthan gum (omit if flour blend already contains this)

¼ cup plus 2 tablespoons (40g) cocoa powder

½ cup plus 1 tablespoon (100g) dairy-free milk chocolate chips

BUTTERCREAM

¾ cup plus 2 tablespoons (200g) vegan buttery sticks

2¾ cups (400g) confectioners' sugar

2 teaspoons peppermint extract

Green gel food coloring

ASSEMBLY

¼ cup (50g) dairy-free milk chocolate chips

MAKES 12

Per Serving (1 cupcake):

Calories	602
Fat	34g
Sodium	354mg
Carbohydrates	74g
Fiber	2g
Sugar	57g
Protein	4g

CUPCAKES

1 Preheat oven to 350°F (180°C) and line a twelve-cup muffin tin with cupcake liners.

2 In a large bowl, add buttery sticks and superfine sugar and beat until light and fluffy. Add eggs one at a time, beating between each addition. Add peppermint and vanilla and beat.

3 In a medium bowl, combine flour, xanthan gum, and cocoa powder and add to batter. Beat until combined. Fold in chocolate chips.

4 Divide mixture between muffin cups. Bake 20–25 minutes or until a skewer inserted in center comes out clean. Cool in tin 5 minutes, then transfer to a wire rack to cool completely, about 30 minutes.

BUTTERCREAM

In a large bowl, beat buttery sticks with an electric mixer at medium speed until soft and fluffy. Gradually add confectioners' sugar, continuing to beat up to 5 minutes until creamy. Add peppermint and beat. Use a wooden skewer or tip of a knife to add 2–3 drops of green food coloring to Buttercream, then beat until combined. Continue until desired color is reached.

ASSEMBLY

Pipe Buttercream onto Cupcakes and sprinkle with chocolate chips. Store in an airtight container at room temperature for up to 3 days.

Gingerbread Cupcakes

MAKES 12

Per Serving (1 cupcake):

Calories	400
Fat	19g
Sodium	339mg
Carbohydrates	57g
Fiber	2g
Sugar	45g
Protein	3g

You'll love these frosted Gingerbread Cupcakes. They are filled with holiday flavors but are delicious any time of the year!

CUPCAKES

- ½ cup plus 1 tablespoon (120g) vegan buttery sticks
- ½ cup plus 1 tablespoon (120g) packed light brown sugar
- 2 large eggs
- ¼ cup plus 2 tablespoons (120g) corn (golden) syrup
- 2 tablespoons (40g) molasses
- ¼ cup plus 3 tablespoons (100ml) unsweetened almond or other dairy-free milk
- 1 teaspoon vanilla extract
- 1¼ cups (200g) gluten-free all-purpose flour
- 1 teaspoon baking powder
- ½ teaspoon baking soda
- ¼ teaspoon salt
- ¼ teaspoon xanthan gum (omit if flour blend already contains this)
- 2 teaspoons ground ginger
- 1 teaspoon ground cinnamon
- ½ teaspoon ground nutmeg

BUTTERCREAM

- ½ cup plus 3 tablespoons (150g) vegan buttery sticks
- 2 cups plus 1 tablespoon (300g) confectioners' sugar
- 1 teaspoon vanilla extract
- 1 teaspoon ground ginger
- 1 teaspoon unsweetened almond or other dairy-free milk

CUPCAKES

1. Preheat oven to 350°F (180°C) and line a twelve-cup muffin tin with cupcake liners.
2. In a large bowl, add buttery sticks and brown sugar and beat until light and fluffy. Add eggs one at a time, continuing to whisk. Add corn syrup, molasses, milk, and vanilla and beat until combined.
3. In a separate large bowl, mix flour, baking powder, baking soda, salt, xanthan gum, ginger, cinnamon, and nutmeg. Add dry ingredients to wet ingredients and fold to combine.
4. Pour mixture into muffin cups and bake 20–25 minutes until a skewer inserted in center comes out clean. Let cool for 1 hour.

BUTTERCREAM

1. In a medium bowl, beat buttery sticks with an electric mixer on medium speed until soft. Gradually add confectioners' sugar, continuing to beat up to 5 minutes until combined and creamy. Add vanilla, ginger, and milk and beat until combined.
2. Pipe Buttercream onto Cupcakes. Store in an airtight container at room temperature for up to 3 days.

Victoria Sponge

This traditional Victoria Sponge showcases a fluffy gluten-free cake with dairy-free buttercream and strawberry jam. It is a simple yet delicious dessert that everyone will love. This recipe is also perfect as a base recipe for any kind of special cake.

CAKE

1 cup (225g) vegan buttery sticks

1 cup plus 2 tablespoons (225g) superfine sugar

4 large eggs

1 teaspoon vanilla extract

1¼ cups plus 2 tablespoons (225g) gluten-free self-rising flour

½ teaspoon baking powder

¼ teaspoon xanthan gum (omit if flour blend already contains this)

FILLING

¾ cup plus 2 tablespoons (200g) vegan buttery sticks

2¾ cups (400g) confectioners' sugar

½ cup strawberry Jam

6 hulled fresh strawberries

SERVES 12	
Per Serving:	
Calories	578
Fat	30g
Sodium	389mg
Carbohydrates	76g
Fiber	1g
Sugar	58g
Protein	3g

CAKE

1. Preheat oven to 350°F (180°C) and line two 8" round springform cake pans with parchment paper.
2. In a large bowl, whisk buttery sticks and superfine sugar until creamy. Add eggs one at a time and continue to whisk until combined. Add vanilla and whisk. Fold in flour, baking powder, and xanthan gum.
3. Divide mixture between prepared pans and bake 20–25 minutes until golden and a skewer inserted in center comes out clean. Let cool completely, about 1 hour.

FILLING

In a medium bowl, beat buttery sticks with an electric mixer on medium speed until soft. Gradually add confectioners' sugar, continuing to beat up to 5 minutes until combined and creamy.

ASSEMBLY

Sandwich Cakes together with Buttercream and jam. Spread remaining Buttercream on top of Cake and decorate with strawberries. Store in an airtight container at room temperature for up to 3 days.

Coffee and Walnut Cake

TOP TIP

To prevent the filling from curdling when adding the coffee, make sure the coffee is cool and add slowly.

This classic recipe pairs a coffee-flavored cake with coffee buttercream and walnuts. It's perfect for dessert or a midmorning snack.

CAKE

1 cup plus 2 tablespoons (250g) vegan buttery sticks

1¼ cups (250g) superfine sugar

4 large eggs

1 teaspoon vanilla extract

¼ cup plus 1 tablespoon (80ml) strong black coffee, cooled

1¾ cups (280g) gluten-free self-rising flour

¼ teaspoon xanthan gum (omit if flour blend already contains this)

1 teaspoon baking powder

1 cup (100g) finely chopped walnuts

BUTTERCREAM

¾ cup plus 2 tablespoons (200g) vegan buttery sticks

2¾ cups (400g) confectioners' sugar

2 teaspoons instant coffee mix

1 tablespoon water

12 walnut halves

CAKE

1 Preheat oven to 350°F (180°C) and line two 8" round springform cake pans with parchment paper.

2 In a large bowl, whisk buttery sticks and superfine sugar until creamy. Add eggs one at a time and continue to whisk until combined. Add vanilla and coffee and whisk. Fold in flour, xanthan gum, and baking powder. Fold in walnuts.

3 Divide mixture between cake pans and bake 20–25 minutes until golden and a skewer inserted in center comes out clean. Let cool completely, about 1 hour.

BUTTERCREAM

In a medium bowl, beat buttery sticks with an electric mixer on medium speed until soft. Gradually add confectioners' sugar, continuing to beat up to 5 minutes until combined and creamy. Mix instant coffee with boiling water, let cool for 10 minutes, then gradually add to buttercream, whisking to combine.

ASSEMBLY

Sandwich Cakes together with a layer of Buttercream. Spread remaining Buttercream on top of Cake and decorate with walnut halves.

Carrot Cake

This two-layer Carrot Cake is sandwiched together with a layer of dairy-free buttercream and filled with warm spices, walnuts, and raisins. It is truly a perfect cake to have with a cup of tea or midafternoon coffee .

CAKE

1¼ cups plus 2 tablespoons (225g) gluten-free all-purpose flour

¼ teaspoon xanthan gum (omit if flour blend already contains this)

1½ teaspoons baking powder

1 teaspoon baking soda

½ teaspoon salt

1 teaspoon ground cinnamon

½ teaspoon pumpkin pie spice

½ teaspoon ground ginger

1 cup plus 2 tablespoons (225g) packed light brown sugar

¼ cup plus 1 tablespoon (50g) raisins

½ cup (50g) chopped walnuts

3 cups (150g) grated carrot

3 large eggs

¾ cup (175ml) vegetable oil

1 teaspoon vanilla extract

BUTTERCREAM

¾ cup (160g) vegan buttery sticks

2 cups plus 3 tablespoons (320g) confectioners' sugar

1 teaspoon vanilla extract

ASSEMBLY

¼ cup whole walnuts

SERVES 12

Per Serving:

Calories	531
Fat	30g
Sodium	395mg
Carbohydrates	63g
Fiber	3g
Sugar	48g
Protein	5g

VEGETABLE OIL

Using vegetable oil in place of butter in this recipe helps the cake to last longer, provides a lovely, moist texture, and also tastes great! If you don't have vegetable oil, you can use sunflower oil.

CAKE

1 Preheat oven to 350°F (180°C) and line two 8" round springform cake pans with parchment paper.

2 In a large bowl, mix flour, xanthan gum, baking powder, baking soda, salt, cinnamon, pumpkin pie spice, and ginger. Add brown sugar, raisins, walnuts, and carrot and mix.

3 In a medium bowl, mix eggs, oil, and vanilla, then add to dry mixture. Stir until fully combined.

4 Divide mixture equally between prepared cake pans and bake 30 minutes or until a skewer inserted in center comes out clean. Let cool for 1 hour.

BUTTERCREAM

In a medium bowl, beat buttery sticks with an electric mixer on medium speed until soft. Gradually add confectioners' sugar, continuing to beat up to 5 minutes until combined and creamy. Add vanilla and whisk.

ASSEMBLY

Sandwich Cakes together with Buttercream and spread a layer on top. Decorate with walnuts. Store in an airtight container in refrigerator for up to 4 days.

Apple, Raisin, and Cinnamon Cake

SERVES 12

Per Serving:

Calories	310
Fat	15g
Sodium	215mg
Carbohydrates	44g
Fiber	2g
Sugar	27g
Protein	3g

This fruity cake is filled with the flavors of autumn and is perfect served with coffee or for breakfast. The cinnamon gives it a really warm quality; it's a cake that your family and friends are certain to love!

¾ cup plus 2 tablespoons (200g) vegan buttery sticks

1 cup (200g) packed light brown sugar

2 teaspoons ground cinnamon

Zest of 1 medium lemon

3 large eggs

1¼ cups (200g) gluten-free self-rising flour

¼ teaspoon xanthan gum (omit if flour blend already contains this)

4 medium apples, 2 peeled, cored, and grated, and 2 peeled, cored, and sliced

¾ cup (110g) raisins

1 Preheat oven to 350°F (180°C) and line an 8" deep round springform cake pan with parchment paper.

2 In a large bowl, add buttery sticks, brown sugar, cinnamon, and lemon zest. Whisk with an electric mixer on medium speed until creamy. Add eggs one at a time and continue to whisk. Stir in flour, xanthan gum, grated apples, and raisins.

3 Pour mixture into lined cake pan, press apple slices into top, and bake 1 hour and 15 minutes or until a skewer inserted in center comes out clean. You may need to cover top with foil toward end of baking time to prevent cake from browning too much.

4 Let cool in pan for at least 1 hour before slicing. Store in an airtight container at room temperature for up to 3 days.

School Pudding Cake

This classic retro dessert combines a vanilla cake with an iced topping. It's simple to make and delicious served with dairy-free custard. You could even use this as the base of a birthday cake, just top with extra sprinkles and gluten-free sweets, and add candles to finish!

CAKE

1 cup plus 2 tablespoons (250g) vegan buttery sticks

1 cup plus 2 tablespoons (225g) superfine sugar

4 large eggs

2 tablespoons unsweetened almond or other dairy-free milk

1 teaspoon vanilla extract

1½ cups plus 1 tablespoon (250g) gluten-free self-rising flour

¼ teaspoon xanthan gum (omit if flour blend already contains this)

½ teaspoon baking powder

ICING

2 cups plus 1 tablespoon (300g) confectioners' sugar

3½ tablespoons boiling water

ASSEMBLY

¼ cup gluten-free sprinkles

SERVES 12

Per Serving:

Calories	426
Fat	19g
Sodium	286mg
Carbohydrates	64g
Fiber	0g
Sugar	47g
Protein	3g

CAKE

1. Preheat oven to 350°F (180°C) and line a 9" square springform cake pan with parchment paper.
2. In a large mixing bowl, whisk buttery sticks and superfine sugar until creamy. Add eggs one at a time and continue to whisk until fully combined. Add milk and vanilla and whisk.
3. Add flour, xanthan gum, and baking powder to wet ingredients. Mix well until combined, then spoon mixture into prepared pan.
4. Bake 40 minutes or until golden brown and a skewer inserted in center comes out clean. Cover top with foil toward end of baking time to prevent cake from browning too much.
5. Let cake cool in pan for 15 minutes before turning out onto a wire rack to cool completely, about 1 hour.

ICING

In a small bowl, combine confectioners' sugar and water until the consistency is fairly runny.

ASSEMBLY

Spread Icing on top of Cake and top with sprinkles. Store in an airtight container at room temperature for up to 3 days.

Lemon-Blueberry Bundt Cake

This stunning Bundt cake is moist and delicious, filled with juicy blueberries and topped with a tasty lemon icing.

GREASING A BUNDT PAN

When baking with a Bundt pan it is important to thoroughly grease the pan, making sure all areas inside the pan are coated. This will ensure the cake comes out of the pan in one piece. You can grease the pan with melted dairy-free butter or a nonstick vegetable oil spray.

1¼ cups (275g) vegan buttery sticks

1¼ cups plus 2 tablespoons (275g) superfine sugar

5 large eggs

1½ cups plus 3 tablespoons (275g) gluten-free self-rising flour

¼ teaspoon xanthan gum (omit if flour blend already contains this)

1 teaspoon baking powder

1 cup (200g) blueberries, divided

2 tablespoons grated lemon zest

4 tablespoons lemon juice, divided

¾ cup plus 2 tablespoons (125g) confectioners' sugar

1. Preheat oven to 350°F (180°C) and grease a Bundt pan with dairy-free vegan butter.
2. In a large mixing bowl, beat buttery sticks and superfine sugar until light and fluffy. Add eggs one at a time, beating in between each addition.
3. In a medium bowl, combine flour, xanthan gum, and baking powder and add to batter. Beat until combined. Fold in ¾ cup blueberries, lemon zest, and 2 tablespoons lemon juice.
4. Pour batter into prepared pan and press remaining ¼ cup blueberries onto top. Bake 50–55 minutes until golden brown and a skewer inserted in center comes out clean.
5. Set aside to cool in pan for 10 minutes, then carefully turn out onto a wire rack to cool completely, about 45 minutes.
6. In a small bowl, mix confectioners' sugar and remaining 2 tablespoons lemon juice. Drizzle over top of cake. Store in an airtight container at room temperature for up to 4 days.

Iced Lemon and Summer Fruits Cake

Take a classic lemon drizzle–style cake to the next level with added summer fruits and a zesty iced topping.

SERVES 12

Per Serving:

Calories	373
Fat	16g
Sodium	235mg
Carbohydrates	56g
Fiber	1g
Sugar	40g
Protein	3g

1 cup (220g) vegan buttery sticks

1 cup plus 1 tablespoon (220g) superfine sugar

4 large eggs

1¼ cups plus 2 tablespoons (220g) gluten-free self-rising flour

¼ teaspoon xanthan gum (omit if flour blend already contains this)

3 tablespoons lemon zest, divided

9 tablespoons lemon juice, divided

1 cup (125g) frozen mixed summer fruits (strawberries, blueberries, raspberries)

¼ cup plus 3 tablespoons (100g) granulated sugar

1 cup (150g) confectioners' sugar

1 Preheat oven to 350°F (180°C) and line an 8" deep round springform cake pan with parchment paper.

2 In a large bowl, beat buttery sticks and superfine sugar until creamy. Add eggs one at a time and continue to beat until combined. Fold in flour, xanthan gum, 2 tablespoons lemon zest, and 2 tablespoons lemon juice. Fold in summer fruits (tossing them in flour beforehand will prevent them from sinking to the bottom of the cake).

3 Transfer mixture to prepared pan and bake 1 hour until golden brown and a skewer inserted in center comes out clean. Cover top with foil toward end of baking to prevent cake from browning too much.

4 In a small bowl, mix 4 tablespoons lemon juice and granulated sugar. Remove cake from oven and, while still warm, poke holes in top of cake with a skewer. Pour topping on top of cake and let cool in pan for about 1 hour.

5 Once cake is cool, in a small bowl, combine confectioners' sugar and remaining 3 tablespoons lemon juice until the consistency is fairly runny.

6 Pour icing over top of cake and sprinkle with remaining 1 tablespoon lemon zest. Let set, about 30 minutes, then store in an airtight container at room temperature for up to 3 days.

Chocolate Bundt Cake

This simple but impressive Chocolate Bundt Cake is perfect for any celebration, combining a moist chocolate cake with a tasty chocolate ganache.

CAKE

1½ cups plus 1 tablespoon (320g) superfine sugar

1½ cups plus 2 tablespoons (260g) gluten-free all-purpose flour

¼ teaspoon xanthan gum (omit if flour blend already contains this)

1 teaspoon baking soda

1 teaspoon baking powder

½ cup plus 3 tablespoons (75g) cocoa powder

½ teaspoon salt

2 large eggs

¾ cup plus 2 tablespoons (200g) dairy-free plain yogurt

¼ cup plus 2 tablespoons (85ml) vegetable oil

¾ cup plus 1 tablespoon (200ml) boiling water

½ cup plus 1 tablespoon (100g) dairy-free milk chocolate chips

GANACHE

½ cup plus 3 tablespoons (120g) dairy-free dark chocolate chips (70% cocoa content or higher)

¼ cup (60ml) dairy-free heavy cream

SERVES 12	
Per Serving:	
Calories	392
Fat	18g
Sodium	257mg
Carbohydrates	55g
Fiber	6g
Sugar	35g
Protein	6g

CAKE

1 Preheat oven to 350°F (180°C) and thoroughly grease a 1.5-liter Bundt pan with buttery spread or nonstick vegetable oil spray.

2 In a large bowl, combine sugar, flour, xanthan gum, baking soda, baking powder, cocoa powder, and salt. In a medium bowl, whisk eggs, yogurt, and oil. Add wet ingredients to dry ingredients, then add boiling water and mix until combined. Fold in milk chocolate chips.

3 Transfer mixture to prepared pan and bake 45–50 minutes or until a skewer inserted in center comes out clean. Let cool in pan for 10 minutes, then carefully turn out onto a wire rack to cool completely, about 1 hour.

GANACHE

1 In a large heatproof bowl, add dark chocolate chips. Add cream to a small saucepan and heat over low heat until it starts to simmer (don't let it boil). Pour cream over chocolate and stir until chocolate is melted and mixture is smooth and glossy.

2 Spread Ganache over cooled Cake and let set 30 minutes. Store in an airtight container at room temperature for up to 3 days.

Chocolate Brownie Cake

SERVES 12

Per Serving:

Calories	269
Fat	14g
Fiber	3g
Carbohydrates	36g
Sodium	175mg
Sugar	25g
Protein	3g

Serve this delicious, fudgy Chocolate Brownie Cake with dairy-free ice cream and fresh raspberries for a memorable dessert.

¾ cup plus 1 tablespoon (185g) vegan buttery spread

½ cup plus 3 tablespoons (75g) cocoa powder

1½ cups (300g) superfine sugar

3 large eggs

¾ cup (120g) gluten-free self-rising flour

¼ teaspoon xanthan gum (omit if flour blend already contains this)

1 Preheat oven to 350°F (180°C) and line an 8" deep round springform cake pan with parchment paper.

2 In a medium saucepan, melt buttery spread over medium heat. Add cocoa powder and sugar and mix until a thick, chocolaty mixture forms. Set aside to cool slightly, about 3 minutes.

3 In a small bowl, beat eggs, then pour into chocolaty mixture. Mix until combined, then fold in flour and xanthan gum. Pour batter into prepared cake pan.

4 Bake 35–40 minutes until firm around the edges with a gentle wobble in center. Let cool completely in pan, about 1–2 hours, then store in an airtight container at room temperature for up to 3 days.

Peanut Butter and Jam Cupcakes

Combining a peanut butter–flavored cake with a jammy center and a peanut butter–flavored buttercream in a cupcake is a no-brainer. This really is such a delicious combination!

CUPCAKES

½ cup plus 1 tablespoon (130g) vegan buttery sticks

¾ cup plus 1 tablespoon (160g) superfine sugar

¼ cup plus 3 tablespoons (100g) smooth peanut butter

3 large eggs

2 tablespoons unsweetened almond or other dairy-free milk

1 cup (160g) gluten-free self-rising flour

¼ teaspoon xanthan gum (omit if flour blend already contains this)

½ teaspoon salt

½ teaspoon baking soda

FILLING AND BUTTERCREAM

12 teaspoons strawberry jam

½ cup plus 3 tablespoons (150g) vegan buttery sticks

¼ cup plus 3 tablespoons (100g) smooth peanut butter

2 cups plus 1 tablespoon (300g) confectioners' sugar

2 tablespoons salted peanuts

6 hulled fresh strawberries

MAKES 12

Per Serving (1 cupcake):

Calories	505
Fat	29g
Sodium	403mg
Carbohydrates	58g
Fiber	1g
Sugar	43g
Protein	6g

CUPCAKES

1 Preheat oven to 350°F (180°C) and line a twelve-cup muffin tin with cupcake liners.

2 In a large bowl, add buttery sticks and superfine sugar and beat until light and fluffy. Add peanut butter and beat. Add eggs and milk and beat. Fold in flour, xanthan gum, salt, and baking soda.

3 Divide mixture between twelve muffin cups and bake 25 minutes or until a skewer inserted in center comes out clean. Let cool completely, about 1 hour.

FILLING AND BUTTERCREAM

1 Once cool, use a serrated knife to cut a small hole in top of each and add 1 teaspoon of jam to each hole.

2 In a medium bowl, beat buttery sticks with an electric mixer on medium speed until soft. Add peanut butter and beat. Gradually add confectioners' sugar, continuing to beat up to 5 minutes until combined and creamy.

ASSEMBLY

Pipe Buttercream onto Cupcakes and top with peanuts and strawberries. Store in an airtight container at room temperature for up to 3 days.

Eton Mess Cake

Inspired by the classic British dessert, Eton Mess, this vanilla- and strawberry-flavored cake is made with fresh dairy-free cream, crushed meringue, and strawberry toppings. A perfect cake for lazy summer afternoons.

SERVES 9

Per Serving:

Calories	513
Fat	30g
Sodium	88mg
Carbohydrates	56g
Fiber	3g
Sugar	40g
Protein	5g

TOP TIP

Tossing the strawberries in gluten-free all-purpose flour before folding them into the cake batter will prevent them from sinking to the bottom of the cake.

CAKE

¾ cup plus 2 tablespoons (200g) vegan buttery sticks

1 cup (200g) superfine sugar

4 large eggs

1 teaspoon vanilla extract

1¼ cups (200g) gluten-free all-purpose flour

3 teaspoons baking powder

½ teaspoon xanthan gum (omit if flour blend already contains this)

1 cup finely hulled and chopped fresh strawberries

TOPPING

1 cup plus 1 tablespoon (250ml) dairy-free heavy cream

¾ cup (110g) confectioners' sugar

ASSEMBLY

3 mini meringue nests, crushed

1 cup fresh hulled and sliced fresh strawberries

CAKE

1   Preheat oven to 350°F (180°C) and line a 9" square springform cake pan with parchment paper.
2   In a large bowl, beat buttery sticks and superfine sugar until creamy. Add eggs one at a time and continue to whisk until combined. Add vanilla and whisk. Fold in flour, baking powder, and xanthan gum.
3   Toss chopped strawberries in gluten-free all-purpose flour and fold into batter. Transfer mixture to prepared pan and bake 35–40 minutes until golden and a skewer inserted in center comes out clean. Let cool completely, about 1 hour.

TOPPING

In a medium bowl, whisk cream to stiff peaks. Add confectioners' sugar and whisk until fully combined.

ASSEMBLY

Spread Topping over cooled Cake and top with crushed meringue pieces and sliced strawberries. Store in an airtight container in the refrigerator for up to 3 days.

Chocolate Cake Pops

These treats feature moist chocolate cake, chocolate frosting, and chocolate coating dipped in sprinkles.

½ cup plus 2 tablespoons (100g) gluten-free all-purpose flour

¼ teaspoon xanthan gum (omit if flour blend already contains this)

¾ cup (150g) superfine sugar

¼ cup (30g) cocoa powder

½ teaspoon baking soda

¼ teaspoon salt

¼ cup plus 3 tablespoons (100ml) vegetable oil

2 large eggs

1 teaspoon vanilla extract

¼ cup plus 3 tablespoons (100ml) hot water

¼ cup plus 1 tablespoon (75g) vegan buttery sticks

½ cup plus 3 tablespoons (100g) confectioners' sugar

¼ cup (30g) cocoa powder

2 tablespoons unsweetened almond or other dairy-free milk

1 teaspoon vanilla extract

1½ cups plus 3 tablespoons (300g) dairy-free milk chocolate, melted

2 tablespoons sprinkles

MAKES 20

Per Serving (1 cake pop):

Calories	227
Fat	14g
Sodium	97mg
Carbohydrates	28g
Fiber	3g
Sugar	21g
Protein	3g

1 Preheat oven to 350°F (180°C) and line a 9" round springform cake pan with parchment paper. Line a baking sheet with parchment paper.

2 In a large bowl, mix flour, xanthan gum, superfine sugar, cocoa powder, baking soda, and salt. In a medium bowl, whisk oil, eggs, and vanilla. Add wet ingredients to dry ingredients, then add hot water and mix until fully incorporated.

3 Transfer mixture to prepared cake pan and bake 30 minutes or until a skewer inserted in center comes out clean. Let cool for 1 hour.

4 In a medium bowl, beat buttery sticks with an electric mixer on medium speed until soft. Add confectioners' sugar, cocoa powder, milk, and vanilla and continue to beat until combined and creamy.

5 In a large bowl, crumble cooled cake and mix in frosting until fully combined. Roll cake mixture into twenty equal-sized balls and place on prepared baking sheet. Refrigerate for 2 hours to set.

6 Once set, remove cake balls from refrigerator one at a time, press a lollipop stick into base, and coat in melted chocolate. Decorate with sprinkles and place back on baking sheet in refrigerator to set for 1 hour. Store in refrigerator for up to 3 days.

Rhubarb and Custard Cake

Enjoy the flavors of rhubarb and custard with this sweet yet tangy cake. This recipe is a great way to use up seasonal rhubarb.

TOP TIP

If you can't find dairy-free ready-made custard in your local grocery store, you can search for the Alpro brand online. Alternatively, substitute it for 1/2 cup of your favorite dairy-free vanilla pudding.

7 ounces (200g) rhubarb stalks, cut into chunks

2 tablespoons granulated sugar

1/4 cup (65ml) water

1 cup (220g) vegan buttery sticks

1 cup plus 1 tablespoon (220g) superfine sugar

4 large eggs

1 teaspoon vanilla extract

1/2 cup (125ml) dairy-free ready-made custard, divided

1 1/4 cups plus 2 tablespoons (220g) gluten-free self-rising flour

1/4 teaspoon xanthan gum (omit if flour blend already contains this)

1/4 teaspoon salt

1. Preheat oven to 350°F (180°C) and line an 8" deep round springform cake pan with parchment paper.
2. In a large saucepan, add rhubarb, granulated sugar, and water. Bring to a simmer over medium heat and cook until water has evaporated, about 10–15 minutes. Remove from heat and set aside.
3. In a large bowl, beat buttery sticks and superfine sugar until creamy. Add eggs one at a time and continue to beat until combined. Add vanilla and 6 tablespoons custard and whisk. Fold in flour, xanthan gum, and salt.
4. Spoon half batter into prepared pan, followed by half rhubarb. Add remaining half batter and top with remaining rhubarb and remaining 2 tablespoons custard.
5. Bake 1 hour until golden brown and a skewer inserted in center comes out clean. Cover top with foil toward end of baking time if cake is browning too quickly.
6. Let cake cool on a wire rack, then store in an airtight container at room temperature for up to 2 days.

Chocolate Mug Cake

Ready in under 5 minutes, this individual Chocolate Mug Cake uses basic pantry ingredients and is great for a quick chocolate fix! Serve with a scoop of dairy-free vanilla ice cream.

3 tablespoons gluten-free all-purpose flour

½ teaspoon baking powder

3 tablespoons sugar

1 tablespoon cocoa powder

⅛ teaspoon salt

2 tablespoons unsweetened almond or other dairy-free milk

1 teaspoon vegetable oil

1 large egg

2 tablespoons dairy-free milk chocolate chips

1 In a microwave-safe mug, add flour, baking powder, sugar, cocoa powder, and salt. Mix well.

2 Add milk, oil, and egg to dry ingredients and whisk until a smooth batter forms. Mix in chocolate chips.

3 Microwave on high 1 minute until cake is risen and cooked through. Serve warm.

SERVES 1

Per Serving:

Calories	498
Fat	21g
Sodium	337mg
Carbohydrates	76g
Fiber	6g
Sugar	53g
Protein	12g

MUG SIZE

Make sure you use a large mug (around 10–15 ounces) for this recipe so the mixture doesn't overflow and make a mess in your microwave!

Orange and Polenta Cake

Make this naturally gluten-free orange-flavored cake using polenta and ground almonds topped with orange syrup.

CAKE

¾ cup plus 1 tablespoon (180g) vegan buttery sticks

¾ cup plus 2 tablespoons (180g) superfine sugar

3 large eggs

1 teaspoon vanilla extract

1¾ cups plus 3 tablespoons (180g) ground almonds

⅔ cup (100g) polenta

Zest of 2 medium oranges

1 teaspoon orange extract

1 teaspoon baking powder

SYRUP

3 cardamon pods

¾ cup plus 1 tablespoon (200ml) pulp-free orange juice

1 teaspoon orange extract

½ cup (100g) superfine sugar

CAKE

1 Preheat oven to 350°F (180°C) and line an 8" deep round springform cake pan with parchment paper.

2 In a large bowl, beat buttery sticks and sugar until creamy. Add eggs one at a time and continue to beat until combined. Add vanilla and beat until combined.

3 In a medium bowl, combine almonds, polenta, orange zest, orange extract, and baking powder. Fold dry ingredients into wet ingredients and transfer mixture to prepared pan.

4 Bake 40 minutes or until a skewer inserted in center comes out clean. Let cool in pan 10 minutes before turning out onto a large plate.

SYRUP

Crush cardamon pods and add them to a small saucepan with orange juice, orange extract, and sugar. Heat over medium heat, stirring continuously, until mixture starts to thicken and reduce, about 10 minutes.

ASSEMBLY

Prick top of Cake all over with a skewer and brush with Syrup. Store in an airtight container at room temperature for up to 3 days.

CHAPTER 7

Quick Breads and Loaf Cakes

Apple Crumble Loaf Cake

This loaf cake combines all the delicious autumn tastes of apple, cinnamon, and raisins, topped with a crunchy topping.

SERVES 12

Per Serving:

Calories	255
Fat	11g
Sodium	134mg
Carbohydrates	37g
Fiber	3g
Sugar	22g
Protein	4g

CRUMBLE TOPPING

2 tablespoons gluten-free all-purpose flour

1 tablespoon (15g) vegan buttery sticks

2 tablespoons granulated sugar

2 tablespoons gluten-free rolled oats

CAKE

1¼ cups (200g) gluten-free self-rising flour

¼ teaspoon xanthan gum (omit if flour blend already contains this)

½ teaspoon baking powder

1 teaspoon pumpkin pie spice

1 teaspoon ground cinnamon

½ cup plus 1 tablespoon (130g) vegan buttery sticks

¼ cup plus 1 tablespoon (75g) packed light brown sugar

¼ cup (60g) granulated sugar

3 large eggs

1 teaspoon vanilla extract

3 tablespoons unsweetened almond or other dairy-free milk

¾ cup (110g) raisins

2 medium Granny Smith apples, peeled, cored, and cut into cubes, divided

CRUMBLE TOPPING

1 Preheat oven to 350°F (180°C) and line a 2-pound loaf pan with parchment paper.

2 In a medium bowl, mix flour, buttery sticks, and granulated sugar. Use your fingers to form a bread crumb consistency and stir in rolled oats.

CAKE

1 In a medium bowl, mix flour, xanthan gum, baking powder, pumpkin pie spice, and cinnamon.

2 In a large bowl, whisk buttery sticks, brown sugar, and granulated sugar until light and fluffy. Add eggs, vanilla, and milk, continuing to whisk until combined.

3 Add dry ingredients to wet ingredients and stir until combined. Stir in raisins and three-quarters of apple.

ASSEMBLY

1 Transfer mixture to prepared pan, sprinkle over Crumble Topping, and top with remaining one-quarter of apple.

2 Bake 50 minutes until golden brown and a skewer inserted in center comes out clean. Let cool for about 1 hour on a wire rack before serving. Store in an airtight container at room temperature for up to 3 days.

Soda Bread

This easy Soda Bread recipe is great for making in a hurry! It's totally yeast-free and takes a matter of minutes to put together. Enjoy warm and fresh out of the oven with dairy-free butter and jam.

1¼ cups (300ml) unsweetened almond or other dairy-free milk

1 tablespoon lemon juice

2½ cups plus 2 tablespoons (420g) gluten-free all-purpose flour

1½ teaspoons xanthan gum (omit if flour blend already contains this)

2 tablespoons granulated sugar

1 teaspoon baking powder

1 teaspoon baking soda

½ teaspoon salt

1 large egg, lightly beaten

4 tablespoons vegan buttery spread, melted

SERVES 10

Per Serving:

Calories	187
Fat	6g
Sodium	365mg
Carbohydrates	31g
Fiber	4g
Sugar	4g
Protein	4g

1 Preheat oven to 375°F (190°C) and lightly grease a baking sheet with vegetable oil or buttery spread. In a large bowl, mix milk and lemon juice to form a dairy-free buttermilk alternative. Set aside for 10 minutes.

2 In a separate large bowl, mix flour, xanthan gum, sugar, baking powder, baking soda, and salt. Add egg, melted buttery spread, and buttermilk mixture and mix until combined. Dough will feel sticky.

3 Turn out dough onto a lightly floured surface and mold into a ball, making sure to not overwork dough. Place on prepared baking sheet and use a knife to score an X into top. Bake 30–35 minutes and serve fresh from oven.

Gin and Tonic Drizzle Cake

This adaptation of a classic drizzle cake is perfect for gin and tonic lovers. Combining a light and fluffy cake with a gin, tonic, and lime drizzle and icing, it's a treat definitely just for the grown-ups!

1 cup (220g) vegan buttery sticks

1 cup plus 1 tablespoon (220g) superfine sugar

4 large eggs

5 teaspoons grated lime zest, divided

1¼ cups plus 2 tablespoons (220g) gluten-free self-rising flour

¼ teaspoon xanthan gum (omit if flour blend already contains this)

4 tablespoons tonic water

¼ cup plus 2 tablespoons (80g) granulated sugar

3 tablespoons lime juice, divided

5 tablespoons gin, divided

1¼ cups plus 2 tablespoons (200g) confectioners' sugar

SERVES 12

Per Serving:

Calories	392
Fat	16g
Sodium	235mg
Carbohydrates	57g
Fiber	0g
Sugar	42g
Protein	3g

1 Preheat oven to 350°F (180°C) and line a 9" × 5" loaf pan with parchment paper.

2 In a large mixing bowl, whisk buttery sticks and superfine sugar until light and fluffy. Add eggs one at a time, beating in between each addition. Add 3 teaspoons lime zest, flour, and xanthan gum. Beat until combined.

3 Pour batter into prepared pan. Bake for 40–45 minutes until golden brown and a skewer inserted in center comes out clean (cover top with foil if cake starts to brown too quickly). Set aside to cool slightly in pan.

4 In a small bowl, whisk together tonic water, granulated sugar, 2 tablespoons lime juice, and 3 tablespoons gin.

5 While cake is still warm, poke holes in top with a skewer. Pour gin and tonic mixture over cake and set aside to cool in pan at least 1 hour.

6 In a small bowl, mix confectioners' sugar with remaining 1 tablespoon lime juice and remaining 2 tablespoons gin. Pour over top of cooled cake and sprinkle with remaining 2 teaspoons lime zest. Set aside 15–30 minutes until icing hardens before serving. Store in an airtight container at room temperature for up to 3 days.

Marble Cake

This cake looks different every time you make it. The patterns of the swirled mixture are always unique and intriguing when the cake is cut!

Per Serving:	
Calories	418
Fat	24g
Sodium	348mg
Carbohydrates	50g
Fiber	4g
Sugar	34g
Protein	5g

CAKE

¾ cup plus 2 tablespoons (200g) vegan buttery sticks

1 cup (200g) superfine sugar

1 teaspoon vanilla extract

4 large eggs

1¼ cups plus 2 tablespoons (225g) gluten-free all-purpose flour

¼ teaspoon xanthan gum (omit if flour blend already contains this)

2 teaspoons baking powder

¼ teaspoon salt

3 tablespoons unsweetened almond or other dairy-free milk, divided

¼ cup (30g) cocoa powder

BUTTERCREAM

½ cup (105g) vegan buttery sticks

1¼ cups (180g) confectioners' sugar

¼ cup (30g) cocoa powder

ASSEMBLY

¼ cup dairy-free milk chocolate chips

CAKE

1 Preheat oven to 350°F (180°C) and line a 2-pound loaf pan with parchment paper.

2 In a large bowl, whisk buttery sticks and superfine sugar together until creamy. Add vanilla and eggs, one at a time, and whisk until fully combined. In a separate large bowl, mix together flour, xanthan gum, baking powder, and salt. Add dry ingredients to wet ingredients and mix well. Add 2 tablespoons milk and mix. In a medium bowl, add one-third of mixture and mix in cocoa powder and remaining 1 tablespoon milk.

3 Spoon half of vanilla batter into prepared loaf pan, followed by half of chocolate mixture. Use a skewer to swirl mixtures together to create a marble effect. Spoon remaining vanilla mixture into pan followed by remaining chocolate mixture and swirl.

4 Bake 45–50 minutes or until a skewer inserted in center comes out clean. Let cool in pan, about 1 hour.

BUTTERCREAM

In a medium bowl, beat buttery sticks with an electric mixer on medium speed until soft. Gradually add confectioners' sugar and cocoa powder, continuing to beat up to 5 minutes until combined and creamy.

ASSEMBLY

Spread Buttercream on top of Cake and decorate with chocolate chips. Store in an airtight container at room temperature for up to 3 days.

Lemon Drizzle Cake

Your friends and family will love this moist and zesty Lemon Drizzle Cake with a crunchy sugar topping. Made with a handful of simple ingredients, this is a recipe you'll want to make again and again!

CAKE

1 cup (220g) vegan buttery sticks

1 cup plus 1 tablespoon (220g) superfine sugar

4 large eggs

Zest of 1 medium lemon

1¼ cups plus 2 tablespoons (220g) gluten-free self-rising flour

¼ teaspoon xanthan gum (omit if flour blend already contains this)

TOPPING

Juice of 2 medium lemons

¾ cup (160g) granulated sugar

SERVES 12

Per Serving:

Calories	337
Fat	16g
Sodium	235mg
Carbohydrates	46g
Fiber	0g
Sugar	32g
Protein	3g

CAKE

1 Preheat oven to 350°F (180°C) and line a 2-pound loaf pan with parchment paper.

2 In a large mixing bowl, whisk buttery sticks and superfine sugar until creamy. Add eggs one at a time and continue to whisk until fully combined. Add lemon zest, flour, and xanthan gum. Mix well until combined, then spoon mixture into prepared pan.

3 Bake 45 minutes until golden brown and a skewer inserted in center comes out clean (cover top with foil if cake starts to brown too quickly).

TOPPING

In a small bowl, combine all Topping ingredients.

ASSEMBLY

While Cake is still warm, poke holes in top with a skewer. Pour Topping on Cake and let cool in pan for 1 hour. Store in an airtight container at room temperature for up to 4 days.

Spiced Honey Cake

Enjoy this tasty honey loaf cake made with warming spices like cinnamon and ginger. Perfect for a midmorning pick-me-up.

SERVES 12

Per Serving:

Calories	234
Fat	11g
Sodium	215mg
Carbohydrates	33g
Fiber	2g
Sugar	22g
Protein	3g

3 large eggs

½ cup plus 2 tablespoons (125g) packed light brown sugar

½ cup (125ml) vegetable oil

½ cup (120ml) clear honey

1¼ cups (200g) gluten-free all-purpose flour

¼ teaspoon xanthan gum (omit if flour blend already contains this)

1 teaspoon baking soda

1 teaspoon baking powder

1½ teaspoons pumpkin pie spice

1 teaspoon ground ginger

1 teaspoon ground cinnamon

¼ teaspoon salt

1 Preheat oven to 350°F (180°C) and line a 2-pound loaf pan with parchment paper.

2 In a large mixing bowl, beat eggs and brown sugar with an electric mixer on medium speed until pale and frothy. Add oil and honey and beat until combined.

3 In a separate large bowl, mix flour, xanthan gum, baking soda, baking powder, pumpkin pie spice, ginger, cinnamon, and salt. Fold dry ingredients into wet ingredients and transfer mixture into prepared pan.

4 Bake 45–50 minutes or until a skewer inserted in center comes out clean. Let cool about 1 hour, then store in an airtight container at room temperature for up to 3 days.

Double Chocolate Loaf Cake

Filled with chocolate chips and topped with a chocolate ganache, this dreamy cake is sure to please chocolate lovers.

CAKE

1¾ cups (280g) gluten-free all-purpose flour

½ teaspoon xanthan gum (omit if flour blend already contains this)

2 teaspoons baking powder

¼ teaspoon salt

½ cup plus 3 tablespoons (75g) cocoa powder

3 large eggs

¾ cup plus 1 tablespoon (160g) packed light brown sugar

¾ cup (160g) granulated sugar

½ cup plus 2 tablespoons (150ml) unsweetened almond or other dairy-free milk

¼ cup (60ml) hot coffee

½ cup (120ml) vegetable oil

2 teaspoons vanilla extract

¾ cup plus 1 tablespoon (150g) dairy-free milk chocolate chips

GANACHE

¾ cup plus 1 tablespoon (150g) dairy-free dark chocolate chips (70% cocoa content or higher)

1 cup plus 1 tablespoon (250ml) dairy-free heavy cream

2 tablespoons granulated sugar

DID YOU KNOW?

Ganache originates from France and is a silky-smooth glaze made from dark chocolate, cream, and sugar. Glossy and rich, it makes a delicious icing or filling.

CAKE

1 Preheat oven to 350°F (180°C) and line a 2-pound loaf pan with parchment paper.

2 In a large bowl, mix together flour, xanthan gum, baking powder, salt, and cocoa powder.

3 In a separate large bowl, beat eggs, brown sugar, and granulated sugar until frothy. Add milk, coffee, oil, and vanilla and beat until combined. Fold dry ingredients into wet ingredients, then add chocolate chips.

4 Transfer mixture to prepared pan and bake 1 hour and 10 minutes or until a skewer inserted in center comes out clean. Let cool for 1 hour.

GANACHE

1 In a large heatproof bowl, add chocolate chips. In a medium saucepan, heat cream and granulated sugar over low heat until mixture starts to simmer (don't let it boil). Remove cream from heat and pour over chocolate chips, stirring until chocolate is melted and mixture is smooth and glossy. Set aside to thicken, about 1 hour.

2 Once thick, spread Ganache on top of cooled Cake. Store in an air-tight container at room temperature for up to 3 days.

Pear and Almond Loaf Cake

SERVES 12

Per Serving:

Calories	296
Fat	17g
Sodium	270mg
Carbohydrates	33g
Fiber	2g
Sugar	20g
Protein	4g

A moist and tasty loaf cake filled with chunks of pear and hints of cinnamon and almonds, this recipe works for breakfast, a midafternoon snack, or dessert.

¾ cup plus 1 tablespoon (180g) vegan buttery sticks

¾ cup plus 2 tablespoons (180g) superfine sugar

3 large eggs

½ teaspoon almond extract

¾ cup plus 3 tablespoons (150g) gluten-free self-rising flour

¼ teaspoon xanthan gum (omit if flour blend already contains this)

1 teaspoon baking powder

1 cup plus 1 tablespoon (100g) ground almonds

1 teaspoon ground cinnamon

¼ teaspoon salt

3 medium pears, peeled, cored, and cut into cubes

1 Preheat oven to 350°F (180°C) and line a 2-pound loaf pan with parchment paper.

2 In a large mixing bowl, whisk buttery sticks and sugar until creamy. Add eggs one at a time and continue to whisk until fully combined. Add almond extract and whisk.

3 In a separate large bowl, mix flour, xanthan gum, baking powder, ground almonds, cinnamon, and salt. Add dry ingredients to wet ingredients and mix well. Fold in pear cubes and transfer mixture to prepared pan.

4 Bake 55 minutes until golden brown and a skewer inserted in center comes out clean (cover top with foil if cake starts to brown too quickly). Let cool about 1 hour, then store in an airtight container at room temperature for up to 3 days.

Lemon and Elderflower Cake

This simple Lemon and Elderflower Cake is a perfect summertime treat. It's light, moist, and beautifully topped with edible flowers.

CAKE

¾ cup plus 1 tablespoon (175g) vegan buttery sticks

¾ cup plus 2 tablespoons (175g) superfine sugar

3 large eggs

Zest of 2 medium lemons

2 tablespoons lemon juice

1½ tablespoons elderflower cordial

1 cup plus 1 tablespoon (175g) gluten-free self-rising flour

¼ teaspoon xanthan gum (omit if flour blend already contains this)

½ teaspoon baking powder

ICING

½ cup plus 3 tablespoons (100g) confectioners' sugar

2½ tablespoons lemon juice

Optional: 8–10 edible flowers such as violets or pansies

SERVES 12

Per Serving:

Calories	261
Fat	13g
Sodium	206mg
Carbohydrates	35g
Fiber	0g
Sugar	23g
Protein	2g

CAKE

1 Preheat oven to 350°F (180°C) and line a 2-pound loaf pan with parchment paper.

2 In a large mixing bowl, whisk buttery sticks and superfine sugar until creamy. Add eggs one at a time and continue to whisk until fully combined. Add lemon zest, lemon juice, cordial, flour, xanthan gum, and baking powder. Mix well until combined, then spoon mixture into prepared pan.

3 Bake 45 minutes until golden brown and a skewer inserted in center comes out clean (cover top with foil if cake starts to brown too quickly).

4 Let cake cool in the pan for 10 minutes before transferring to a wire rack for 1 hour to cool completely.

ICING

In a small bowl, combine confectioners' sugar with lemon juice to form a runny consistency. Drizzle over Cake and top with edible flowers. Store in an airtight container at room temperature for up to 3 days.

Battenberg Cake

SERVES 12

Per Serving:

Calories	419
Fat	17g
Sodium	216mg
Carbohydrates	64g
Fiber	3g
Sugar	42g
Protein	5g

ENSURE YOUR PAN IS PREPPED

To ensure this recipe works correctly, make sure your pan is fully prepped with foil and parchment paper so there's no chance of different-colored mixtures leaking into each other.

A classic pink-and-yellow checkerboard cake, this traditional British Battenberg Cake is the ultimate sweet treat. Although it's easy to make, the finished product looks seriously impressive.

¾ cup plus 1 tablespoon (180g) vegan buttery sticks

¾ cup plus 2 tablespoons (180g) superfine sugar

3 large eggs

¾ cup plus 1 tablespoon (130g) gluten-free self-rising flour

¼ teaspoon xanthan gum (omit if flour blend contains this)

½ cup plus 1 tablespoon (50g) ground almonds

½ teaspoon baking powder

1 teaspoon vanilla extract

1 teaspoon almond extract

Pink gel food coloring

1 block (400g) marzipan

1 cup apricot jam, melted

1 Preheat oven to 350°F (180°C) and grease a 9" × 9" baking dish with buttery spread or vegetable oil. Use foil to make a barrier down center of pan to split it in half. Line each compartment with parchment paper.

2 In a large bowl, beat buttery sticks and sugar until light and fluffy. Add eggs one at a time. Add flour, xanthan gum, ground almonds, baking powder, and vanilla and almond extracts. Beat until combined.

3 Split mixture into two medium bowls. Use a wooden skewer or tip of a knife to add a few drops of food coloring to one bowl and mix until combined. Continue until desired color is reached.

4 Pour one mixture into each side of pan and smooth tops. Bake for 20–25 minutes or until a skewer inserted in center comes out clean.

5 Transfer pan to a wire rack and cool cake completely, at least 1 hour.

6 Remove cakes from pan and place on top of each other on a cutting board. Trim edges as needed so cakes are uniform. Cut down middle of both cakes lengthwise. You will now have four equal-sized pieces of cake (two pink and two yellow).

7 Place marzipan on a work surface dusted with confectioners' sugar. Roll out into a rectangle shape large enough to fit around outside of cake. Brush middle of marzipan rectangle with melted jam. Brush outsides of one pink and one yellow cake piece and place side-by-side on top of jam. Brush outsides of remaining two pieces of cake and stack them on top of other two pieces. Alternate colors in a checkerboard pattern. Wrap cake stack with marzipan, leaving short edges open.

8 Turn cake over so seam is on bottom. Trim short edges so you can see pattern of cake. Serve immediately or store in an airtight container at room temperature for up to 3 days.

Chocolate Orange Loaf Cake

SERVES 12

Per Serving:

Calories	455
Fat	27g
Sodium	293mg
Carbohydrates	54g
Fiber	3g
Sugar	38g
Protein	4g

DAIRY-FREE BUTTERCREAM

When making dairy-free buttercream, be sure to use hard vegan buttery sticks formulated for baking instead of a soft buttery spread, as some dairy-free soft spreads can curdle when beaten.

If you are a fan of chocolate oranges, you will absolutely love this recipe.

CAKE

¾ cup plus 2 tablespoons (200g) vegan buttery sticks

1 cup (200g) superfine sugar

4 large eggs

2 teaspoons orange extract

1 tablespoon unsweetened almond or other dairy-free milk

1 cup plus 1 tablespoon (170g) gluten-free self-rising flour

¼ teaspoon xanthan gum (omit if flour blend already contains this)

½ teaspoon baking powder

¼ cup (30g) cocoa powder

½ cup plus 1 tablespoon (100g) dairy-free milk chocolate chips

BUTTERCREAM

½ cup (105g) vegan buttery sticks

1¼ cups (180g) confectioners' sugar

¼ cup (30g) cocoa powder

1 teaspoon orange extract

ASSEMBLY

¼ cup dairy-free milk chocolate chips

Zest of 1 medium orange

CAKE

1   Preheat oven to 350°F (180°C) and line a 2-pound loaf pan with parchment paper.

2   In a large bowl, whisk buttery sticks and superfine sugar until creamy. Add eggs one at a time and continue to whisk until fully combined. Add orange extract and milk and whisk.

3   In a separate large bowl, mix flour, xanthan gum, baking powder, and cocoa powder. Add dry ingredients to wet ingredients and mix well. Fold in chocolate chips.

4   Transfer mixture to prepared pan and bake 45–50 minutes or until a skewer inserted in center comes out clean. Let cool in pan for 10 minutes before transferring to a wire rack to cool for an additional 1 hour.

BUTTERCREAM

In a medium bowl, beat buttery sticks with an electric mixer on medium speed until soft. Gradually add confectioners' sugar and cocoa powder, continuing to beat up to 5 minutes until creamy. Whisk in orange extract.

ASSEMBLY

Spread Buttercream on top of Cake and decorate with chocolate chips and orange zest. Store in an airtight container at room temperature for up to 3 days.

Simple Banana Bread

Add chocolate chips, walnuts, pecans, or raisins if you fancy something a little different!

½ cup plus 2 tablespoons (140g) vegan buttery sticks

½ cup plus 3 tablespoons (140g) superfine sugar

2 large eggs

¾ cup plus 2 tablespoons (140g) gluten-free self-rising flour

¼ teaspoon xanthan gum (omit if flour blend already contains this)

1 teaspoon baking powder

½ teaspoon ground cinnamon

2 large ripe bananas, peeled and mashed

SERVES 12	
Per Serving:	
Calories	196
Fat	10g
Sodium	187mg
Carbohydrates	25g
Fiber	1g
Sugar	14g
Protein	2g

1 Preheat oven to 350°F (180°C) and line a 2-pound loaf pan with parchment paper.

2 In a large mixing bowl, whisk buttery sticks and sugar until creamy. Add eggs one at a time and continue to whisk. Mix in flour, xanthan gum, baking powder, and cinnamon, then banana.

3 Transfer mixture to prepared pan and bake 30–35 minutes or until a skewer inserted in center comes out clean. Store in an airtight container at room temperature for up to 3 days.

Honey Corn Bread

Serve this sweet and buttery bread warm with a big bowl of chili.

1 cup (150g) cornmeal

¾ cup (125g) gluten-free all-purpose flour

¼ teaspoon xanthan gum (omit if flour blend already contains this)

½ teaspoon salt

1 teaspoon baking powder

¼ cup plus 1 tablespoon (75g) buttery spread, melted and cooled

1 tablespoon vegetable oil

1 large egg

¼ cup (80g) clear honey

¾ cup plus 1 tablespoon (200ml) unsweetened almond or other dairy-free milk

SERVES 9	
Per Serving:	
Calories	212
Fat	10g
Sodium	276mg
Carbohydrates	30g
Fiber	3g
Sugar	8g
Protein	3g

1 Preheat oven to 350°F (180°C) and line a 9" square springform cake pan with parchment paper.

2 In a large bowl, mix together dry ingredients. In a medium bowl, whisk together wet ingredients. Mix wet ingredients into dry ingredients and pour into prepared pan.

3 Bake 20–25 minutes until golden brown and a skewer inserted in center comes out clean. Store in an airtight container at room temperature for up to 3 days.

Sticky Toffee Loaf Cake

SERVES 12

Per Serving:

Calories	335
Fat	16g
Sodium	270mg
Carbohydrates	47g
Fiber	1g
Sugar	34g
Protein	2g

All the tastes of a sticky toffee pudding in a loaf cake, this recipe features comforting ginger and cinnamon spices and is served with a homemade toffee sauce.

CAKE

1 cup (200g) Medjool dates

¾ cup plus 1 tablespoon (200ml) boiling water

1 teaspoon baking soda

¼ cup plus 3 tablespoons (100g) vegan buttery sticks

¾ cup (150g) packed light brown sugar

2 large eggs

1 teaspoon vanilla extract

1 teaspoon ground cinnamon

1 teaspoon ground ginger

1 cup plus 1 tablespoon (175g) gluten-free self-rising flour

¼ teaspoon xanthan gum (omit if flour blend already contains this)

TOFFEE SAUCE

½ cup (100g) packed light brown sugar

¾ cup plus 1 tablespoon (200ml) dairy-free soy cream

½ teaspoon vanilla extract

3 tablespoons (40g) vegan buttery spread

2 tablespoons (40g) corn (golden) syrup

CAKE

1 Preheat oven to 350°F (180°C) and line a 2-pound loaf pan with parchment paper.

2 In a small bowl, add dates. Pour boiling water and baking soda over dates. Let sit 10 minutes. After 10 minutes add date and water mixture to a food processor and blitz to form a paste.

3 In a large bowl, beat buttery sticks and brown sugar until creamy, then add eggs one at a time, continuing to beat until combined. Add vanilla and beat. Fold in cinnamon, ginger, flour, xanthan gum, and date mixture.

4 Transfer mixture to prepared pan. Bake 45–50 minutes or until a skewer inserted in center comes out clean. Remove from oven and let cool, about 1 hour.

TOFFEE SAUCE

1 In a medium saucepan, add brown sugar, soy cream, vanilla, buttery spread, and corn syrup. Bring to boil over high heat, then simmer over medium heat about 3 minutes until mixture starts to thicken slightly. Remove from heat.

2 Slice Cake and drizzle Toffee Sauce over Cake to serve. Store Cake in an airtight container at room temperature for up to 3 days, and Toffee Sauce in a jar in refrigerator for up to 3 days.

Tea Loaf

Enjoy this fruity Tea Loaf packed full of tea-infused raisins and sultanas. It's perfect sliced and slathered with vegan buttery spread.

SERVES 12

Per Serving:

Calories	235
Fat	3g
Sodium	103mg
Carbohydrates	51g
Fiber	1g
Sugar	29g
Protein	3g

1 cup (150g) raisins

1 cup (150g) sultanas

Zest of 1 large orange

1¼ cups (300ml) boiling tea (made with 2 English Breakfast teabags)

1½ cups plus 1 tablespoon (250g) gluten-free self-rising flour

¼ teaspoon xanthan gum (omit if flour blend already contains this)

¾ cup plus 2 tablespoons (180g) packed light brown sugar

1 teaspoon pumpkin pie spice

1 teaspoon ground cinnamon

2 large eggs

2 tablespoons vegetable oil

1 In a medium bowl, add raisins, sultanas, and orange zest. Pour boiling tea over this and let sit 6 hours to soak.

2 Preheat oven to 350°F (180°C) and line a 2-pound loaf pan with parchment paper. In a large bowl, add flour, xanthan gum, brown sugar, pumpkin pie spice, and cinnamon and mix until combined. In a medium bowl, beat eggs and oil.

3 Mix wet ingredients into dry ingredients and stir in tea-soaked fruit, including any leftover liquid.

4 Transfer mixture to prepared pan and bake 1 hour and 15 minutes until firm to touch. Let cool for 1 hour, then store in an airtight container at room temperature for up to 2 days.

Coconut and Lime Cake

Featuring refreshing lime and coconut flavors, this tropical-tasting loaf cake is finished off with a crunchy lime and sugar topping.

SERVES 12

Per Serving:

Calories	304
Fat	17g
Sodium	199mg
Carbohydrates	35g
Fiber	1g
Sugar	22g
Protein	3g

CAKE

¾ cup plus 1 tablespoon (180g) vegan buttery sticks

¾ cup plus 2 tablespoons (180g) superfine sugar

4 large eggs

Zest of 2 small limes

1 tablespoon lime juice

1 tablespoon unsweetened almond or other dairy-free milk

1 cup plus 2 tablespoons (180g) gluten-free self-rising flour

¼ teaspoon xanthan gum (omit if flour blend already contains this)

1 cup (70g) desiccated coconut

DRIZZLE TOPPING

Juice of 2 small limes

¼ cup plus 2 tablespoons (85g) granulated sugar

CAKE

1 Preheat oven to 350°F (180°C) and line a 2-pound loaf pan with parchment paper.

2 In a large mixing bowl, whisk buttery sticks and superfine sugar until creamy. Add eggs one at a time and continue to whisk until fully combined. Add lime zest, lime juice, and milk and whisk until combined. Fold in flour, xanthan gum, and coconut.

3 Transfer mixture to prepared pan and bake 40–45 minutes until golden brown and a skewer inserted in center comes out clean (cover top with foil if cake starts to brown too quickly).

DRIZZLE TOPPING

In a small bowl, mix lime juice and granulated sugar.

ASSEMBLY

While still warm, poke top of Cake with a skewer. Pour Drizzle Topping over Cake and let cool in pan for 1 hour. Store in an airtight container at room temperature for up to 3 days.

CHAPTER 8

Celebration Cakes

Lemon and Berry Celebration Cake

SERVES 16

Per Serving:

Calories	601
Fat	32g
Sodium	420mg
Carbohydrates	77g
Fiber	1g
Sugar	59g
Protein	3g

A festive lemon-flavored cake topped with dairy-free buttercream, zesty lemon curd, and fresh berries is your new favorite dessert!

CAKE

1½ cups (335g) vegan buttery sticks

1½ cups plus 3 tablespoons (335g) superfine sugar

6 large eggs

1 teaspoon vanilla extract

Zest of 2 medium lemons

1 tablespoon lemon juice

2 cups plus 1 tablespoon (335g) gluten-free self-rising flour

½ teaspoon xanthan gum (omit if flour blend already contains this)

1 teaspoon baking powder

BUTTERCREAM

1 cup plus 2 tablespoons (250g) vegan buttery sticks

3¼ cups plus 3 tablespoons (500g) confectioners' sugar

ASSEMBLY

5 ounces lemon curd

1 cup fresh blueberries

1 cup fresh raspberries

1 cup hulled fresh strawberries

CAKE

1 Preheat oven to 350°F (180°C) and line three 8" round springform cake pans with parchment paper.

2 In a large bowl, whisk buttery sticks and superfine sugar until creamy. Add eggs one at a time and continue to whisk until combined. Add vanilla, lemon zest, and lemon juice and whisk. Fold in flour, xanthan gum, and baking powder.

3 Divide mixture between prepared pans and bake 20–25 minutes until golden brown and a skewer inserted in center comes out clean. Let cool completely, about 1 hour.

BUTTERCREAM

In a medium bowl, beat buttery sticks with an electric mixer on medium speed until soft. Gradually add confectioners' sugar, continuing to beat up to 5 minutes until combined and creamy.

ASSEMBLY

Sandwich Cake layers together with Buttercream and lemon curd. Spread remaining Buttercream on top and decorate with fresh berries.

Funfetti Cake

Take your birthday cake to the next level with this deliciously light and fluffy vanilla-flavored cake filled with brightly colored Funfetti sprinkles. It's topped with a decadent dairy-free vanilla buttercream.

CAKE

1¼ cups plus 2 tablespoons (300g) vegan buttery sticks

1½ cups (300g) superfine sugar

5 large eggs

2 teaspoons vanilla extract

1¾ cups plus 2 tablespoons (300g) gluten-free self-rising flour

½ teaspoon xanthan gum (omit if flour blend already contains this)

¾ cup (130g) rainbow sprinkles

BUTTERCREAM

1 cup plus 2 tablespoons (250g) vegan buttery sticks

3¼ cups plus 3 tablespoons (500g) confectioners' sugar

1 teaspoon vanilla extract

1 teaspoon unsweetened almond or other dairy-free milk

ASSEMBLY

¾ cup (130g) rainbow sprinkles

SERVES 16

Per Serving:

Calories	573
Fat	31g
Sodium	356mg
Carbohydrates	78g
Fiber	0g
Sugar	62g
Protein	3g

RAINBOW SPRINKLES

For this cake recipe it is important to use larger rainbow sprinkles instead of small ball or strand sprinkles to prevent them from disappearing into the cake batter once cooked. There is plenty of information online about the best sprinkles to use in Funfetti cakes. Make sure they are gluten-free too!

CAKE

1 Preheat oven to 350°F (180°C) and line three 8" round springform cake pans with parchment paper.

2 In a large bowl, whisk buttery sticks and superfine sugar until creamy. Add eggs one at a time and continue to whisk until combined. Add vanilla and whisk. Fold in flour, xanthan gum, and sprinkles.

3 Divide mixture between prepared pans and bake 20–25 minutes until golden brown and a skewer inserted in center comes out clean. Let cool completely, about 1 hour.

BUTTERCREAM

In a medium bowl, beat buttery sticks with an electric mixer on medium speed until soft. Gradually add confectioners' sugar, continuing to beat up to 5 minutes until combined and creamy. Add vanilla and milk and beat.

ASSEMBLY

Sandwich Cake layers together with Buttercream and spread remaining Buttercream on top. Decorate with sprinkles and store in an airtight container at room temperature for up to 3 days.

Prosecco and Strawberry Cake

This impressive adult celebration cake combines three layers of vanilla cake infused with Prosecco syrup with dairy-free buttercream and Prosecco-soaked strawberries. It's a real crowd-pleaser, perfect for birthdays or any other celebrations.

TOPPING

1 cup (200g) hulled and halved fresh strawberries

¼ cup (60ml) Prosecco

PROSECCO SYRUP

¾ cup plus 1 tablespoon (200ml) Prosecco

½ cup (100g) superfine sugar

CAKE

1¼ cups plus 2 tablespoons (300g) vegan buttery sticks

1½ cups (300g) superfine sugar

5 large eggs

1 teaspoon vanilla extract

1¾ cups plus 2 tablespoons (300g) gluten-free self-rising flour

½ teaspoon xanthan gum (omit if flour blend already contains this)

BUTTERCREAM

1 cup plus 2 tablespoons (250g) vegan buttery sticks

3¼ cups plus 3 tablespoons (500g) confectioners' sugar

Preheat oven to 350°F (180°C) and line three 8" round cake pans with parchment paper.

TOPPING

In a medium bowl, add strawberry slices. Pour Prosecco over strawberries and set aside to soak for 1 hour.

PROSECCO SYRUP

In a medium saucepan, heat Prosecco and superfine sugar over medium heat, stirring constantly, until sugar is dissolved and mixture starts to thicken, about 5 minutes. Set aside.

SERVES 16	
Per Serving:	
Calories	554
Fat	29g
Sodium	356mg
Carbohydrates	72g
Fiber	1g
Sugar	56g
Protein	3g

continued on next page

continued

CAKE

1 In a large bowl, beat buttery sticks and superfine sugar until light and fluffy. Add eggs one at a time, beating in between each addition. Add vanilla and beat until combined. Stir in flour and xanthan gum.

2 Divide batter among prepared pans and bake 20–25 minutes until golden brown and a skewer inserted in center comes out clean.

3 Remove pans from oven and poke holes in top of cakes with a skewer. Spoon Prosecco Syrup over Cakes. Set aside to cool at least 1 hour.

BUTTERCREAM

In a large bowl, beat buttery sticks with an electric mixer at medium speed until soft and fluffy. Gradually add confectioners' sugar, continuing to beat for up to 5 minutes until combined and creamy.

ASSEMBLY

Sandwich Cake layers together with Buttercream and spread a layer on top. Press Prosecco-soaked strawberry halves onto top. Store in an airtight container at room temperature for up to 3 days.

Christmas Cake

This classic Christmas Cake is full of the beloved spices and flavors of the holidays, and it keeps for weeks. It's perfect with midmorning coffee after all the festivities have passed. You can leave it undecorated as a simple fruit cake or top with marzipan and icing in any design.

2¾ cups plus 1 tablespoon (450g) gluten-free all-purpose flour

½ teaspoon salt

1 teaspoon pumpkin pie spice

½ teaspoon ground nutmeg

1 cup (225g) vegan buttery sticks

1 cup plus 2 tablespoons (225g) lightly packed light brown sugar

4 large eggs

3 cups plus 1 tablespoon (450g) currants

1¼ cups plus 2 tablespoons (200g) sultanas

1¼ cups plus 2 tablespoons (200g) raisins

¼ cup (50g) chopped glacé cherries

1 tablespoon treacle

Zest of 1 medium lemon

Zest of 1 medium orange

4 tablespoons brandy

SERVES 16

Per Serving:

Calories	369
Fat	13g
Sodium	203mg
Carbohydrates	59g
Fiber	5g
Sugar	34g
Protein	5g

FEEDING CAKE

Usually this cake is made at least one month before it is served and is "fed" with brandy each week until then. This ensures a lovely, rich taste and extremely moist texture.

1. Preheat oven to 300°F (150°C) and line a 7" square cake pan with parchment paper.
2. In a large bowl, mix flour, salt, pumpkin pie spice, and nutmeg.
3. In a separate large bowl, whisk buttery sticks and brown sugar until light and fluffy. Add eggs, one at a time, whisking in between each egg, until combined.
4. Gently fold dry ingredients into wet ingredients. Add currants, sultanas, raisins, cherries, and treacle and stir until well combined. Add lemon and orange zests.
5. Transfer mixture to prepared pan and cover with parchment paper, cutting a small hole in center of parchment to allow air to escape. Bake 4 hours or until a skewer inserted in center comes out clean. Let cool completely, about 2 hours, in pan.
6. Once cooled, remove from pan and cut six knife slits in cake. Pour 1 tablespoon brandy into holes, wrap cake in parchment paper, and place in an airtight container. Store at room temperature and feed with brandy weekly for up to 3 weeks before serving.

Rainbow Cake

SERVES 16

Per Serving:

Calories	724
Fat	39g
Sodium	469mg
Carbohydrates	92g
Fiber	0g
Sugar	74g
Protein	3g

You'll love cutting into this stunning cake with its six rainbow-colored layers and luscious dairy-free buttercream. Rainbow sprinkles finish the look, and you can just add candles to make this an impressive birthday cake!

CAKE

1½ cups plus 1 tablespoon (350g) vegan buttery sticks, divided in half

1¾ cups (350g) superfine sugar, divided in half

6 large eggs, divided

2 teaspoons vanilla extract, divided

2 cups plus 3 tablespoons (350g) gluten-free self-rising flour, divided in half

½ teaspoon xanthan gum (omit if flour blend already contains this), divided

2 tablespoons (30ml) unsweetened almond or other dairy-free milk, divided

Yellow, orange, red, green, blue, and purple gel food coloring

BUTTERCREAM

1¾ cups plus 1 tablespoon (400g) vegan buttery sticks

5½ cups (800g) confectioners' sugar

1½ teaspoons unsweetened almond or other dairy-free milk

ASSEMBLY

¼ cup rainbow sprinkles

CAKE

1 Preheat oven to 350°F (180°C) and line three 8" round springform cake pans with parchment paper.

2 In a large bowl, whisk half of buttery sticks and half of sugar until creamy. Add 3 eggs, one at a time, and continue to whisk until combined. Add 1 teaspoon vanilla and whisk until combined. Fold in half of flour, ¼ teaspoon xanthan gum, and 1 tablespoon milk.

3 Divide mixture between three separate medium bowls. Add yellow food coloring to first bowl, orange to second bowl, and red to third bowl, adding ¼ teaspoon gel at a time until you reach desired color. Pour batters into 3 prepared pans and spread to level. Bake 15 minutes or until a skewer inserted in center comes out clean. Let cool in the pans for 10 minutes before transferring to a wire rack to cool for 1 hour.

4 Wipe out pans and regrease. Repeat the above steps with remaining ingredients to make three additional cakes with green, blue, and purple food coloring. Pour into prepared pans and bake 15 minutes or until a skewer inserted in center comes out clean. Let cool in the pans for 10 minutes before transferring to a wire rack to cool for 1 hour.

BUTTERCREAM

In a medium bowl, beat buttery sticks with an electric mixer on medium speed until soft. Gradually add confectioners' sugar, continuing to beat up to 5 minutes until combined and creamy. Add milk and beat until combined.

ASSEMBLY

Sandwich Cake layers together with thin layers of Buttercream to form a rainbow pattern. Spread remaining Buttercream around sides and top of Cake. Decorate with rainbow sprinkles. Store in an airtight container at room temperature for up to 3 days.

Devil's Food Chocolate Cake

Two layers of rich and decadent chocolate cake, enriched with cocoa powder and coffee, are joined together with chocolate buttercream frosting for the ultimate chocolaty treat.

SERVES 12

Per Serving:

Calories	544
Fat	27g
Sodium	300mg
Carbohydrates	77g
Fiber	5g
Sugar	60g
Protein	5g

CAKE

1¼ cups (200g) gluten-free all-purpose flour

¼ teaspoon xanthan gum (omit if flour blend already contains this)

1 teaspoon baking powder

½ teaspoon baking soda

¾ cup plus 1 tablespoon (160g) superfine sugar

½ cup plus 1 tablespoon (120g) packed light brown sugar

¼ cup plus 3 tablespoons (50g) cocoa powder

2 large eggs

1 tablespoon vegetable oil

¼ cup plus 3 tablespoons (100g) vegan buttery spread, melted

1 teaspoon vanilla extract

1 cup plus 1 tablespoon (250ml) boiling coffee

BUTTERCREAM

¾ cup plus 2 tablespoons (200g) vegan buttery sticks

2½ cups plus 1 tablespoon (375g) confectioners' sugar

¼ cup (30g) cocoa powder

¾ cup plus 1 tablespoon (150g) dairy-free dark chocolate, melted and cooled

CAKE

1 Preheat oven to 350°F (180°C) and line two 8" round springform cake pans with parchment paper.

2 In a large bowl, mix flour, xanthan gum, baking powder, baking soda, superfine sugar, brown sugar, and cocoa powder. In a medium bowl, mix eggs, oil, buttery spread, and vanilla. Add wet ingredients and boiling coffee to dry ingredients and mix well.

3 Divide mixture between two prepared pans and bake 25–30 minutes or until a skewer inserted in center comes out clean. Let cool completely, about 1 hour.

BUTTERCREAM

1 In a medium bowl, beat buttery sticks with an electric mixer on medium speed until soft. Gradually add confectioners' sugar and cocoa powder, continuing to beat up to 5 minutes until combined and creamy. Add melted chocolate and whisk until combined.

2 Sandwich Cakes together with Buttercream and spread remaining Buttercream on top. Store in an airtight container at room temperature for up to 3 days.

Peanut Butter Layer Cake

A delicious peanut butter–flavored cake is sandwiched together with peanut butter frosting and topped with crushed peanuts. It's a peanut butter lover's dream!

CAKE

1 cup plus 2 tablespoons (250g) vegan buttery sticks

1½ cups (300g) superfine sugar

¾ cup plus 1 tablespoon (180g) smooth peanut butter

6 large eggs

4 tablespoons unsweetened almond or other dairy-free milk

1¾ cups plus 2 tablespoons (300g) gluten-free self-rising flour

½ teaspoon xanthan gum (omit if flour blend already contains this)

½ teaspoon salt

½ teaspoon baking soda

BUTTERCREAM

¾ cup plus 2 tablespoons (200g) vegan buttery sticks

½ cup plus 3 tablespoons (150g) smooth peanut butter

2¾ cups (400g) confectioners' sugar

ASSEMBLY

¼ cup salted peanuts

SERVES 16	
Per Serving:	
Calories	595
Fat	35g
Sodium	439mg
Carbohydrates	63g
Fiber	2g
Sugar	46g
Protein	8g

CAKE

1. Preheat oven to 350°F (180°C) and line three 8" round springform cake pans with parchment paper.
2. In a large bowl, whisk buttery sticks and superfine sugar until creamy. Add peanut butter and whisk until combined. Add eggs one at a time and continue to whisk until combined. Fold in milk, flour, xanthan gum, salt, and baking soda.
3. Divide mixture between prepared pans and bake 25–30 minutes until golden brown and a skewer inserted in center comes out clean. Let cool completely, about 1 hour.

BUTTERCREAM

In a medium bowl, beat buttery sticks with an electric mixer on medium speed until creamy. Add peanut butter and beat until combined. Gradually add confectioners' sugar, continuing to beat up to 5 minutes until combined.

ASSEMBLY

Sandwich Cakes together with Buttercream and spread remaining Buttercream on top. Decorate with peanuts and store in an airtight container at room temperature for up to 3 days.

Almond Layer Cake

SERVES 16

Per Serving:

Calories	591
Fat	33g
Sodium	305mg
Carbohydrates	69g
Fiber	2g
Sugar	59g
Protein	5g

SOFT-BALL STAGE

Test whether your sugar syrup is at the soft-ball stage by dropping a small amount in a bowl of cold water. It should form a soft ball when pressed together.

This delicious celebration cake combines three layers of almond-flavored cake with almond buttercream and candied almonds. A tasty, nutty treat!

CAKE

1 cup plus 3 tablespoons (260g) vegan buttery sticks

1½ cups (300g) superfine sugar

6 large eggs, separated

1½ teaspoons almond extract

¾ cup plus 3 tablespoons (150g) gluten-free self-rising flour

½ teaspoon xanthan gum (omit if flour blend already contains this)

1 cup plus 3 tablespoons (110g) ground almonds

CANDIED ALMONDS

1 cup (100g) blanched almonds

½ cup plus 2 tablespoons (150ml) water

¾ cup (150g) superfine sugar

BUTTERCREAM

1 cup plus 2 tablespoons (250g) dairy-free vegan buttery sticks

3¼ cups plus 3 tablespoons (500g) confectioners' sugar

1 teaspoon almond extract

CAKE

1 Preheat oven to 350°F (180°C) and line three 8" round springform cake pans with parchment paper.

2 In a large bowl, whisk buttery sticks and superfine sugar until creamy. Add egg yolks one at a time and continue to whisk until combined. Add almond extract and whisk to combine. Fold in flour, xanthan gum, and ground almonds.

3 In a medium bowl, whisk egg whites to stiff peaks. Fold into cake mixture until combined.

4 Divide mixture equally between prepared pans and bake 25–30 minutes until cooked through and a skewer inserted in center comes out clean. Let cool completely, about 1 hour.

CANDIED ALMONDS

1 Spread blanched almonds out on a baking sheet lined with parchment paper and bake 10 minutes until golden brown. Set aside.

2 In a medium saucepan, heat water and superfine sugar over medium heat, stirring regularly until mixture starts to thicken and reaches soft-ball stage, about 10–15 minutes. Stir in almonds, then immediately pour back onto baking sheet and set aside to solidify, about 15 minutes.

BUTTERCREAM

In a medium bowl, beat buttery sticks with an electric mixer on medium speed until soft. Gradually add confectioners' sugar, continuing to beat up to 5 minutes until combined and creamy. Add almond extract and beat until combined.

ASSEMBLY

Sandwich Cake layers together with Buttercream and spread remaining Buttercream on top. Decorate with Candied Almonds and store in an airtight container at room temperature for up to 3 days.

Triple Chocolate Layer Cake

Everyone will be delighted with this impressive-looking triple chocolate cake. It features layers of dairy-free dark chocolate, milk chocolate, and white chocolate cake to create an ombre pattern. Sandwiched together with chocolate buttercream and decorated with chocolate chips, it's a real chocolate lover's treat.

CAKE

2½ ounces (75g) chopped dairy-free dark chocolate

2½ ounces (75g) dairy-free milk chocolate

2½ ounces (75g) dairy-free white chocolate

1¼ cups plus 2 tablespoons (300g) vegan buttery sticks

1½ cups (300g) superfine sugar

6 large eggs

1 teaspoon vanilla extract

1¾ cups plus 2 tablespoons (300g) gluten-free self-rising flour

½ teaspoon xanthan gum (omit if flour blend already contains this)

2 teaspoons baking powder

¼ cup plus 3 tablespoons (100ml) unsweetened almond or other dairy-free milk

BUTTERCREAM

1¼ cups plus 2 tablespoons (300g) vegan buttery sticks

3¾ cups (550g) confectioners' sugar

¼ cup plus 3 tablespoons (50g) cocoa powder

2 tablespoons unsweetened almond or other dairy-free milk

ASSEMBLY

¼ cup (50g) dairy-free white chocolate chips

¼ cup (50g) dairy-free milk chocolate chips

CAKE

1 Preheat oven to 350°F (180°C) and line three 8" round cake pans with parchment paper.

2 In three separate large microwave-safe bowls, melt dark chocolate, milk chocolate, and white chocolate in microwave on high and set aside.

continued on next page

continued

3 In a large bowl, beat buttery sticks and superfine sugar until light and fluffy. Add eggs one at a time, beating in between each addition. Add vanilla and beat until combined. Stir in flour, xanthan gum, baking powder, and milk.

4 Divide mixture equally between three bowls containing dark, milk, and white chocolate. Beat until fully combined and transfer to prepared pans.

5 Bake 25–30 minutes or until a skewer inserted in center comes out clean. Remove from oven, cool in pans 5 minutes, then remove from pans and cool on a wire rack at least 45 minutes.

BUTTERCREAM

In a large bowl, beat buttery sticks with an electric mixer at medium speed until soft and fluffy. Gradually add confectioners' sugar and cocoa powder, continuing to beat for up to 5 minutes until creamy. Add milk and beat until combined.

ASSEMBLY

Sandwich 3 Cake layers together with Buttercream (starting with dark chocolate layer, followed by milk chocolate, and finally white chocolate) and spread a thin layer of Buttercream around outside and top of Cake. Decorate top with white and milk chocolate chips. Store in an airtight container at room temperature for up to 3 days.

Red Velvet Cake

This classic Red Velvet Cake is soft and moist, flavored with a hint of cocoa powder and a homemade dairy-free buttermilk, and topped with a silky-smooth dairy-free cream cheese frosting.

CAKE

3/4 cup plus 3 tablespoons (220ml) unsweetened almond or other dairy-free milk

1 tablespoon apple cider vinegar

2 1/4 cups plus 1 tablespoon (375g) gluten-free all-purpose flour

1/2 teaspoon xanthan gum (omit if flour blend already contains this)

1 teaspoon baking soda

1/2 teaspoon salt

2 teaspoons cocoa powder

1/4 cup plus 3 tablespoons (100g) vegan buttery sticks

1 3/4 cups (350g) superfine sugar

2 large eggs

2 teaspoons red gel food coloring

1 teaspoon vanilla extract

1/4 cup plus 3 tablespoons (100ml) boiling water

BUTTERCREAM

3/4 cup plus 2 tablespoons (200g) vegan buttery sticks

3/4 cup plus 2 tablespoons (200g) dairy-free cream cheese

4 cups plus 2 tablespoons (600g) confectioners' sugar

SERVES 12

Per Serving:

Calories	643
Fat	26g
Sodium	544mg
Carbohydrates	103g
Fiber	3g
Sugar	80g
Protein	5g

CREAM CHEESE FROSTING

Different brands of dairy-free cream cheese can work in different ways, so you may need to add a little more confectioners' sugar to the frosting to thicken it up slightly.

CAKE

1 Preheat oven to 350°F (180°C) and line two 8" round springform cake pans with parchment paper.

2 In a large bowl, add milk and vinegar. Mix and let sit for 3 minutes to form a dairy-free buttermilk alternative.

3 In a separate large bowl, mix flour, xanthan gum, baking soda, salt, and cocoa powder. In a medium bowl, beat buttery sticks and superfine sugar until creamy. Add eggs one at a time and continue to beat until combined. Add red food coloring and vanilla and beat until combined.

4 Mix wet ingredients into dry ingredients, then pour in buttermilk and boiling water and whisk until combined.

5 Divide mixture between prepared pans and bake 25–30 minutes or until a skewer inserted in center comes out clean. Let cool for 1 hour.

BUTTERCREAM

1 In a medium bowl, beat buttery sticks and cream cheese with an electric mixer on medium speed until soft. Gradually add confectioners' sugar, continuing to beat up to 5 minutes until combined and creamy.

2 Sandwich Cakes together with Buttercream and spread remaining Buttercream on top. Store in an airtight container at room temperature for up to 3 days.

Summary Party Cake

Wow your guests with this epic-looking Summer Party Cake, which features three vanilla cake layers, vanilla buttercream, and strawberry jam, and is topped with white chocolate–covered strawberries, homemade meringue kisses, and fresh berries.

SERVES 16

Per Serving:

Calories	606
Fat	31g
Sodium	370mg
Carbohydrates	80g
Fiber	1g
Sugar	64g
Protein	4g

CAKE
1¼ cups plus 2 tablespoons (300g) vegan buttery sticks

1½ cups (300g) superfine sugar

5 large eggs

1 teaspoon vanilla extract

1¾ cups plus 2 tablespoons (300g) gluten-free self-rising flour

½ teaspoon xanthan gum (omit if flour blend already contains this)

MERINGUE KISSES
¼ cup fresh raspberries

2 large egg whites

½ cup plus 2 tablespoons (120g) superfine sugar

WHITE CHOCOLATE–COVERED STRAWBERRIES
½ cup plus 1 tablespoon (100g) dairy-free white chocolate chips

10 hulled fresh strawberries

BUTTERCREAM
1 cup plus 2 tablespoons (250g) vegan buttery sticks

3¼ cups plus 3 tablespoons (500g) confectioners' sugar

1 teaspoon vanilla extract

1 teaspoon unsweetened almond or other dairy-free milk

ASSEMBLY
¼ cup strawberry jam

¼ cup fresh raspberries

CAKE

1 Preheat oven to 350°F (180°C) and line three 8" round springform cake pans with parchment paper.

2 In a large bowl, whisk buttery sticks and superfine sugar until creamy. Add eggs one at a time and continue to whisk until combined. Add vanilla and whisk until combined. Fold in flour and xanthan gum.

3 Divide mixture between prepared pans and bake 20–25 minutes until golden and a skewer inserted in center comes out clean. Let cool completely, about 1 hour.

MERINGUE KISSES

1 In a medium bowl, add raspberries and use a spoon to press down to form a purée. Press purée through a sieve to form a raspberry liquid, discard pips, and set aside.
2 Preheat oven to 250°F (120°C) and line a baking sheet with parchment paper.
3 In a large bowl, add egg whites and mix with an electric mixer on low speed until mixture starts to foam, turn up to medium speed and whisk to stiff peaks. Add superfine sugar 1 tablespoon at a time and continue to whisk until stiff and glossy.
4 Spoon raspberry juice into a piping bag. Swirl bag so juice covers entire inside of bag. Spoon meringue mixture into bag. Pipe Meringue Kisses onto baking sheet and bake 1 hour until crisp on outside. Turn off oven and leave baking sheet in oven with door open 1 hour.

WHITE CHOCOLATE–COVERED STRAWBERRIES

In a small saucepan, melt chocolate chips over low heat, then dip strawberries in chocolate. Place on a baking sheet lined with parchment paper and refrigerate 1 hour.

BUTTERCREAM

In a medium bowl, beat buttery sticks with an electric mixer at medium speed until soft. Gradually add confectioners' sugar, continuing to beat up to 5 minutes until combined and creamy. Add vanilla and milk and beat until combined.

ASSEMBLY

Sandwich Cake layers together with Buttercream and jam and spread remaining Buttercream on top. Decorate with Meringue Kisses, White Chocolate–Covered Strawberries, and fresh raspberries. Store in an airtight container at room temperature for up to 3 days.

Black Forest Cake

SERVES 12

Per Serving:

Calories	539
Fat	29g
Sodium	227mg
Carbohydrates	67g
Fiber	5g
Sugar	47g
Protein	6g

COCONUT CREAM

The coconut milk in this recipe needs to be stored in the refrigerator overnight, which will allow the milk to separate, forming a solid layer of cream at the top of the can. Once whipped, putting the cream back in the refrigerator before spreading on the cake will create a sturdier structure.

A truly delicious dessert with two layers of tasty chocolate cake sandwiched together with whipped coconut cream and a Kirsch cherry filling, then topped with grated chocolate and fresh cherries. You'll love this take on a Black Forest gâteau.

CAKE

½ cup plus 3 tablespoons (150g) vegan buttery sticks

½ cup plus 1 tablespoon (100g) dairy-free dark chocolate chips

1½ cups plus 3 tablespoons (275g) gluten-free all-purpose flour

½ teaspoon xanthan gum (omit if flour blend already contains this)

1¾ cup (350g) superfine sugar

¼ cup (30g) cocoa powder

1 teaspoon baking soda

2 large eggs

¾ cup (175g) dairy-free plain yogurt

¼ cup plus 3 tablespoons (100ml) boiling water

CHERRY FILLING

1 can (15-ounce or 425g) black pitted cherries in syrup

3 tablespoons Kirsch (or substitute with juice from cherries)

¼ cup plus 1 tablespoon (75ml) water

1 teaspoon cornstarch

COCONUT CREAM

2 (14-ounce or 400ml) cans chilled full-fat coconut milk

3 tablespoons confectioners' sugar

1 teaspoon vanilla extract

ASSEMBLY

¼ cup fresh cherries

¼ cup (50g) grated dairy-free dark chocolate

CAKE

1 Preheat oven to 350°F (180°C) and line two 8" round springform cake pans with parchment paper.

2 In a small saucepan, heat buttery sticks and chocolate chips over low heat until melted and combined. Set aside.

3　In a large bowl, mix flour, xanthan gum, superfine sugar, cocoa powder, and baking soda. In a medium bowl, whisk eggs and yogurt. Add egg mixture and melted chocolate to dry ingredients along with boiling water. Whisk with an electric mixer at low speed until fully combined.

4　Divide mixture between prepared pans and bake 30 minutes or until a skewer inserted in center comes out clean. Let cool completely, about 1 hour.

CHERRY FILLING

1　In a small saucepan, combine cherries with Kirsch and water. Bring to a simmer over medium-low heat and cook 10–15 minutes until cherries start to soften and release some juices.

2　In a small bowl, combine 1 tablespoon liquid from saucepan with 1 teaspoon cornstarch and whisk until well mixed. Add back into saucepan. Simmer another 2 minutes until thickened, adding a little more syrup from cherries if it thickens too much. Set aside.

COCONUT CREAM

Remove 2 cans coconut milk from refrigerator and scoop solid cream layer at top of each can into a large bowl. Beat with an electric mixer on medium speed to form stiff peaks. Add confectioners' sugar and vanilla and beat until thick and creamy. Place in refrigerator to firm up until ready to assemble cake.

ASSEMBLY

Sandwich Cakes together with Coconut Cream and Cherry Filling. Top with remaining Coconut Cream, cherries, and grated chocolate. Store in refrigerator for up to 3 days.

Salted Caramel Popcorn Cake

Two layers of brown sugar cake are surround by salted caramel buttercream and topped with toffee popcorn and salted caramel sauce. If you've got a sweet tooth, this cake is for you!

CAKE

1 cup plus 2 tablespoons (250g) vegan buttery sticks

1¼ cups (250g) packed light brown sugar

5 large eggs

1 teaspoon vanilla extract

2 tablespoons unsweetened almond or other dairy-free milk

1½ cups plus 1 tablespoon (250g) gluten-free self-rising flour

¼ teaspoon xanthan gum (omit if flour blend already contains this)

1½ teaspoons baking powder

¼ teaspoon salt

SALTED CARAMEL SAUCE

1 can (14-ounce or 400ml) full-fat coconut milk

¾ cup plus 2 tablespoons (175g) packed light brown sugar

1 teaspoon vanilla extract

1 teaspoon salt

BUTTERCREAM

½ cup plus 3 tablespoons (150g) vegan buttery sticks

2 cups plus 1 tablespoon (300g) confectioners' sugar

2 tablespoons Salted Caramel Sauce

ASSEMBLY

½ cup toffee popcorn

CAKE

1 Preheat oven to 350°F (180°C) and line two 8" round springform cake pans with parchment paper.

2 In a large bowl, whisk buttery sticks and brown sugar until creamy. Add eggs one at a time and continue to whisk until combined. Add vanilla and milk and whisk until combined. Fold in flour, xanthan gum, baking powder, and salt.

3 Divide mixture between prepared pans and bake 25–30 minutes until golden brown and a skewer inserted in center comes out clean. Let cool completely, about 1 hour.

SALTED CARAMEL SAUCE

In a medium saucepan, cook coconut milk, brown sugar, and vanilla over medium heat. Stir until mixture comes to a boil; continue to stir 20 minutes until slightly thickened. Remove from heat and stir in salt. Set aside to cool completely, about 1 hour.

BUTTERCREAM

In a medium bowl, beat buttery sticks with an electric mixer on medium speed until soft. Gradually add confectioners' sugar, continuing to beat up to 5 minutes until combined and creamy. Add cooled Salted Caramel Sauce and mix until combined.

ASSEMBLY

Sandwich Cakes together with a layer of Buttercream. Spread remaining Buttercream on top of Cake. Top with toffee popcorn and drizzle with Salted Caramel Sauce. Store in an airtight container at room temperature for up to 3 days.

Chocolate Yule Log

SERVES 10

Per Serving:

Calories	410
Fat	20g
Sodium	163mg
Carbohydrates	58g
Fiber	3g
Sugar	49g
Protein	5g

SWISS ROLL TIN

A Swiss roll tin is a baking pan, usually nonstick, that has been designed to make thin rectangular cakes. It can be found at most supermarkets or baking equipment shops.

This festive Chocolate Yule Log is an impressive-looking Christmas dessert that is great for the whole family. It combines a tasty, fluffy chocolate cake with delicious chocolate buttercream.

CAKE

5 large eggs

½ cup plus 2 tablespoons (120g) superfine sugar

¼ cup plus 3 tablespoons (75g) gluten-free all-purpose flour

¼ teaspoon baking powder

¼ teaspoon xanthan gum (omit if flour blend already contains this)

¼ cup plus 1 tablespoon (35g) cocoa powder

BUTTERCREAM

½ cup plus 3 tablespoons (150g) vegan buttery sticks

2 cups plus 1 tablespoon (300g) confectioners' sugar

¾ cup plus 1 tablespoon (150g) dairy-free milk chocolate, melted

1 tablespoon unsweetened almond or other dairy-free milk

CAKE

1 Preheat oven to 350°F (180°C) and line a 9" × 13" Swiss roll tin with parchment paper.

2 In a large bowl, whisk eggs and superfine sugar with an electric mixer on medium speed until pale and frothy. In a separate large bowl, mix flour, baking powder, xanthan gum, and cocoa powder. Gently fold dry ingredients into wet ingredients.

3 Pour mixture into prepared tin, spreading it out to edges. Bake 10 minutes until firm but still springy.

4 Remove from oven and, while still warm, turn out onto a large sheet of parchment paper sprinkled with confectioners' sugar. Carefully peel paper off bottom of cake and trim edges so they are straight.

5 While Cake is still warm, tightly roll it up from short end with parchment paper inside it. Let cool completely, about 1 hour.

BUTTERCREAM

1 In a medium bowl, beat buttery sticks with an electric mixer on medium speed until soft. Gradually add confectioners' sugar, continuing to beat up to 5 minutes until combined and creamy. Add melted chocolate and milk and beat until combined.

2 Carefully unroll Cake and spread with a layer of Buttercream. Roll back up and cover with remaining Buttercream. Use a fork to create a log pattern to serve. Store in an airtight container at room temperature for up to 3 days.

CHAPTER 9

Pies and Tarts

Sweet Short-Crust Pastry

KEEP IN THE REFRIGERATOR

If you don't want to use the dough right away, it will keep in the refrigerator for up to 48 hours until you are ready to bake with it. Just add a few drops of water if it's a little hard.

This Sweet Short-Crust Pastry recipe is flaky and buttery and a great base to all sorts of desserts, sweet pies, and tarts. Gluten-free pastry is thought to be really difficult to work with, but you'll be surprised at how easy this recipe is to make and how workable the dough is! The trick is to have cool hands and lots of flour on your work surface when you roll it out to use.

1¾ cups plus 2 tablespoons (300g) gluten-free all-purpose flour

1½ teaspoons xanthan gum (omit if flour blend already contains this)

¼ teaspoon salt

2 tablespoons granulated sugar

¾ cup plus 1 tablespoon (175g) vegan buttery sticks, cold and cubed

1 large egg

3–4 tablespoons cold water

1 In a large bowl, add flour, xanthan gum, salt, and sugar. Mix well.
2 Add cubed buttery sticks and rub into flour using a fork until mixture resembles bread crumbs. Stir in egg.
3 Add cold water 1 tablespoon at a time and mix well until mixture starts to form a firm dough (about 3–4 tablespoons total).
4 Turn out dough onto a lightly floured surface and knead until smooth. Wrap dough in plastic wrap and refrigerate at least 1 hour before using.

Apple Pie

Dessert doesn't get much better than this warm Apple Pie with dairy-free vanilla ice cream or custard. It's the perfect winter treat to impress any dinner guests. Most supermarkets stock dairy-free ice cream too, so there is no need to feel like you are missing out!

6 medium Granny Smith apples, peeled, cored, and sliced

Juice of 1/2 medium lemon

1/4 cup plus 2 tablespoons (80g) superfine sugar

1 tablespoon gluten-free all-purpose flour

1 1/2 teaspoons ground cinnamon

1 batch Sweet Short-Crust Pastry (see recipe in this chapter)

1 large egg, beaten

1 Preheat oven to 350°F (180°C).

2 In a large bowl, add apples, lemon juice, sugar, flour, and cinnamon. Mix well.

3 Remove pastry from refrigerator and cut off one-third for topping. Roll out remaining dough on a lightly floured surface to slightly larger than pie dish. Carefully line dish with pastry and trim excess pastry from edges.

4 Spoon apple mixture into a 9" round springform pie dish.

5 Roll out remaining pastry on a lightly floured surface to slightly larger than pie dish and carefully lay over top of pie, pressing edges together to seal. Use a fork to crimp edges.

6 Brush top with egg and cut three slits for steam to escape. Bake 45 minutes until golden brown and cooked through. Serve warm or store in refrigerator for up to 2 days.

SERVES 12

Per Serving:

Calories	267
Fat	13g
Sodium	172mg
Carbohydrates	37g
Fiber	4g
Sugar	18g
Protein	4g

NOT A FAN OF APPLES?

Swap out the apples for cherries, peaches, blackberries, or pears for a different flavor.

Individual Custard Tarts

SERVES 12

Per Serving (1 tart):

Calories	212
Fat	13g
Sodium	177mg
Carbohydrates	22g
Fiber	3g
Sugar	7g
Protein	4g

It couldn't be easier to make these delicious tarts, which combine a Sweet Short-Crust Pastry base with a sweet and creamy dairy-free custard filling.

1 batch Sweet Short-Crust Pastry (see recipe in this chapter)

1½ cups plus 3 tablespoons (400ml) unsweetened almond or other dairy-free milk

4 large egg yolks

¼ cup (50g) superfine sugar

¼ teaspoon ground nutmeg

1 Preheat oven to 400°F (200°C).

2 Remove pastry from refrigerator and roll out on a lightly floured surface. Use a cookie cutter to cut out twelve circles slightly larger than cavities of a twelve-cup muffin tin. Press a circle into each cup, ensuring pastry is pressed up side of cup.

3 In a small saucepan, heat milk over medium heat until it starts to simmer (don't let it boil). Set aside. In a medium bowl, beat egg yolks and sugar until pale and creamy. Slowly pour warm milk into egg mixture, mixing well.

4 Pour custard into pastry cups and sprinkle with nutmeg. Bake 10 minutes, reduce heat to 360°F (180°C), and bake another 15 minutes. Let cool completely, about 1 hour in tin until set. Store in refrigerator for up to 2 days.

Frangipane Mince Pies

This adaptation of classic mince pies features a pastry base with fruity mincemeat filling and frangipane topping for a delicious and festive treat to enjoy around Christmas.

1 batch Sweet Short-Crust Pastry (see recipe in this chapter)

½ cup (110g) vegan buttery sticks

½ cup plus 1 tablespoon (110g) superfine sugar

1 large egg

1 tablespoon gluten-free all-purpose flour

1 cup plus 1 tablespoon (100g) ground almonds

1 (14-ounce) jar mincemeat

2 tablespoons flaked almonds

2 tablespoons confectioners' sugar, to dust

1 Preheat oven to 350°F (180°C).

2 Remove pastry from refrigerator and roll out on a lightly floured surface. Use a cookie cutter to cut out twelve circles slightly larger than cavities of a twelve-cup muffin tin. Press a circle into each cup, ensuring pastry is pressed up side of cup.

3 In a large bowl, whisk buttery sticks and superfine sugar until creamy. Add egg and continue to whisk until combined. Stir in flour and ground almonds.

4 Spoon 1 tablespoon mincemeat into each pastry cup, followed by 1 tablespoon almond frangipane mixture. Sprinkle with flaked almonds and bake 25–30 minutes until golden brown and cooked through. Dust with confectioners' sugar and store in an airtight container at room temperature for up to 3 days.

SERVES 12

Per Serving (1 pie):

Calories	389
Fat	25g
Sodium	323mg
Carbohydrates	38g
Fiber	4g
Sugar	15g
Protein	6g

MINCEMEAT

Mincemeat is a sweet mixture of dried fruit, spirits, and spices, traditionally used in recipes around Christmas. This recipe calls for a ready-made jar, which can be bought online or in some supermarkets. If you can't find ready-made mincemeat, there are plenty of delicious recipes online.

Pear and Blackberry Crumble Pie

SERVES 12

Per Serving:

Calories	326
Fat	17g
Sodium	201mg
Carbohydrates	44g
Fiber	6g
Sugar	19g
Protein	4g

Combining pear and blackberry filling with a crunchy crumble topping makes this fruity pie a sweet and tart treat. It's delicious on its own or served with a scoop of dairy-free ice cream.

PIE

1 batch Sweet Short-Crust Pastry (see recipe in this chapter)

4 medium pears, peeled and sliced

1 cup (150g) fresh blackberries

¼ cup (55g) granulated sugar

2 teaspoons ground cinnamon

1 teaspoon orange zest

CRUMBLE TOPPING

½ cup plus 2 tablespoons (100g) gluten-free all-purpose flour

¼ cup (55g) vegan buttery sticks

¼ cup (55g) granulated sugar

PIE

1 Preheat oven to 350°F (180°C).

2 Remove pastry from refrigerator and roll out on a lightly floured surface to slightly larger than a 9" round springform pie dish. Carefully line dish with rolled-out pastry, trimming excess pastry from edges.

3 In a small saucepan, heat pears, blackberries, sugar, cinnamon, and orange zest over medium heat 5 minutes, mixing well during heating. Transfer filling to pie shell.

CRUMBLE TOPPING

In a medium bowl, combine flour and buttery sticks. Rub mixture together with your fingertips until it resembles bread crumbs and stir through sugar.

ASSEMBLY

Sprinkle Crumble Topping over pie filling. Bake 45 minutes until Pie is steaming hot and cooked through. Serve warm or store in refrigerator for up to 3 days.

Rhubarb and Strawberry Galette

This quick and easy-to-make galette is perfect for using up seasonal fruit. The recipe calls for rhubarb and strawberries, but you can use any fruit you have on hand.

1 cup fresh rhubarb chunks

1 cup hulled and sliced fresh strawberries

½ cup (100g) sugar

1 batch Sweet Short-Crust Pastry (see recipe in this chapter)

1 large egg, beaten

SERVES 6	
Per Serving:	
Calories	477
Fat	26g
Sodium	345mg
Carbohydrates	57g
Fiber	6g
Sugar	24g
Protein	7g

1 In a large mixing bowl, add rhubarb, strawberries, and sugar. Mix well and leave to sit 1 hour.

2 Preheat oven to 350°F (180°C).

3 Remove pastry from refrigerator and roll out on a lightly floured surface into an oval shape. Drain any liquid from fruit mixture and spoon into middle of pastry, leaving about a 2" gap around outside.

4 Fold edges of pastry to slightly overlap fruit, leaving a large open space in center. Brush pastry with egg and bake 40–45 minutes until golden brown and cooked through. Serve warm.

Pumpkin Pie

Bursting with flavor, this traditional American treat is rich and delicious.

1 batch Sweet Short-Crust Pastry (see recipe in this chapter)

1 can (14-ounce or 400g) pumpkin purée

1 can (14-ounce or 400ml) full-fat coconut milk

¾ cup (150g) packed light brown sugar

2 large eggs

1 teaspoon ground cinnamon

½ teaspoon ground ginger

¼ teaspoon ground nutmeg

SERVES 12	
Per Serving:	
Calories	333
Fat	20g
Sodium	187mg
Carbohydrates	35g
Fiber	4g
Sugar	16g
Protein	5g

1 Preheat oven to 428°F (220°C).

2 Remove pastry from refrigerator and roll out on a lightly floured surface to slightly larger than a 9" round springform pie dish. Carefully line dish with rolled-out pastry, trimming excess pastry from edges.

3 In a food processor, pulse remaining ingredients until fully combined and pour into piecrust.

4 Bake 15 minutes, reduce oven temperature to 350°F (180°C), and bake another 45 minutes until filling is just set. Remove from oven and cool for 2 hours before slicing. Store in refrigerator for up to 2 days.

Summer Peach Galette

Just as tasty as a pie but much simpler to make, this rustic Summer Peach Galette recipe combines a delicious pastry base with sweet cinnamon peaches. The best part is you can change up this recipe depending on what fruit is in season.

4 medium peaches, pitted and sliced

¼ cup (50g) packed light brown sugar

1 tablespoon lemon juice

2 teaspoons vanilla extract

1 tablespoon cornstarch

1 teaspoon ground cinnamon

1 batch Sweet Short-Crust Pastry (see recipe in this chapter)

2 tablespoons ground almonds

1 large egg, beaten

1 tablespoon demerara sugar

1. Preheat oven to 350°F (180°C) and line a baking sheet with parchment paper.
2. In a large bowl, combine peaches, light brown sugar, lemon juice, vanilla, cornstarch, and cinnamon.
3. Roll pastry dough out on a lightly floured surface into an oval shape. Transfer oval to prepared baking sheet. Sprinkle dough with almonds, then spoon peach mixture onto middle of dough, leaving a 2" gap around outside.
4. Fold in edges of pastry to slightly overlap filling, leaving a large open space in center. Brush pastry with egg and sprinkle with demerara sugar.
5. Bake 40–45 minutes until golden brown and cooked through. Serve warm.

SERVES 6

Per Serving:

Calories	501
Fat	27g
Sodium	347mg
Carbohydrates	60g
Fiber	8g
Sugar	25g
Protein	8g

DID YOU KNOW?

Galettes originated in France and combine a pastry base and sweet or savory filling with the edges roughly folded inward to create a rustic-looking dish.

Cherry Bakewells

Individual Cherry Bakewells combine a homemade Sweet Short-Crust Pastry base with a cherry jam and frangipane filling, topped with icing and a glacé cherry. A classic and nostalgic British treat.

1 batch Sweet Short-Crust Pastry (see recipe in this chapter)

½ cup (110g) vegan buttery sticks

½ cup plus 1 tablespoon (110g) superfine sugar

1 large egg

1 tablespoon gluten-free all-purpose flour

1 cup plus 1 tablespoon (100g) ground almonds

12 teaspoons cherry jam

½ cup plus 3 tablespoons (100g) confectioners' sugar

2–3 teaspoons water

12 glacé cherries

1 Preheat oven to 350°F (180°C).

2 Remove pastry from refrigerator and roll out on a lightly floured surface. Use a cookie cutter to cut out twelve circles slightly larger than cavities of a twelve-cup muffin tin. Press a circle into each cup, ensuring pastry is pressed up side of cup.

3 Add parchment paper and pastry weights to each pastry cup. Blind bake 10 minutes. Remove paper and weights and bake an additional 5 minutes. Remove from oven and let cool while making frangipane mixture.

4 In a large bowl, whisk buttery sticks and superfine sugar until creamy. Add egg and continue to whisk until combined. Stir in flour and almonds.

5 Add 1 teaspoon jam to bottom of each of pastry cup, followed by 1 tablespoon frangipane mixture. Bake 20 minutes until golden brown and cooked through. Let cool while you make icing.

6 In a small bowl, combine confectioners' sugar with water, adding 1 teaspoon water at a time until desired consistency is reached.

7 Pour icing over Bakewells and top each with a cherry. Store in an airtight container at room temperature for up to 3 days.

Pecan Pie

What would the holidays be without Pecan Pie! With a buttery pastry base and sweet pecan filling, this pie is delicious served with dairy-free cream.

1 batch Sweet Short-Crust Pastry (see recipe in this chapter)

3 large eggs

¾ cup (150g) packed light brown sugar

¼ cup plus 3 tablespoons (150g) light corn (golden) syrup

¼ teaspoon salt

1 teaspoon vanilla extract

¼ cup (55g) vegan buttery spread, melted

1 tablespoon gluten-free all-purpose flour

2 cups (200g) pecan halves

SERVES 12

Per Serving:

Calories	445
Fat	29g
Sodium	277mg
Carbohydrates	44g
Fiber	4g
Sugar	25g
Protein	6g

1 Preheat oven to 350°F (180°C).

2 Remove pastry from refrigerator and roll out on a lightly floured surface to slightly larger than a 9" round springform pie dish. Carefully line dish with rolled-out pastry, trimming excess pastry from edges.

3 Place parchment paper or foil tightly against crust and fill with pastry weights or baking beans. Blind bake 10 minutes. Remove paper and weights and bake another 5 minutes. Remove from oven and set aside.

4 In a large bowl, whisk eggs and brown sugar until combined. Add corn syrup, salt, vanilla, and melted buttery spread and whisk until combined. Add flour and stir to combine. Stir in pecans and pour mixture into pastry crust.

5 Bake 40–45 minutes until center no longer feels wobbly. Cool in pan on a wire rack about 2 hours, then store in an airtight container at room temperature for up to 2 days.

Lemon Meringue Pie

SERVES 12

Per Serving:

Calories	412
Fat	17g
Sodium	217mg
Carbohydrates	63g
Fiber	3g
Sugar	41g
Protein	5g

ASSEMBLING THE PIE

When assembling the pie, be sure to reheat the lemon curd filling and add the meringue on top right away, making sure that the meringue mixture attaches to the crust with no gaps. This will stop any steam from forming inside the pie and prevent a watery filling.

Don't be intimidated. This Lemon Meringue Pie looks impressive, but it's much easier to make than you might think! The sweet pastry base is the perfect match for a tangy lemon curd filling and fluffy toasted meringue topping.

PIE

1 batch Sweet Short-Crust Pastry (see recipe in this chapter)

¾ cup (175ml) lemon juice

¾ cup plus 1 tablespoon (200ml) water

Zest of 5 medium lemons

½ cup (60g) cornstarch

1 cup plus 2 tablespoons (225g) superfine sugar

5 large egg yolks

3 tablespoons (40g) vegan buttery spread

MERINGUE TOPPING

5 large egg whites

2 teaspoons cornstarch

1 cup plus 2 tablespoons (225g) superfine sugar

PIE

1 Preheat oven to 350°F (180°C).

2 Remove pastry from refrigerator and roll out on a lightly floured surface to slightly larger than a 9" round springform pie dish. Carefully line dish with rolled-out pastry, trimming excess pastry from edges.

3 Place parchment paper or foil tightly against crust and fill with pastry weights or baking beans. Blind bake 15 minutes. Remove paper and weights and bake another 10 minutes. Remove from oven and set aside. Reduce oven temperature to 320°F (160°C).

4 In a large bowl, mix lemon juice and water. In a medium saucepan, heat lemon zest, cornstarch, and sugar over medium heat.

5 Gradually add lemon juice and water mixture to saucepan while constantly whisking until mixture starts to simmer. Once simmering and all lemon juice mixture is added, cook another 2 minutes until thickened and smooth. Remove from heat and stir in egg yolks followed by buttery spread. Set aside.

MERINGUE TOPPING

In a medium bowl, whisk egg whites with an electric mixer at high speed to form stiff peaks, starting on low speed, then increasing speed to medium. Add cornstarch and continue to whisk until combined. Add sugar 1 teaspoon at a time and keep whisking until mixture is glossy and thick.

ASSEMBLY

1. In a medium saucepan, reheat lemon curd filling over low heat about 2–3 minutes until warm, then spoon into pastry filling. Immediately spoon meringue mixture on top, starting around edges and moving to center. Use the back of a spoon to create peaks over meringue.
2. Bake pie 30 minutes until meringue is set and crisp. Remove from oven and let sit at least 30 minutes before serving. Store in refrigerator for up to 2 days.

Lemon Tart

SERVES 12

Per Serving:

Calories	343
Fat	20g
Sodium	195mg
Carbohydrates	36g
Fiber	3g
Sugar	20g
Protein	5g

This classic Lemon Tart combines a light, buttery pastry crust with a tangy lemon filling. You won't believe it is both gluten- and dairy-free!

1 batch Sweet Short-Crust Pastry (see recipe in this chapter)

5 large eggs

1 cup (200g) superfine sugar

¾ cup plus 1 tablespoon (200ml) dairy-free heavy cream

Zest and juice of 4 medium lemons

1 Preheat oven to 350°F (180°C).

2 Remove pastry from refrigerator and roll out on a lightly floured surface to slightly larger than a 9" round springform tart pan. Carefully line dish with rolled-out pastry, trimming excess pastry from edges.

3 Place parchment paper or foil tightly against crust and fill with pastry weights or baking beans. Blind bake 10 minutes. Remove paper and weights and bake another 5 minutes. Remove from oven and set aside.

4 In a large bowl, beat eggs and sugar until pale and frothy. Add cream and lemon zest and juice, and beat until fully combined.

5 Pour mixture into pastry crust and bake 30 minutes until filling is firm to touch but still slightly wobbly. Let cool completely, about 2 hours, then store in refrigerator for up to 3 days.

No-Bake Chocolate Tart

This decadent No-Bake Chocolate Tart has a gluten-free graham cracker crust with a rich and creamy chocolate filling. It has just six ingredients and couldn't be easier to make.

3¼ cups (320g) gluten-free graham crackers (or gluten-free digestive biscuits), crushed to fine crumbs

½ cup plus 3 tablespoons (150g) vegan buttery spread, melted

1 cup (240ml) dairy-free heavy cream

1½ cups plus 3 tablespoons (300g) dairy-free dark chocolate chips (70% cocoa content or higher)

1 teaspoon vanilla extract

1 tablespoon pure maple syrup

1 In a medium bowl, mix cracker crumbs and buttery spread. Press into base and up sides of a 9" round springform tart pan greased with buttery spread or vegetable oil.

2 In a medium saucepan, heat cream over medium heat until it starts to simmer, about 2–3 minutes. Remove from heat and stir in chocolate chips until melted. Add vanilla and maple syrup and mix well.

3 Pour chocolate mixture into tart pan over crust and leave in refrigerator to set 2 hours before serving. Store in refrigerator for up to 3 days.

SERVES 12

Per Serving:

Calories	457
Fat	34g
Sodium	182mg
Carbohydrates	32g
Fiber	3g
Sugar	15g
Protein	3g

CRUSH YOUR COOKIES

An easy way to crush cookies or crackers is to place them in a sealed bag and use a rolling pin to bang them into crumbs. You can decide whether you want fine or larger crumbs. Alternatively, you can put the cookies in a food processor and pulse into crumbs.

Key Lime Pie

SERVES 12

Per Serving:

Calories	414
Fat	26g
Sodium	210mg
Carbohydrates	43g
Fiber	1g
Sugar	28g
Protein	2g

Yes, you can eat Key Lime Pie on a gluten- and dairy-free diet! This traditional pie features a buttery biscuit base and a tasty baked lime-flavored filling topped with dairy-free whipped cream.

PIE

3¼ cups (320g) gluten-free graham crackers (or gluten-free digestive biscuits), crushed to fine crumbs

½ cup plus 3 tablespoons (150g) vegan buttery spread, melted

4 large egg yolks

1¼ cups (400ml) vegan sweetened condensed coconut milk

Zest and juice of 4 medium limes

TOPPING

½ cup plus 2 tablespoons (150ml) dairy-free heavy cream

2 tablespoons confectioners' sugar

1 teaspoon lime zest, to decorate

PIE

1 Preheat oven to 320°F (160°C).

2 In a medium bowl, mix cracker crumbs and buttery spread. Press into base and up sides of a 9" round springform tart pan greased with buttery spread or vegetable oil. Bake 15 minutes.

3 In a large bowl, beat egg yolks with an electric mixer 2 minutes on medium speed. Add coconut milk and lime zest and juice, and mix 1 more minute until combined.

4 Pour lime mixture into crust and bake another 15 minutes. Remove from oven (filling will still be wobbly) and place in refrigerator to set at least 3 hours or overnight.

TOPPING

Before serving, in a medium bowl, whisk cream to stiff peaks then add confectioners' sugar and whisk until combined. Spread on top of Pie and sprinkle with remaining lime zest. Store in refrigerator up to 2 days.

No-Bake Chocolate and Salted Caramel Tart

This decadent no-bake tart is filled with an oozy salted caramel sauce and a rich chocolate filling. It's the perfect combination of flavors and textures in a tart.

SERVES 12

Per Serving:	
Calories	542
Fat	37g
Sodium	382mg
Carbohydrates	46g
Fiber	3g
Sugar	29g
Protein	3g

CRUST

3¼ cups (320g) gluten-free graham crackers (or gluten-free digestive biscuits), crushed to fine crumbs

½ cup plus 3 tablespoons (150g) vegan buttery spread, melted

SALTED CARAMEL FILLING

1 can (14-ounce or 400ml) full-fat coconut milk

¾ cup plus 2 tablespoons (175g) packed light brown sugar

1 teaspoon vanilla extract

1 teaspoon salt

CHOCOLATE FILLING

1 cup (240ml) dairy-free heavy cream

1½ cups plus 3 tablespoons (300g) dairy-free dark chocolate chips (70% cocoa content or higher)

1 teaspoon vanilla extract

1 tablespoon pure maple syrup

CRUST

In a medium bowl, mix cracker crumbs and buttery spread. Press into base and up sides of a 9" round springform tart pan greased with buttery spread or vegetable oil. Set aside.

SALTED CARAMEL FILLING

In a small saucepan, heat coconut milk, brown sugar, and vanilla over medium heat. Stir until mixture comes to a boil, then continue to stir 20 minutes until slightly thickened. Remove from heat and stir in salt. Pour into crust and refrigerate 1 hour.

CHOCOLATE FILLING

1 In a small saucepan, heat cream over medium heat until it starts to simmer. Remove from heat and stir in dark chocolate until melted. Add vanilla and maple syrup and mix well.

2 Pour Chocolate Filling over Salted Caramel Filling and refrigerate 2 hours before serving. Store in refrigerator for up to 3 days.

Strawberry Hand Tarts

SERVES 8

Per Serving:

Calories	404
Fat	19g
Sodium	264mg
Carbohydrates	54g
Fiber	4g
Sugar	26g
Protein	5g

You'll love this homemade version of frosted Pop-Tarts filled with straw-berry jam. This fun childhood classic is simple to make and tastes great! They can even be decorated with colorful gluten-free sprinkles.

1 batch Sweet Short-Crust Pastry (see recipe in this chapter)

8 tablespoons strawberry jam

1 large egg, beaten

½ cup plus 3 tablespoons (100g) confectioners' sugar

1 Preheat oven to 350°F (180°C) and line a baking sheet with parchment paper.

2 Roll pastry dough out on a lightly floured surface to approximately ¼" thick. Using a sharp knife, cut dough into sixteen (3" × 5") rectangles.

3 Place eight rectangles on prepared baking sheet. Spoon 1 tablespoon jam in center of each rectangle. Brush outside edges with egg and place one rectangle on top of another, repeating to make eight tarts. Gently pinch edges to seal and crimp with a fork. Prick tops with a fork to allow steam to escape and brush top with egg.

4 Bake 15–20 minutes until golden brown and cooked through. Remove from oven and cool on wire racks at least 30 minutes.

5 In a small bowl, mix confectioners' sugar with 2–3 teaspoons water until it reaches drizzling consistency. Drizzle icing over tarts. Store in an airtight container at room temperature for up to 2 days.

Cherry and Chocolate Frangipane Tart

Per Serving:

Calories	410
Fat	27g
Sodium	242mg
Carbohydrates	38g
Fiber	5g
Sugar	18g
Protein	6g

SAVE THE LEFTOVER PASTRY

Any leftover pastry from this recipe can be kept in the refrigerator for up to 2 days and used to make individual pies or tarts.

This recipe combines sweet pastry crust filled with a chocolate frangipane cake and fresh cherries for a chocolaty adaptation of the classic Bakewell tart.

1 batch Sweet Short-Crust Pastry (see recipe in this chapter)

½ cup (110g) vegan buttery sticks

½ cup plus 1 tablespoon (110g) superfine sugar

1 large egg

1 tablespoon gluten-free all-purpose flour

1 cup plus 1 tablespoon (100g) ground almonds

½ cup plus 1 tablespoon (100g) dairy-free dark chocolate, melted and cooled

1¾ cups (170g) fresh cherries

2 tablespoons flaked almonds

1 Preheat oven to 350°F (180°C).

2 Remove pastry from refrigerator and roll out on a lightly floured surface to slightly larger than a 9" round springform tart pan. Carefully line dish with rolled-out pastry, trimming excess pastry from edges.

3 Place parchment paper or foil tightly against crust and fill with pastry weights or baking beans. Blind bake 10 minutes. Remove paper and weights and bake another 5 minutes. Remove from oven and set aside.

4 In a large bowl, whisk buttery sticks and sugar until creamy, then add egg and beat until combined. Add flour, ground almonds, and chocolate and beat until combined.

5 Pour mixture into crust and press cherries and flaked almonds into top. Bake 40–45 minutes until brown and cooked through. Remove from oven and let cool for 1 hour before serving or store in an airtight container at room temperature for up to 2 days.

CHAPTER 10

Cookies, Brownies, and Bars

White Chocolate and Cranberry Cookies

Combining the flavors of white chocolate and cranberries, these soft and chewy cookies are ideal for anyone with a sweet tooth!

½ cup plus 2 tablespoons (140g) vegan buttery sticks

½ cup plus 3 tablespoons (140g) packed light brown sugar

½ cup plus 1 tablespoon (120g) granulated sugar

1 large egg

1 teaspoon vanilla extract

1½ cups plus 3 tablespoons (270g) gluten-free all-purpose flour

¼ teaspoon xanthan gum (omit if flour blend already contains this)

1 teaspoon baking powder

¼ teaspoon salt

½ cup plus 1 tablespoon (100g) dairy-free white chocolate chips

½ cup (75g) dried cranberries

1 In a large bowl, add buttery sticks, brown sugar, and granulated sugar and beat with an electric mixer on medium speed until light and fluffy. Add egg and vanilla and beat until combined.

2 In a medium bowl, combine flour, xanthan gum, baking powder, and salt and add to batter. Beat until smooth. Stir in chocolate chips and cranberries.

3 Cover and refrigerate dough 30 minutes.

4 Preheat oven to 350°F (180°C) and line two baking sheets with parchment paper.

5 Roll dough into twelve large balls and place on prepared baking sheets, spaced at least 2" apart. Press down slightly on top of each ball.

6 Bake 10–12 minutes until golden brown; cookies will continue to cook and firm up once out of oven. Cool on baking sheets 10 minutes before transferring to a wire rack and cooling completely, about 1 hour. Store in an airtight container at room temperature for up to 3 days.

MAKES 12

Per Serving (1 cookie):

Calories	304
Fat	13g
Sodium	193mg
Carbohydrates	46g
Fiber	2g
Sugar	31g
Protein	3g

ADAPT THE COOKIES

Switch up this recipe by adding any chocolate, fruit, or nuts for a different flavor. Any of the cookie recipes in this book would make a lovely gift for someone. Just wrap six cookies in see-through bags and tie with some brown string or colorful ribbon.

Oatmeal and Raisin Cookies

MAKES 10

Per Serving (1 cookie):

Calories	316
Fat	12g
Sodium	275mg
Carbohydrates	50g
Fiber	4g
Sugar	26g
Protein	5g

You will love these classic Oatmeal and Raisin Cookies with coffee, as a snack, or right before bed with a glass of dairy-free milk.

½ cup plus 1 tablespoon (125g) vegan buttery sticks

½ cup plus 1 tablespoon (110g) packed light brown sugar

¼ cup (55g) granulated sugar

1 large egg

1 teaspoon vanilla extract

1 teaspoon ground cinnamon

1 cup (160g) gluten-free all-purpose flour

1¾ cups (160g) gluten-free rolled oats

1 teaspoon baking powder

½ teaspoon baking soda

¼ teaspoon salt

¼ teaspoon xanthan gum (omit if flour blend already contains this)

1 cup (150g) raisins

1 In a large bowl, add buttery sticks, brown sugar, and granulated sugar. Beat with an electric mixer on medium speed until light and fluffy, then add egg, vanilla, and cinnamon and beat until combined.

2 Stir in flour, oats, baking powder, baking soda, salt, and xanthan gum. Fold in raisins. Roll into ten equal-sized balls and refrigerate on a baking sheet lined with parchment paper 30 minutes.

3 Preheat oven to 350°F (180°C) and line two baking sheets with fresh parchment paper.

4 Place five cookies evenly across each baking sheet and flatten slightly. Bake 12 minutes. Remove from oven and leave to cool on a wire rack for 1 hour. Store in an airtight container at room temperature for up to 3 days.

Chocolate Chip Cookies

These soft and chewy cookies are filled with dairy-free chocolate chips. With golden brown edges and a gooey center, they taste just like bakery-style cookies.

½ cup plus 2 tablespoons (140g) vegan buttery sticks

½ cup plus 3 tablespoons (140g) packed light brown sugar

½ cup plus 1 tablespoon (120g) granulated sugar

1 large egg

1 teaspoon vanilla extract

1½ cups plus 3 tablespoons (270g) gluten-free all-purpose flour

¼ teaspoon xanthan gum (omit if flour blend already contains this)

1 teaspoon baking powder

¼ teaspoon salt

1 cup (180g) dairy-free milk chocolate chips

1 In a large bowl, add buttery sticks, brown sugar, and granulated sugar. Mix with an electric mixer on medium speed until creamy. Add egg and vanilla and whisk until combined.

2 Add flour, xanthan gum, baking powder, and salt. Mix to form a sticky dough and stir in chocolate chips. Cover and refrigerate dough 30 minutes.

3 Preheat oven to 350°F (180°C) and line two baking sheets with parchment paper.

4 Remove dough from refrigerator and roll into twelve equal-sized balls. Transfer balls to prepared baking sheets (ensuring they are evenly spaced apart) and press down slightly.

5 Bake 12 minutes or until golden brown; cookies will continue to cook and firm up once out of oven. Let cool on tray 10 minutes before transferring to a wire rack and cooling completely, about 1 hour. Store in an airtight container at room temperature for up to 3 days.

MAKES 12

Per Serving (1 cookie):

Calories	315
Fat	15g
Sodium	186mg
Carbohydrates	45g
Fiber	3g
Sugar	29g
Protein	4g

FREEZE THE DOUGH

This cookie dough is suitable for freezing. Simply freeze the dough in balls and cook from frozen for a few minutes longer than the recipe states for warm and gooey Chocolate Chip Cookies on demand.

Triple Chocolate Cookies

MAKES 12

Per Serving (1 cookie):

Calories	268
Fat	15g
Sodium	166mg
Carbohydrates	34g
Fiber	3g
Sugar	23g
Protein	4g

A chewy chocolate-flavored cookie filled with dairy-free milk and white chocolate chips: What more could you want?!

¼ cup plus 3 tablespoons (100g) vegan buttery sticks

¼ cup plus 2 tablespoons (75g) packed light brown sugar

¼ cup (55g) granulated sugar

1 large egg

1 teaspoon vanilla extract

½ cup (90g) dairy-free milk chocolate, melted and cooled

1 cup (160g) gluten-free all-purpose flour

¼ teaspoon xanthan gum (omit if flour blend already contains this)

1 teaspoon baking powder

¼ cup (30g) cocoa powder

¼ teaspoon salt

½ cup (90g) dairy-free milk chocolate chips

½ cup (90g) dairy-free white chocolate chips

1 In a large bowl, add buttery sticks, brown sugar, and granulated sugar. Mix with an electric mixer on medium speed until creamy. Add egg and vanilla and whisk until combined. Add melted chocolate and mix to combine.

2 Add flour, xanthan gum, baking powder, cocoa powder, and salt. Mix to form a sticky dough, then stir in chocolate chips. Cover and refrigerate dough 30 minutes.

3 Preheat oven to 350°F (180°C) and line two baking sheets with parchment paper.

4 Roll dough into twelve equal-sized balls and evenly space on prepared baking sheets. Flatten slightly. Bake 10–12 minutes until soft. Let cool on tray 10 minutes before transferring to a wire rack and cooling completely, about 1 hour. Store in an airtight container at room temperature for up to 3 days.

Chocolate Lava Cookies

These rich chocolate cookies are stuffed with a dairy-free chocolate spread for a gooey surprise when you bite into them! They really are a chocolate lover's dream.

10 tablespoons dairy-free chocolate hazelnut spread

½ cup plus 1 tablespoon (120g) vegan buttery sticks

2 tablespoons plus 1 teaspoon (30g) packed light brown sugar

¼ cup (60g) granulated sugar

1 large egg

1 teaspoon vanilla extract

¾ cup plus 2 tablespoons (140g) gluten-free all-purpose flour

¼ teaspoon xanthan gum (omit if flour blend already contains this)

½ teaspoon baking powder

¼ cup plus 2 tablespoons (40g) cocoa powder

½ teaspoon salt

1 teaspoon cornstarch

¼ cup plus 3 tablespoons (75g) dairy-free milk chocolate chips

MAKES 10

Per Serving (1 cookie):

Calories	316
Fat	19g
Sodium	247mg
Carbohydrates	37g
Fiber	4g
Sugar	23g
Protein	4g

CHOCOLATE SPREAD CENTER

When adding the chocolate spread center to the cookies, make sure to work quickly, as it will melt fast, making it difficult to handle.

1 Dollop tablespoons of chocolate spread onto a baking sheet lined with parchment paper. Freeze at least 1 hour until solid.

2 While chocolate spread freezes, in a large bowl, whisk buttery sticks, brown sugar, and granulated sugar with an electric mixer on medium speed until creamy. Add egg and vanilla and whisk until combined.

3 In a separate large bowl, combine flour, xanthan gum, baking powder, cocoa powder, salt, and cornstarch. Mix until fully combined. Add dry ingredients to wet ingredients and mix until combined. Fold in chocolate chips.

4 Roll dough into ten equal-sized balls and refrigerate on a baking sheet lined with parchment paper 1 hour.

5 Preheat oven to 375°F (190°C).

6 Working quickly, flatten each cookie dough ball, add chocolate spread to middle, then fold cookie dough around chocolate spread.

7 Place cookies on baking sheets lined with fresh parchment paper and bake 12 minutes. Remove from oven and let cool for 1 hour. Store in an airtight container at room temperature for up to 3 days.

Almond, Pistachio, and Dark Chocolate Biscotti

MAKES 14

Per Serving (1 biscotti):

Calories	177
Fat	6g
Sodium	88mg
Carbohydrates	27g
Fiber	3g
Sugar	15g
Protein	4g

These traditional Italian biscotti are twice baked for a delicious crunch. Filled with tasty almonds and pistachios and dunked in dark chocolate, they may become a new favorite.

¼ cup (50g) chopped almonds, divided

¼ cup (50g) chopped pistachios, divided

2 large eggs

1 teaspoon vanilla extract

1¼ cups plus 1 tablespoon (210g) gluten-free all-purpose flour

½ teaspoon ground cinnamon

1 teaspoon baking powder

¼ teaspoon xanthan gum (omit if flour blend already contains this)

¼ teaspoon salt

½ cup plus 3 tablespoons (150g) granulated sugar

3½ ounces (100g) dairy-free dark chocolate, melted

1 Preheat oven to 350°F (180°C) and line two baking sheets with parchment paper.

2 Place almonds and pistachios on one prepared baking sheet. Roast 5 minutes. Finely chop nuts and set aside.

3 In a large bowl, beat eggs with an electric mixer at medium speed until frothy. Add vanilla and beat until combined. In a medium bowl, combine flour, cinnamon, baking powder, xanthan gum, salt, and sugar. Add to egg mixture and beat until smooth. Reserve 2 tablespoons chopped nuts and add remaining nuts to dough. Stir to mix.

4 Shape dough into a long log shape and place on second prepared baking sheet. Bake 25–30 minutes until golden brown. Remove baking sheet from oven and leave oven on.

5 Transfer log to a cutting board and cool 10 minutes. Using a large, sharp knife, carefully cut into ½" slices and place slices back on baking sheet.

6 Bake slices 5 minutes, flip with a pair of tongs, and bake another 5 minutes. Remove from oven and transfer to a wire rack to cool completely, at least 30 minutes.

7 Dip one end of each biscotti piece into melted chocolate and sprinkle with remaining nuts. Store in an airtight container at room temperate for up to 3 days.

Cranberry, Pistachio, and White Chocolate Shortbread

MAKES 12

Per Serving (1 cookie):

Calories	246
Fat	14g
Sodium	74mg
Carbohydrates	27g
Fiber	2g
Sugar	16g
Protein	4g

Combining all the festive flavors of cranberries, pistachios, and white chocolate, these yummy shortbread cookies make a delicious homemade gift. Just wrap them up in pretty paper for family or friends.

¼ cup plus 3 tablespoons (100g) vegan buttery sticks
¼ cup (55g) superfine sugar
1 cup plus 1 tablespoon (175g) gluten-free all-purpose flour
¼ teaspoon xanthan gum (omit if flour blend already contains this)
¼ cup (50g) finely chopped dried cranberries
½ cup (100g) finely chopped pistachios, divided
¼ cup (50g) dairy-free white chocolate chips
½ cup (100g) dairy-free white chocolate, melted

1 In a large bowl, beat buttery sticks and sugar with an electric mixer on medium speed until creamy. Sift in flour and xanthan gum. Mix until mixture resembles bread crumbs.

2 Add cranberries, ¼ cup pistachios, and chocolate chips and mix well. Use your hands to squeeze mixture together into a ball. Cover and refrigerate 30 minutes.

3 Turn chilled dough out onto a lightly floured surface and roll out to about ½" thick. Using a cookie cutter, cut rounds out of dough and place on a large baking sheet lined with parchment paper. Refrigerate 60 minutes.

4 Preheat oven to 350°F (180°C) and bake cookies about 20 minutes until just golden on top. Let cool 30 minutes before decorating with melted chocolate and remaining ¼ cup pistachios. Store in an airtight container at room temperature for up to 3 days.

Gingerbread People

With a soft center and crisp edges, these delicately spiced Gingerbread People are great fun to make and decorate with children. Place some on a tray and wrap with clear plastic wrap for an extra special edible holiday gift.

¼ cup plus 3 tablespoons (100g) vegan buttery sticks

3 tablespoons (60g) corn (golden) syrup

¾ cup (150g) packed light brown sugar

1¾ cups plus 2 tablespoons (300g) gluten-free all-purpose flour

¼ teaspoon xanthan gum (omit if flour blend already contains this)

1 teaspoon baking soda

2 teaspoons ground ginger

½ teaspoon ground cinnamon

½ teaspoon ground nutmeg

¼ teaspoon salt

1 large egg, lightly beaten

1 In a medium saucepan, heat buttery sticks, corn syrup, and sugar over low heat until melted and sugar has dissolved, about 3–4 minutes. Set aside to cool while you prepare the rest of the ingredients.

2 In a large bowl, combine flour, xanthan gum, baking soda, ginger, cinnamon, nutmeg, and salt. Add ingredients from saucepan and egg, stirring to form a sticky dough. Cover and refrigerate for 1 hour.

3 Preheat oven to 375°F (190°C) and line two baking sheets with parchment paper.

4 Roll dough out on a lightly floured surface to about ½" thick. Stamp out gingerbread people shapes with a cookie cutter and place on prepared baking sheets. Bake 10–12 minutes until golden, remove from oven, and let cool completely, about 1 hour, before decorating as you please. Store in an airtight container at room temperature for up to 3 days.

MAKES 16

Per Serving (1 cookie):

Calories	151
Fat	6g
Sodium	171mg
Carbohydrates	25g
Fiber	2g
Sugar	13g
Protein	2g

GINGERBREAD DOUGH

This gingerbread dough will be very sticky; however, do not add any extra flour to the mixture, as it will dry out the cookies. Chilling the dough for at least an 1 hour will make it easier to roll out and cut.

Peanut Butter Sandwich Cookies

MAKES 8

Per Serving (1 cookie):

Calories	613
Fat	35g
Sodium	405mg
Carbohydrates	70g
Fiber	3g
Sugar	52g
Protein	8g

Soft and golden peanut butter-flavored cookies are sandwiched together with a peanut butter frosting.

COOKIES

- ½ cup plus 1 tablespoon (120g) vegan buttery sticks
- ¼ cup plus 3 tablespoons (100g) granulated sugar
- ½ cup (100g) packed light brown sugar
- ½ cup plus 1 tablespoon (120g) smooth peanut butter
- 1 large egg
- 1 teaspoon vanilla extract
- 1 cup plus 2 tablespoons (180g) gluten-free all-purpose flour
- 1 teaspoon cornstarch
- ½ teaspoon baking powder
- ½ teaspoon baking soda
- ¼ teaspoon xanthan gum (omit if flour blend already contains this)
- ¼ teaspoon salt

FROSTING

- ¼ cup plus 3 tablespoons (100g) vegan buttery sticks
- ¼ cup plus 1 tablespoon (75g) smooth peanut butter
- 1¼ cups plus 2 tablespoons (200g) confectioners' sugar

COOKIES

1. In a large bowl, beat buttery sticks, granulated sugar, and brown sugar until creamy. Add peanut butter, egg, and vanilla and beat until combined.
2. In a separate large bowl, mix flour, cornstarch, baking powder, baking soda, xanthan gum, and salt. Add dry ingredients to wet ingredients and mix until combined. Cover dough and refrigerate 1 hour.
3. Preheat oven to 350°F (180°C) and line three baking sheets with parchment paper.
4. Roll dough into sixteen equal-sized balls and space evenly across prepared baking sheets. Press down slightly and bake 12–14 minutes. Remove from oven and let cool completely on sheets, about 1 hour.

FROSTING

In a medium bowl, beat buttery sticks with an electric mixer on medium speed until soft. Add peanut butter and beat until combined. Gradually add confectioners' sugar and beat up to 5 minutes until creamy.

ASSEMBLY

Sandwich two Cookies together with a layer of Frosting. Repeat with remaining Cookies and Frosting. Store in an airtight container at room temperature for up to 3 days.

Jam Thumbprint Cookies

These delicious cookies combine a simple vanilla cookie base with raspberry jam for a tasty treat everyone will enjoy.

¾ cup plus 1 tablespoon (180g) vegan buttery sticks

¾ cup plus 2 tablespoons (180g) superfine sugar

1 large egg

1 teaspoon vanilla extract

1¾ cups plus 2 tablespoons (300g) gluten-free all-purpose flour

¼ teaspoon xanthan gum (omit if flour blend already contains this)

½ teaspoon baking powder

½ teaspoon salt

6 tablespoons raspberry jam

MAKES 18	
Per Serving (1 cookie):	
Calories	181
Fat	9g
Sodium	159mg
Carbohydrates	26g
Fiber	2g
Sugar	14g
Protein	2g

1 Preheat oven to 350°F (180°C) and line three baking sheets with parchment paper.

2 In a large bowl, beat buttery sticks and sugar until creamy. Add egg and vanilla and beat until combined.

3 Stir in flour, xanthan gum, baking powder, and salt to form a soft dough. Roll dough into balls and spread out over prepared baking sheets.

4 Gently press your thumb into center of each cookie to create a small indent. Spoon 1 teaspoon jam into each indent and bake 12–14 minutes until golden brown. Remove from oven and let cool for 1 hour. Store in an airtight container at room temperature for up to 3 days.

Chocolate-Dipped Florentines

Packed full of almonds, pistachios, and cranberries, these chewy Florentines have a sinful dairy-free dark chocolate base.

MAKES ABOUT 14

Per Serving (1 Florentine):

Calories	192
Fat	11g
Sodium	57mg
Carbohydrates	22g
Fiber	2g
Sugar	16g
Protein	3g

SPREAD OUT ON YOUR BAKING SHEET

These Florentines will spread a lot in the oven, so be sure to add no more than four cookies to each baking sheet. You may have to bake them in two separate batches.

¼ cup plus 1 tablespoon (75g) vegan buttery spread

¼ cup plus 2 tablespoons (75g) dark brown sugar

3 tablespoons plus 2 teaspoons (75g) corn (golden) syrup

¼ cup plus 3 tablespoons (75g) gluten-free all-purpose flour

1 cup (80g) flaked almonds

¼ cup (50g) finely chopped pistachios

¼ cup (50g) finely chopped dried cranberries

1⁄16 teaspoon salt

½ cup plus 1 tablespoon (100g) dairy-free dark chocolate, melted

1. Preheat oven to 350°F (180°C) and line three baking sheets with parchment paper.

2. In a medium saucepan, heat buttery spread, sugar, and corn syrup over low heat until melted and combined. Stir in flour, almonds, pistachios, cranberries, and salt.

3. Spoon mixture onto prepared baking sheets 1 teaspoon at a time, ensuring they are spread out, and flatten slightly. Bake 10 minutes until golden brown and let cool completely, about 30 minutes.

4. Dip cooled Florentines into melted chocolate and let set, about 1 hour. Store in an airtight container at room temperature for up to 4 days.

Ginger Nut Cookies

These fiery Ginger Nut Cookies are supereasy to bake and taste great served with a hot drink. They are crisp on the outside and chewy on the inside. Despite the name, they don't contain nuts!

½ cup plus 2 tablespoons (100g) gluten-free all-purpose flour

1 teaspoon baking powder

¼ teaspoon xanthan gum (omit if flour blend already contains this)

1 teaspoon baking soda

2 teaspoons ground ginger

¼ cup (50g) superfine sugar

¼ cup (55g) vegan buttery sticks, melted

2 tablespoons (40g) corn (golden) syrup

1 Preheat oven to 375°F (190°C) and line a baking sheet with parchment paper.
2 In a large bowl, add flour, baking powder, xanthan gum, baking soda, ginger, and sugar. Mix well.
3 Make a well in center of bowl and add melted buttery sticks and corn syrup. Mix to form a soft dough. Roll into eight balls, cover, and refrigerate 30 minutes.
4 Spread balls out evenly on prepared baking sheet, flatten slightly, and bake 12 minutes. Let cool 1 hour, then store in an airtight container at room temperature for up to 3 days.

MAKES 8

Per Serving (1 cookie):

Calories	127
Fat	6g
Sodium	273mg
Carbohydrates	19g
Fiber	1g
Sugar	11g
Protein	1g

BAKING COOKIES

Cookies will always appear soft when first taken out of the oven, but they will continue to cook and firm up as they cool.

NYC Chocolate Chip Cookies

These giant NYC cookies are filled with three kinds of dairy-free chocolate and are certainly not your average cookie!

½ cup plus 1 tablespoon (120g) vegan buttery sticks

½ cup (100g) packed light brown sugar

¼ cup (60g) granulated sugar

1 large egg

1 teaspoon vanilla extract

1½ cups plus 1 tablespoon (250g) gluten-free all-purpose flour

¼ teaspoon xanthan gum (omit if flour blend already contains this)

1½ teaspoons baking powder

½ teaspoon salt

½ teaspoon baking soda

1 tablespoon cornstarch

½ cup plus 1 tablespoon (100g) dairy-free white chocolate chips

½ cup plus 1 tablespoon (100g) dairy-free milk chocolate chips

½ cup plus 1 tablespoon (100g) dairy-free dark chocolate chips

MAKES 8

Per Serving (1 cookie):

Calories	489
Fat	25g
Sodium	454mg
Carbohydrates	64g
Fiber	5g
Sugar	40g
Protein	6g

1 In a large bowl, add buttery sticks, brown sugar, and granulated sugar and beat with an electric mixer on medium speed until light and fluffy. Add egg and vanilla and beat until combined.

2 In a medium bowl, combine flour, xanthan gum, baking powder, salt, baking soda, and cornstarch and add to batter. Beat until smooth. Stir in chocolate chips.

3 Line two baking sheets with parchment paper.

4 Roll dough into eight large balls and place on prepared baking sheets. Refrigerate 1 hour.

5 Preheat oven to 350°F (180°C).

6 Remove baking sheets from refrigerator and transfer to oven. Bake 12–14 minutes until golden brown; cookies will continue to cook and firm up once out of oven. Cool on baking sheets 10 minutes before transferring to a wire rack and cooling completely, about 1 hour. Store in an airtight container at room temperature for up to 3 days.

Chocolate Chip Shortbread

MAKES 12

Per Serving (1 cookie):

Calories	140
Fat	8g
Sodium	62mg
Carbohydrates	17g
Fiber	2g
Sugar	7g
Protein	2g

COOKIE GIFTS

These cookies make yummy presents for friends and family, especially around the holiday season. Just wrap in cellophane and tie off with a pretty ribbon.

A classic buttery shortbread filled with dairy-free chocolate chips, this recipe is made with just five ingredients!

¼ cup plus 3 tablespoons (100g) vegan buttery sticks

¼ cup (55g) superfine sugar

1 cup plus 1 tablespoon (175g) gluten-free all-purpose flour

¼ teaspoon xanthan gum (omit if flour blend already contains this)

¼ cup (50g) dairy-free milk chocolate chips

1 Preheat oven to 350°F (180°C) and line a baking sheet with parchment paper.

2 In a large bowl, beat buttery sticks and sugar with an electric mixer on medium speed until creamy. Sift in flour and xanthan gum. Mix until mixture resembles bread crumbs.

3 Add chocolate chips and mix well. Use your hands to squeeze mixture together into a ball. Cover and refrigerate 30 minutes.

4 Turn out dough onto a lightly floured surface and roll out to about ½" thick. Using a cookie cutter, cut rounds out of dough and place on prepared baking sheet. Refrigerate 60 minutes.

5 Bake cookies about 20 minutes until just golden on top. Let cool for 1 hour, then store in an airtight container at room temperature for up to 3 days.

Coconut Macaroons

Soft and chewy on the inside and crisp on the outside, these easy-to-make, naturally gluten-free macaroons use just a handful of simple ingredients.

2 large egg whites

¼ cup plus 2 tablespoons (75g) superfine sugar

1 teaspoon vanilla extract

1¾ cups plus 2 tablespoons (130g) desiccated coconut

½ cup plus 1 tablespoon (100g) dairy-free dark chocolate, melted

1 Preheat oven to 350°F (180°C) and line two baking sheets with parchment paper.

2 In a large bowl, whisk egg whites, sugar, and vanilla on medium speed with an electric mixer, about 3 minutes, until foamy and light. Fold in coconut and let sit 10 minutes.

3 Scoop even-sized teaspoons of mixture onto prepared baking sheets and bake 15 minutes until golden brown. Let cool completely, about 1 hour.

4 Dip bottom of each of cooled macaroon into melted chocolate. Arrange on a baking sheet lined with fresh parchment paper chocolate-side up and refrigerate 30 minutes until set. Store in an airtight container at room temperature for up to 4 days.

MAKES 10

Per Serving (1 macaroon):

Calories	173
Fat	11g
Sodium	18mg
Carbohydrates	17g
Fiber	3g
Sugar	13g
Protein	2g

Snickerdoodle Cookies

MAKES 10

Per Serving (1 cookie):

Calories	227
Fat	10g
Sodium	271mg
Carbohydrates	34g
Fiber	2g
Sugar	21g
Protein	2g

A timeless classic and real crowd-pleaser, these soft and chewy Snickerdoodle Cookies are like a sugar cookie wrapped in a cinnamon sugar coating.

½ cup (110g) vegan buttery sticks

½ cup plus 3 tablespoons (155g) granulated sugar, divided

¼ cup (50g) packed light brown sugar

1 large egg

1 teaspoon vanilla extract

1 teaspoon cream of tartar

½ teaspoon baking soda

½ teaspoon salt

1¼ cups (200g) gluten-free all-purpose flour

2 teaspoons ground cinnamon, divided

½ teaspoon xanthan gum (omit if flour blend already contains this)

1 In a medium bowl, add buttery sticks, all but ¼ cup granulated sugar, and brown sugar. Mix until creamy. Add egg and vanilla and mix until combined.

2 In a large bowl, mix cream of tartar, baking soda, salt, flour, 1 teaspoon cinnamon, and xanthan gum. Mix wet ingredients into dry ingredients to form a thick dough. Cover and refrigerate 1 hour.

3 Preheat oven to 338°F (170°C) and line two baking sheets with parchment paper.

4 In a small bowl, mix remaining ¼ cup granulated sugar and remaining 1 teaspoon cinnamon. Roll cookies into balls and dip in cinnamon sugar mixture. Spread out evenly on prepared baking sheets and gently press down, leaving them quite thick.

5 Bake cookies 11–12 minutes until they start to crack on top, then transfer to a wire rack to cool for 1 hour. Store in an airtight container at room temperature for up to 3 days.

Chocolate Sandwich Cookies

These soft and fudgy sandwich cookies are filled with a dairy-free butter-cream and make for a delicious homemade treat. They can be stored for up to 3 days, but they will probably be devoured long before then!

COOKIES

½ cup plus 1 tablespoon (120g) vegan buttery sticks

½ cup plus 3 tablespoons (150g) granulated sugar

¼ cup (50g) packed light brown sugar

1 large egg

1 teaspoon vanilla extract

1 cup (160g) gluten-free all-purpose flour

¼ teaspoon xanthan gum (omit if flour blend already contains this)

½ teaspoon baking powder

½ teaspoon salt

¼ cup plus 3 tablespoons (50g) cocoa powder

BUTTERCREAM

¼ cup plus 3 tablespoons (100g) vegan buttery sticks

1¼ cups plus 2 tablespoons (200g) confectioners' sugar

1 teaspoon vanilla extract

MAKES 10

Per Serving (1 cookie):

Calories	379
Fat	19g
Sodium	316mg
Carbohydrates	53g
Fiber	3g
Sugar	40g
Protein	3g

COOKIES

1 In a large bowl, beat buttery sticks, granulated sugar, and brown sugar until creamy. Add egg and vanilla and beat until combined.

2 In a separate large bowl, mix flour, xanthan gum, baking powder, salt, and cocoa powder. Add dry ingredients to wet ingredients and mix until combined. Cover dough and refrigerate 1 hour.

3 Preheat oven to 350°F (180°C) and line two baking sheets with parchment paper.

4 Roll dough into small balls (about ⅓ cup each) and place ten cookies on each prepared baking sheet. Press dough down slightly to flatten and bake 8–10 minutes until the tops just look set. Remove from oven and let cool completely, about 1 hour.

BUTTERCREAM

In a medium bowl, beat buttery sticks with an electric mixer on medium speed until soft. Gradually add confectioners' sugar, continuing to beat up to 5 minutes until combined and creamy. Add vanilla and beat until combined.

ASSEMBLY

Sandwich two Cookies together with a layer of Buttercream. Repeat with remaining Cookies and Buttercream. Store in an airtight container at room temperature for up to 3 days.

Sugar Cookies

MAKES ABOUT 18

Per Serving (1 cookie):

Calories	115
Fat	6g
Sodium	104mg
Carbohydrates	14g
Fiber	1g
Sugar	7g
Protein	1g

Simple and versatile, these Sugar Cookies have soft centers and crisp edges, and the dough is easy to work with. Use your favorite cookie cutter and decorate with icing and sprinkles.

½ cup plus 1 tablespoon (130g) vegan buttery sticks

½ cup plus 1 tablespoon (120g) granulated sugar

1 large egg

1 teaspoon vanilla extract

½ teaspoon almond extract

1¼ cups (200g) gluten-free all-purpose flour

¼ teaspoon xanthan gum (omit if flour blend already contains this)

½ teaspoon baking powder

¼ teaspoon salt

1 In a large bowl, add buttery sticks and granulated sugar. Mix with an electric mixer on medium speed until creamy. Add egg, vanilla and almond extracts and whisk until combined.

2 Add flour, xanthan gum, baking powder, and salt. Mix to form a thick dough and split into two separate pieces. Mold each piece into a disc shape. Wrap discs in plastic wrap and refrigerate for 2 hours.

3 Preheat oven to 350°F (180°C) and line two baking sheets with parchment paper.

4 Roll out each disc on a lightly floured surface with a floured rolling pin to about ¼" thick. Cut cookies out using a cookie cutter, rerolling leftover dough when required.

5 Spread cookies out on prepared baking sheets and bake 10 minutes until edges are golden brown. Let cool completely, about 1 hour, before decorating.

Classic Chocolate Brownies

These Classic Chocolate Brownies have a crunchy top and fudgy middle filled with gooey chocolate chips. It's everything a proper brownie should be!

¾ cup plus 1 tablespoon (185g) vegan buttery spread

½ cup plus 3 tablespoons (75g) cocoa powder

1½ cups (300g) superfine sugar

3 large eggs

¾ cup (120g) gluten-free all-purpose flour

¼ teaspoon xanthan gum (omit if flour blend already contains this)

¾ cup plus 1 tablespoon (150g) dairy-free milk chocolate chips

1 Preheat oven to 350°F (180°C) and line a 9" square springform cake pan with parchment paper.

2 In a medium saucepan, melt buttery spread over medium heat. Add cocoa powder and sugar and mix until a thick, chocolaty mixture forms. Set to one side to cool slightly, about 3 minutes.

3 In a small bowl, beat eggs and add to chocolaty mixture. Mix, then add flour and xanthan gum. Stir in chocolate chips and pour into prepared pan.

4 Bake 25–35 minutes to desired texture. Remove from oven and let cool completely (see Top Tip) in pan before cutting into squares. Store in an airtight container at room temperature for up to 3 days.

MAKES 9

Per Serving (1 brownie):

Calories	437
Fat	25g
Sodium	180mg
Carbohydrates	57g
Fiber	5g
Sugar	42g
Protein	6g

TOP TIP

Adapt the cooking time depending on how you like your brownies. For a very fudgy brownie, take them out of the oven after 25 minutes, leaving them in the refrigerator overnight to prevent them from falling apart when you cut them. For a cakier brownie, bake for 35 minutes.

Strawberry White Chocolate Blondies

MAKES 9

Per Serving (1 blondie):

Calories	329
Fat	15g
Sodium	107mg
Carbohydrates	44g
Fiber	2g
Sugar	34g
Protein	4g

These blondies are the perfect treat for anyone with a sweet tooth. They are fudgy and indulgent, with chunks of white chocolate in the middle and juicy strawberries on top.

¼ cup plus 2 tablespoons (85g) vegan buttery sticks

1 cup plus 2 tablespoons (200g) dairy-free white chocolate chips, divided

2 large eggs

¾ cup plus 1 tablespoon (160g) superfine sugar

1 teaspoon vanilla extract

¾ cup plus 3 tablespoons (140g) gluten-free all-purpose flour, divided

¼ teaspoon xanthan gum (omit if flour blend already contains this)

1 pint (250g) hulled and quartered fresh strawberries

1 tablespoon confectioners' sugar

1 Preheat oven to 350°F (180°C) and line a 9" × 9" baking dish with parchment paper.

2 In a medium saucepan, melt buttery sticks and ½ cup plus 1 tablespoon chocolate chips over low heat. Stir continuously until melted, 3–4 minutes. Set aside to cool slightly.

3 In a large bowl, beat eggs, superfine sugar, and vanilla until creamy. Add melted chocolate mixture and beat until smooth.

4 Fold in ¾ cup plus 2 tablespoons flour and xanthan gum. Stir in remaining ½ cup plus 1 tablespoon chocolate chips. Transfer batter to prepared pan.

5 In a large bowl, toss strawberries with remaining 1 tablespoon flour. Press over top of batter.

6 Bake 35–40 minutes until golden brown. Cool in pan 45 minutes.

7 Dust blondies with confectioners' sugar and cut into squares. Store in an airtight container at room temperature for up to 3 days.

Holiday Brownies

MAKES 9

Per Serving (1 brownie):

Calories	411
Fat	20g
Sodium	235mg
Carbohydrates	62g
Fiber	5g
Sugar	45g
Protein	5g

This adaptation of Classic Chocolate Brownies (see recipe in this chapter) is perfect for the holidays, combining a chocolate brownie with mincemeat.

¾ cup plus 1 tablespoon (185g) vegan buttery spread

½ cup plus 3 tablespoons (75g) cocoa powder

1½ cups (300g) superfine sugar

3 large eggs

¾ cup (120g) gluten-free all-purpose flour

¼ teaspoon xanthan gum (omit if flour blend already contains this)

½ (14-ounce) jar mincemeat

3 tablespoons festive sprinkles

1 Preheat oven to 350°F (180°C) and line a 9" square springform cake pan with parchment paper.

2 In a medium saucepan, melt buttery spread over medium heat. Add cocoa powder and sugar and mix until a thick, chocolaty mixture forms. Set aside to cool slightly, about 3 minutes.

3 In a small bowl, beat eggs and add to chocolaty mixture. Mix, then add flour and xanthan gum. Stir in mincemeat and pour mixture into prepared pan. Top with sprinkles.

4 Bake 25–35 minutes to desired texture. Remove from oven and let cool completely in pan before cutting into squares (see Top Tip sidebar with Classic Chocolate Brownies recipe in this chapter). Store in an airtight container at room temperature for up to 3 days.

Salted Caramel Brownies

These classic brownies have a decadent fudgy middle and are topped with a delicious four-ingredient dairy-free salted caramel sauce. Store any extra sauce in the refrigerator for up to 2 weeks and use to drizzle on desserts!

SALTED CARAMEL SAUCE

1 can (14-ounce or 400ml) full-fat coconut milk

¾ cup plus 2 tablespoons (175g) packed light brown sugar

1 teaspoon vanilla extract

1 teaspoon salt

BROWNIES

¾ cup plus 1 tablespoon (185g) vegan buttery spread

½ cup plus 3 tablespoons (75g) cocoa powder

1½ cups (300g) superfine sugar

3 large eggs

¾ cup (120g) gluten-free all-purpose flour

¼ teaspoon xanthan gum (omit if flour blend already contains this)

¾ cup plus 1 tablespoon (150g) dairy-free milk chocolate chips

MAKES 9

Per Serving (1 brownie):

Calories	558
Fat	34g
Sodium	446mg
Carbohydrates	67g
Fiber	5g
Sugar	50g
Protein	7g

SALTED CARAMEL SAUCE

In a medium saucepan, heat coconut milk, brown sugar, and vanilla over medium heat and stir until mixture comes to a boil. Continue to stir about 20 minutes until mixture is slightly thick and is a dark brown color. Stir in salt and set aside.

BROWNIES

1 Preheat oven to 350°F (180°C) and line a 9" square springform cake pan with parchment paper.

2 In a medium saucepan, melt buttery spread over medium heat. Add cocoa powder and sugar and mix until a thick, chocolaty mixture forms. Set to one side to cool slightly, about 3 minutes.

3 In a small bowl, beat eggs and add to chocolaty mixture. Mix, then add flour and xanthan gum. Stir in chocolate chips and pour into prepared pan.

ASSEMBLY

Drizzle Salted Caramel Sauce on top of Brownies and swirl with a knife. Bake 25–30 minutes to desired texture. Remove from oven and let cool completely in pan before cutting into squares (see Top Tip sidebar with Classic Chocolate Brownies recipe in this chapter). Store in an airtight container at room temperature for up to 3 days.

Peanut Butter Blondies

MAKES 9

Per Serving (1 blondie):

Calories	381
Fat	21g
Sodium	177mg
Carbohydrates	44g
Fiber	2g
Sugar	34g
Protein	6g

These simple, mouthwatering blondies are packed with creamy peanut butter and dairy-free white chocolate chips. You will definitely want to go back for more!

¼ cup plus 3 tablespoons (100g) vegan buttery sticks

½ cup plus 1 tablespoon (120g) smooth peanut butter

½ cup plus 1 tablespoon (120g) packed light brown sugar

¼ cup plus 2 tablespoons (80g) superfine sugar

1 large egg

1 teaspoon vanilla extract

¾ cup (120g) gluten-free all-purpose flour

¼ teaspoon xanthan gum (omit if flour blend already contains this)

¼ teaspoon salt

¾ cup plus 1 tablespoon (150g) dairy-free white chocolate chips

1 Preheat oven to 350°F (180°C) and line a 9" square springform cake pan with parchment paper.

2 In a large bowl, beat buttery sticks and peanut butter until creamy. Add brown sugar and superfine sugar and beat until combined. Add egg and vanilla and beat until combined.

3 Add flour, xanthan gum, and salt. Mix well and stir in chocolate chips. Transfer mixture to prepared pan and bake 25–30 minutes until golden brown around edges and a skewer inserted in center comes out clean. Let cool in the pan for 1–2 hours and store in an airtight container at room temperature for up to 3 days.

S'mores Cookie Bars

If you love cookies, you are going to love these S'mores Cookie Bars, which combine giant slabs of fudgy cookie with a marshmallow and chocolate chip filling.

½ cup (110g) vegan buttery sticks

½ cup (100g) packed light brown sugar

¼ cup plus 2 tablespoons (75g) granulated sugar

1 large egg

1 teaspoon vanilla extract

1¼ cups plus 2 tablespoons (220g) gluten-free self-rising flour

¼ teaspoon xanthan gum (omit if flour blend already contains this)

¼ teaspoon salt

1 tablespoon cornstarch

½ cup plus 1 tablespoon (100g) dairy-free milk chocolate chips

2 cups (100g) mini marshmallows

1 Preheat oven to 350°F (180°C) and line a 9" square springform cake pan with parchment paper.

2 In a large bowl, add buttery sticks, brown sugar, and granulated sugar. Mix with an electric mixer on medium speed until creamy. Add egg and vanilla and whisk until combined.

3 Add flour, xanthan gum, salt, and cornstarch. Mix to form a sticky dough and stir in chocolate chips and marshmallows.

4 Transfer mixture to prepared pan, ensuring it is pressed into corners. Bake 25 minutes until golden brown. Let cool completely, about 2 hours, in pan. Carefully remove from pan and cut into squares. Store in an airtight container at room temperature for up to 3 days.

MAKES 9

Per Serving (1 cookie bar):

Calories	337
Fat	15g
Sodium	176mg
Carbohydrates	52g
Fiber	3g
Sugar	31g
Protein	4g

Brookie Bars

A layer of chewy chocolate chip cookie dough topped with a fudgy chocolate brownie—what's not to love?! This recipe really is the best of both worlds.

COOKIE LAYER

½ cup (110g) vegan buttery sticks

¼ cup plus 2 tablespoons (75g) granulated sugar

½ cup (100g) packed light brown sugar

1 large egg

1 teaspoon vanilla extract

1¼ cups plus 2 tablespoons (220g) gluten-free self-rising flour

¼ teaspoon xanthan gum (omit if flour blend already contains this)

¼ teaspoon salt

1 tablespoon cornstarch

½ cup plus 1 tablespoon (100g) dairy-free milk chocolate chips

BROWNIE LAYER

½ cup plus 1 tablespoon (125g) vegan buttery spread

½ cup (55g) cocoa powder

1 cup plus 1 tablespoon (220g) superfine sugar

2 large eggs

½ cup (80g) gluten-free self-rising flour

¼ teaspoon xanthan gum (omit if flour blend already contains this)

½ cup plus 1 tablespoon (100g) dairy-free milk chocolate chips

MAKES 12

Per Serving (1 bar):	
Calories	456
Fat	23g
Sodium	195mg
Carbohydrates	63g
Fiber	5g
Sugar	41g
Protein	5g

COOKIE LAYER

1 Preheat oven to 350°F (180°C) and line a 9" × 9" baking dish with parchment paper.

2 In a large bowl, add buttery sticks, granulated sugar, and brown sugar and beat until light and fluffy. Add egg and vanilla and beat until combined.

3 In a medium bowl, combine flour, xanthan gum, salt, and cornstarch and add to batter. Beat until combined. Stir in chocolate chips. Press into prepared pan and refrigerate 10 minutes.

BROWNIE LAYER

1 In a medium saucepan, melt buttery spread over medium heat. Add cocoa powder and superfine sugar and stir until combined.

2 In a small bowl, beat eggs and add to chocolate mixture. Stir in flour and xanthan gum. Add chocolate chips and stir to combine.

3 Spread batter over cookie layer. Bake 35–40 minutes until mostly set but slightly wobbly in center.

4 Cool in pan 30 minutes, then refrigerate 1 hour before cutting and serving. Store in an airtight container at room temperature for up to 3 days.

Millionaire Shortbread

MAKES 9

Per Serving (1 shortbread):

Calories	483
Fat	26g
Sodium	186mg
Carbohydrates	63g
Fiber	4g
Sugar	41g
Protein	4g

CHECKING YOUR CARAMEL SAUCE

Test whether your caramel is ready by dropping a small amount in a bowl of cold water. It should form a soft caramel ball when pressed together.

With a homemade shortbread base, a gooey five-ingredient caramel center, and a dairy-free chocolate topping, this is an indulgent treat that everyone will love.

SHORTBREAD

¾ cup plus 1 tablespoon (175g) vegan buttery sticks

¼ cup plus 2 tablespoons (75g) superfine sugar

1½ cups plus 1 tablespoon (250g) gluten-free all-purpose flour

¼ teaspoon xanthan gum (omit if flour blend already contains this)

CARAMEL SAUCE

½ cup plus 2 tablespoons (120g) superfine sugar

¼ cup plus 1 tablespoon (100g) corn (golden) syrup

1 teaspoon vanilla extract

½ cup plus 1 tablespoon (130g) dairy-free soy cream

2 tablespoons (30g) vegan buttery spread

CHOCOLATE TOPPING

1 cup plus 2 tablespoons (200g) dairy-free milk chocolate

SHORTBREAD

1 Preheat oven to 350°F (180°C) and line a 9" square springform cake pan with parchment paper.

2 In a large bowl, add buttery sticks and sugar and cream together with an electric mixer on medium speed until smooth. Add flour and xanthan gum and mix until combined and a crumbly dough is formed.

3 Press dough into prepared pan and bake 25–30 minutes until slightly golden on top and firm to touch. Cool in tin on a wire rack.

CARAMEL SAUCE

1 In a medium saucepan, heat sugar, corn syrup, vanilla, and soy cream over low heat. Stir until combined, then stir in buttery spread and bring to a simmer over medium heat. Simmer 15–20 minutes until sauce thickens but is slightly runny; continue to stir constantly so it doesn't stick or burn.

2 Pour Caramel Sauce on top of Shortbread and refrigerate 1 hour to set.

CHOCOLATE TOPPING

1 In a small saucepan, melt chocolate over low heat, stirring regularly so it doesn't burn.

2 Pour Chocolate Topping on top of Caramel Sauce. Refrigerate 1 hour before cutting and serving. Store in an airtight container at room temperature for up to 3 days.

Mixed Berry Crumble Bars

This simple recipe uses the same mixture for the crust and topping, sandwiched together with a layer of fresh mixed berries. It's perfect for snacking on.

BERRY LAYER

1 cup fresh raspberries

1 cup fresh blackberries

1 cup hulled and quartered fresh strawberries

1 tablespoon lemon juice

¼ cup plus 3 tablespoons (100g) granulated sugar

2 tablespoons cornstarch

CRUMBLE

¼ cup plus 2 tablespoons (75g) packed light brown sugar

¼ cup plus 2 tablespoons (75g) granulated sugar

1¾ cups plus 2 tablespoons (300g) gluten-free all-purpose flour

1 teaspoon baking powder

1 teaspoon ground cinnamon

¼ teaspoon salt

½ cup plus 3 tablespoons (150g) vegan buttery sticks, cubed

1 large egg

MAKES 9	
Per Serving (1 bar):	
Calories	358
Fat	15g
Sodium	254mg
Carbohydrates	56g
Fiber	5g
Sugar	31g
Protein	4g

BERRY LAYER

1 Preheat oven to 350°F (180°C) and line a 9" square springform cake pan with parchment paper.

2 In a large bowl, add raspberries, blackberries, and strawberries with lemon juice, granulated sugar, and cornstarch. Mix well and set aside.

CRUMBLE

In a large bowl, add brown sugar, granulated sugar, flour, baking powder, cinnamon, and salt. Mix, then add cubed buttery sticks and rub in with a fork until it resembles bread crumbs. Add egg and mix well until fully incorporated.

ASSEMBLY

Press half Crumble into prepared pan followed by Berry Layer mixture. Sprinkle remaining Crumble over Berry Layer and bake 45 minutes until golden brown and cooked through. Let cool for 1 hour before slicing. Store in an airtight container at room temperature for up to 2 days.

Chocolate Flapjacks

SERVES 10

Per Serving:

Calories	356
Fat	19g
Sodium	133mg
Carbohydrates	42g
Fiber	4g
Sugar	20g
Protein	5g

TOP TIP

As soon as you have taken these flapjacks out of the oven, score squares into the top with a serrated knife. This will make it easier to cut when they are cool.

These easy-to-bake flapjacks are great as a midmorning snack. Substitute the chocolate chips for any dried fruit or nuts of your choice to change the flavor.

¾ cup (170g) vegan buttery spread

2 tablespoons corn (golden) syrup

½ cup plus 1 tablespoon (120g) packed light brown sugar

3½ cups (320g) gluten-free rolled oats

½ cup plus 1 tablespoon (100g) dairy-free milk chocolate chips

1 Preheat oven to 350°F (180°C) and line a 9" square springform cake pan with parchment paper.

2 In a large saucepan, gently melt buttery spread, corn syrup, and brown sugar over low to medium heat until buttery spread is melted and sugar is dissolved, about 3–4 minutes.

3 Remove from heat and add oats. Mix well. Stir in chocolate chips. Pour mixture into prepared pan and press down with the back of a spoon until packed and level.

4 Bake 30–35 minutes until golden brown on top. Remove from oven and leave to fully cool, about 2 hours, in pan before removing and cutting. Store in an airtight container at room temperature for up to 4 days.

Raspberry, Peach, and Almond Traybake

This simple almond-flavored cake is topped with fresh peaches and raspberries. A delicious treat that's perfect served with coffee.

¾ cup plus 1 tablespoon (180g) vegan buttery sticks

¾ cup plus 2 tablespoons (180g) superfine sugar

3 large eggs

1 teaspoon almond extract

1 cup plus 2 tablespoons (180g) self-rising flour

¼ teaspoon xanthan gum (omit if flour blend already contains this)

¾ cup plus 2 tablespoons (80g) ground almonds

1 teaspoon baking powder

¼ teaspoon salt

2 tablespoons unsweetened almond or other dairy-free milk

2 medium peaches, pitted and sliced

¾ cup (100g) fresh raspberries

1 Preheat oven to 350°F (180°C) and line a 9" square springform cake pan with parchment paper.

2 In a large bowl, beat buttery sticks and sugar until creamy. Add eggs one at a time and continue to whisk until combined. Add almond extract and whisk until combined. Fold in flour, xanthan gum, ground almonds, baking powder, and salt. Beat in milk.

3 Transfer mixture to prepared pan and press in peaches and raspberries. Bake 40 minutes or until a skewer inserted in center comes out clean. Store in an airtight container at room temperature for up to 3 days.

SERVES 9

Per Serving:

Calories	380
Fat	22g
Sodium	375mg
Carbohydrates	42g
Fiber	3g
Sugar	24g
Protein	5g

Granola Bars

You'll never need to buy granola bars again! This easy-to-make recipe is packed full of oats, almonds, sunflower seeds, and raisins and is a great lunchbox filler.

MAKES 9

Per Serving (1 bar):

Calories	378
Fat	19g
Sodium	196mg
Carbohydrates	47g
Fiber	5g
Sugar	25g
Protein	8g

ADAPT THE RECIPE

This granola bar recipe can be easily adapted depending on which nuts, seeds, and dried fruits you have in the cupboard. It works really well with dried cranberries or apricots.

2½ cups (220g) gluten-free rolled oats

½ cup (100g) roughly chopped almonds

½ cup (60g) sunflower seeds

¼ cup plus 3 tablespoons (100g) vegan buttery spread

3 tablespoons (60g) amber honey

¼ teaspoon salt

½ cup (100g) packed light brown sugar

1 teaspoon ground cinnamon

¾ cup (110g) raisins

1. Preheat oven to 350°F (180°C) and line a baking sheet with parchment paper.
2. In a medium bowl, mix oats, almonds, and sunflower seeds and spread out on prepared baking sheet. Bake 10 minutes until golden. Remove from oven and set aside.
3. Line a 9" square springform cake pan with parchment paper. In a medium saucepan, heat buttery spread, honey, salt, sugar, and cinnamon over low heat, stirring continuously, until melted and combined.
4. Add oat mixture and raisins to saucepan and mix until fully coated.
5. Press mixture into prepared pan and bake 20–25 minutes until golden brown and set. Let cool completely, about 2 hours, before cutting. Store in an airtight container at room temperature for up to 4 days.

CHAPTER 11

Simple Desserts and No-Bake Treats

Madeleines

MAKES 16

Per Serving (1 Madeleine):

Calories	94
Fat	6g
Sodium	107mg
Carbohydrates	10g
Fiber	1g
Sugar	6g
Protein	1g

Light and delicate, these classic French Madeleines are flavored with lemon zest.

¼ cup plus 3 tablespoons (100g) vegan buttery sticks

¼ cup plus 2 tablespoons (80g) granulated sugar

2 large eggs

1 teaspoon lemon zest

1 teaspoon vanilla extract

½ cup plus 2 tablespoons (100g) gluten-free all-purpose flour

¼ teaspoon xanthan gum (omit if flour blend already contains this)

½ teaspoon baking powder

¼ teaspoon salt

1 tablespoon confectioners' sugar, to dust

1 In a small saucepan, heat buttery sticks on medium heat until melted. Set aside to cool, about 10 minutes. In a large bowl, beat granulated sugar and eggs on medium speed with an electric mixer 4–5 minutes until thick and pale. Add lemon zest and vanilla and beat until combined.

2 Fold in flour, xanthan gum, baking powder, and salt. Stir in melted buttery sticks a little at a time to form a thick pale batter. Cover with plastic wrap and refrigerate for 1 hour.

3 Preheat oven to 350°F (180°C) and grease a Madeleine tray with melted buttery sticks.

4 Spoon 1 tablespoon batter into center of each Madeleine mold. Bake 10–12 minutes until risen and golden brown.

5 Cool on a wire rack for 30 minutes before dusting with confectioners' sugar. Store in an airtight container at room temperature for up to 2 days.

Berry Meringue Nests

These meringue nests are served with a dairy-free cream and fresh berries. They are the perfect dessert for a warm day.

MERINGUE NESTS

2 large egg whites

½ cup (100g) superfine sugar

TOPPINGS

½ cup (120ml) dairy-free heavy cream

¼ pint (50g) hulled fresh strawberries

¼ pint (50g) fresh raspberries

SERVES 6

Per Serving:

Calories	141
Fat	7g
Sodium	18mg
Carbohydrates	18g
Fiber	1g
Sugar	18g
Protein	1g

MERINGUE NESTS

1 Preheat oven to 210°F (100°C) and line a baking sheet with parchment paper.

2 In a large bowl, add egg whites. Using an electric mixer, whisk on low until mixture starts to foam. Turn up to medium speed and whisk to stiff peaks.

3 Add sugar 1 tablespoon at a time and continue to whisk until mixture is stiff and glossy.

4 Spoon mixture into a piping bag and snip top off with scissors. Pipe six circular nest shapes onto prepared baking sheet.

5 Bake 1 hour and 45 minutes. Once cooked, turn off oven and leave nests in closed oven until oven is completely cool.

TOPPINGS

In a medium bowl, add cream and whisk on medium speed using an electric mixer until thick. Serve meringue nests topped with whipped cream, strawberries, and raspberries.

STIFF PEAKS

Stiff peaks stand up straight when the electric mixer is lifted. You should be able to hold the bowl upside down over your head, and the mixture will stay inside the bowl.

Strawberry, Elderflower, and Mint Pavlova

Pavlova is always impressive looking, and this dessert is no exception. Perfect for summertime and much easier to make than you might think! It's topped with strawberries, elderflower cordial, lime juice, and fresh mint.

5 large egg whites

1¼ cups (250g) superfine sugar

½ teaspoon vanilla extract

1 tablespoon cornstarch

1 pint (250g) hulled and halved fresh strawberries

2 tablespoons elderflower cordial

2 teaspoons lime juice

½ cup fresh mint leaves

½ cup (120ml) dairy-free heavy cream

1 Preheat oven to 300°F (150°C) and line a baking sheet with parchment paper. Place a large dinner plate on parchment paper and trace a circle around outside of plate using a dark pencil or marker. Turn parchment paper so circle is facing baking sheet.

2 In a large bowl, beat egg whites with an electric mixer on low speed until foamy. Increase speed to high and beat until stiff peaks form.

3 Add sugar 1 tablespoon at a time and continue to beat until mixture is stiff and glossy. Add vanilla and cornstarch and beat until incorporated.

4 Spoon meringue mixture onto prepared baking sheet, using traced circle as a guide. With the back of a large spoon, form an indentation in the middle so sides are higher than center.

5 Bake 1 hour until firm. Turn off oven, leaving meringue inside and let cool in oven with door closed 1 hour.

6 In a medium bowl, stir together strawberries, cordial, lime juice, and mint leaves. Set aside.

7 In a separate medium bowl, beat cream until soft peaks form. Spoon whipped cream over meringue and top with strawberry mixture. Serve immediately.

Individual Apple and Blackberry Crumbles

SERVES 6

Per Serving (1 crumble):

Calories	318
Fat	12g
Sodium	106mg
Carbohydrates	53g
Fiber	5g
Sugar	34g
Protein	3g

These Individual Apple and Blackberry Crumbles are the perfect dessert when you don't want a lot of leftovers. Serve with dairy-free ice cream or custard.

FILLING

1 teaspoon vegan buttery spread

1 pound (500g) peeled, cored, and sliced Bramley apples

1 cup (150g) fresh blackberries

1 teaspoon lemon juice

¼ cup (50g) granulated sugar

¼ teaspoon ground cinnamon

TOPPING

½ cup plus 2 tablespoons (100g) gluten-free all-purpose flour

¼ cup plus 1 tablespoon (75g) vegan buttery sticks

½ cup (100g) superfine sugar

½ cup (50g) gluten-free rolled oats

FILLING

1 Preheat oven to 350°F (180°C).

2 In a large saucepan, heat buttery spread on medium heat until melted. Add apples, blackberries, lemon juice, sugar, and cinnamon. Mix well until combined and continue to heat 5 minutes, stirring regularly. Divide between six ramekins greased with buttery spread.

TOPPING

In a large bowl, add flour and buttery sticks and rub mixture together with your fingertips until it resembles bread crumbs. Stir in sugar and oats.

ASSEMBLY

Sprinkle Topping over Filling. Bake 25–30 minutes until Filling is hot and Topping is golden brown. Serve warm or refrigerate for up to 2 days and reheat before eating.

Pineapple Upside Down Cake

Soft and tender, this Pineapple Upside Down Cake is topped with car-amelized pineapples. It's delicious served with dairy-free ice cream or custard.

TOPPING

¼ cup (55g) vegan buttery sticks

¼ cup (50g) packed light brown sugar

7 canned pineapple rings in syrup

CAKE

½ cup plus 3 tablespoons (150g) vegan buttery sticks

¾ cup (150g) superfine sugar

3 large eggs

1 teaspoon vanilla extract

¾ cup plus 3 tablespoons (150g) gluten-free self-rising flour

¼ teaspoon xanthan gum (omit if flour blend already contains this)

1 teaspoon baking powder

SERVES 10

Per Serving:

Calories	320
Fat	18g
Sodium	285mg
Carbohydrates	39g
Fiber	1g
Sugar	26g
Protein	3g

TOPPING

1 Preheat oven to 350°F (180°C) and grease an 8" deep round cake pan with buttery spread or vegetable oil.

2 In a small saucepan, heat buttery sticks and brown sugar over medium heat about 3 minutes until sugar dissolves and mixture bubbles. Pour into bottom of cake pan and arrange pineapple rings in a single layer on top (saving syrup from pineapple).

CAKE

1 In a large bowl, add buttery sticks and superfine sugar. Whisk with an electric mixer on medium speed until creamy. Add eggs one at a time and continue to whisk into mixture along with vanilla.

2 Stir in flour, xanthan gum, baking powder, and 2 tablespoons pineapple syrup. Spoon over pineapple rings and level with a knife.

3 Bake 35–40 minutes or until a skewer inserted in center comes out clean. Let stand in pan 5 minutes, then turn out onto a large plate. Slice and serve, or store in an airtight container at room temperature for up to 3 days.

Sticky Toffee Pudding

SERVES 6

Per Serving:

Calories	603
Fat	18g
Sodium	667mg
Carbohydrates	103g
Fiber	2g
Sugar	72g
Protein	5g

Sweet, warming, and delicious, this Sticky Toffee Pudding is the ultimate dessert recipe, combining a light cake with toffee sauce. Serve with a scoop of dairy-free ice cream.

CAKE

1 cup (175g) pitted and roughly chopped dates

½ cup plus 2 tablespoons (150ml) boiling water

¼ cup plus 1 tablespoon (75g) vegan buttery sticks

¾ cup (150g) packed light brown sugar

3 large eggs

1 teaspoon vanilla extract

2 tablespoons plus 1 teaspoon (50g) molasses

1¼ cups (200g) gluten-free self-rising flour

1 teaspoon baking soda

¼ teaspoon salt

¼ cup plus 1 tablespoon (75ml) unsweetened almond or other dairy-free milk

TOFFEE SAUCE

½ cup (100g) packed light brown sugar

¾ cup plus 1 tablespoon (200ml) dairy-free soy cream

½ teaspoon vanilla extract

3 tablespoons (40g) vegan buttery spread

2 tablespoons (40g) corn (golden) syrup

CAKE

1 In a medium bowl, add dates and water and let sit 15 minutes. Then add to a food processor and pulse until smooth. Set aside.

2 Preheat oven to 350°F (180°C) and grease an 8" × 8" baking dish with buttery spread or vegetable oil.

3 In a large bowl, beat buttery sticks and sugar until creamy, then add eggs one at a time, continuing to beat until combined. Add vanilla and molasses and beat until combined.

4 Fold in flour, baking soda, salt, and date mixture. Fold in milk a little at a time until fully combined.

5 Transfer mixture to prepared dish and bake 35–40 minutes or until a skewer inserted in center comes out clean.

TOFFEE SAUCE

1 In a small saucepan, add sugar, soy cream, vanilla, buttery spread, and corn syrup. Bring to a boil over high heat, then simmer over medium heat about 3 minutes until mixture starts to thicken slightly. Remove from heat and set aside.

2 Pour Toffee Sauce over Cake and let soak 20 minutes. Serve or store in refrigerator for up to 3 days and reheat prior to serving.

Cookie Dough Skillet

Bake this restaurant-style gooey cookie in a cast iron skillet and serve warm and fresh straight out of the oven! A great sharing dessert for two served with dairy-free ice cream.

¼ cup (60g) vegan buttery sticks

¼ cup plus 2 tablespoons (80g) packed light brown sugar

¼ cup plus 1 tablespoon (65g) granulated sugar

1 teaspoon vanilla extract

2 tablespoons unsweetened almond or other dairy-free milk

1 cup plus 1 tablespoon (175g) gluten-free all-purpose flour

½ teaspoon baking powder

¼ teaspoon salt

½ cup (85g) dairy-free milk chocolate chips

1 Preheat oven to 350°F (180°C) and lightly grease a 6.5" cast iron skillet with buttery spread or vegetable oil.

2 In a large bowl, add buttery sticks, brown sugar, and granulated sugar. Mix with an electric mixer on medium speed until creamy. Add vanilla and milk and whisk until combined.

3 Add flour, baking powder, and salt. Mix to form a sticky dough and stir in chocolate chips. Spoon into prepared skillet and press until even.

4 Bake 25 minutes until golden brown and cooked through. Serve warm.

SERVES 2

Per Serving:

Calories	969
Fat	41g
Sodium	695mg
Carbohydrates	155g
Fiber	11g
Sugar	94g
Protein	11g

DON'T HAVE A CAST IRON SKILLET?

You can easily make this cookie dough skillet in a small cake pan. It will taste just as great!

Melt-in-the-Middle Chocolate Pots

These rich and indulgent chocolaty puddings have a gooey melt in the middle of their chocolaty center. They are made in individual ramekins, making them the perfect dessert for a dinner party. Serve with dairy-free vanilla ice cream and fresh berries.

2 tablespoons (30g) vegan buttery sticks

¼ cup plus 2 tablespoons (75g) superfine sugar

2 large eggs

½ teaspoon vanilla extract

2 tablespoons plus 1 teaspoon (25g) gluten-free all-purpose flour

5 ounces (150g) dairy-free dark chocolate, melted

1 Preheat oven to 350°F (180°C) and grease four 4-ounce ramekins with buttery spread or vegetable oil and place on a baking sheet.

2 In a large bowl, beat buttery sticks and sugar until light and fluffy. Add eggs one at a time, beating in between each addition. Add vanilla and beat until combined.

3 Fold in flour and melted chocolate. Divide mixture between prepared ramekins and bake 10 minutes for a runny middle or 12 minutes for a slightly cakier middle. Serve warm.

SERVES 4

Per Serving (1 chocolate pot):

Calories	387
Fat	19g
Sodium	100mg
Carbohydrates	46g
Fiber	3g
Sugar	36g
Protein	6g

Flourless Chocolate and Almond Torte

SERVES 12

Per Serving:

Calories	360
Fat	25g
Sodium	142mg
Carbohydrates	28g
Fiber	3g
Sugar	23g
Protein	6g

Classy and delicious, this rich chocolaty torte is made with almonds instead of flour and is a naturally gluten-free indulgent treat. Serve for dessert with dairy-free ice cream and fresh berries.

¾ cup plus 1 tablespoon (180g) vegan buttery sticks

1 cup (180g) dairy-free dark chocolate chips

4 large eggs, yolks and whites divided

¾ cup plus 2 tablespoons (180g) superfine sugar

1¼ cups (180g) blanched almonds

1 tablespoon confectioners' sugar

1 Preheat oven to 350°F (180°C) and line an 8" deep round springform cake pan with parchment paper.

2 In a large saucepan, heat buttery sticks and chocolate chips over medium heat until melted and combined. Remove from heat and let cool 3 minutes.

3 Whisk egg yolks and superfine sugar until combined and pour into chocolate mixture. Mix to combine.

4 In a food processor, pulse almonds until fine, then stir into chocolate mixture.

5 In a medium bowl, whisk egg whites to form stiff peaks, then fold into chocolate mixture. Pour into prepared pan.

6 Bake 35–40 minutes until a crust has formed around outside of torte but center is still wobbly. Let cool in pan for 1 hour, then refrigerate until fully set, about 2 hours. Once set, dust with confectioners' sugar to serve. Store in an airtight container in refrigerator for up to 3 days.

Self-Saucing Chocolate Pudding

A dessert everyone will love, this Self-Saucing Chocolate Pudding is made by pouring boiling water over chocolate cake batter before baking it in the oven. The result is a delicious chocolate cake with a rich chocolate sauce. Serve with dairy-free ice cream and fresh berries.

¼ cup plus 1 tablespoon (75g) vegan buttery spread, melted and cooled

3 large eggs

1 teaspoon vanilla extract

¼ cup plus 3 tablespoons (100ml) unsweetened almond or other dairy-free milk

¾ cup plus 3 tablespoons (150g) gluten-free all-purpose flour

1 teaspoon baking soda

¼ teaspoon salt

1¼ cups (250g) packed light brown sugar, divided

¼ cup plus 3 tablespoons (50g) cocoa powder, divided

¾ cup plus 3 tablespoons (225ml) boiling water

1 tablespoon confectioners' sugar, for dusting

1 Preheat oven to 320°F (160°C) and grease an 8" × 8" baking dish with buttery spread.

2 In a large bowl, whisk buttery spread, eggs, vanilla, and milk. In a separate large bowl, mix flour, baking soda, salt, 1 cup brown sugar, and half of cocoa powder.

3 Fold wet ingredients into dry ingredients, then transfer mixture to prepared baking dish. Level with a knife.

4 In a medium bowl, mix remaining ¼ cup brown sugar with remaining half of cocoa powder. Using a spoon, sprinkle over chocolate cake batter, making sure entire top is covered. Pour boiling water over top of pudding and carefully transfer to oven.

5 Bake 30 minutes until firm. Dust with confectioners' sugar and serve warm.

SERVES 6

Per Serving:

Calories	385
Fat	14g
Sodium	462mg
Carbohydrates	64g
Fiber	5g
Sugar	43g
Protein	7g

Trifle

Trifle is traditionally made during the holidays, but this recipe is so delicious, it would be a shame not to make it all year-round! This tasty dessert is packed full of custard, cream, and fruit, with sherry-soaked cake, and it looks impressive served in a glass dish.

TRIFLE

½ cup plus 2 tablespoons (100g) gluten-free all-purpose flour

½ cup (100g) superfine sugar

¼ cup plus 3 tablespoons (100g) vegan buttery sticks

1 large egg

3 tablespoons strawberry jam

2 tablespoons sherry

1 (15-ounce or 425g) can pear halves, drained

1 (15-ounce or 425g) can fruit cocktail, drained

1 (15-ounce or 425g) can peach slices, drained

CUSTARD

2 cups plus 1 tablespoon (500ml) unsweetened almond or other dairy-free milk

1 teaspoon vanilla extract

5 large egg yolks

2 tablespoons (15g) cornstarch

1 tablespoon plus 1 teaspoon (15g) gluten-free all-purpose flour

3 tablespoons plus 2 teaspoons (50g) granulated sugar

TOPPING

1 cup plus 1 tablespoon (250ml) dairy-free heavy cream

¼ cup (50g) grated dairy-free milk chocolate

SERVES 12

Per Serving:

Calories	326
Fat	17g
Sodium	117mg
Carbohydrates	41g
Fiber	3g
Sugar	30g
Protein	3g

MIX IT UP

This trifle can be made with any fruit you have in the cupboard, canned or fresh. Once made, it can be kept in the refrigerator for up to 4 days. If you would prefer, this recipe can also be made into individual trifles in small dishes. It would make between six and eight lovely individual desserts, depending on the size of your dishes!

TRIFLE

1 Preheat oven to 350°F (180°C) and line an 8" round cake pan with parchment paper.

2 In a large bowl, add flour, superfine sugar, buttery sticks, and egg and beat until smooth.

3 Transfer batter to prepared pan and bake 15–20 minutes until golden brown and a skewer inserted in center comes out clean. Cool 5 minutes in pan, then transfer to a wire rack and cool completely, at least 45 minutes.

continued on next page

continued

4 Cut cake into cubes, spread each cube with jam, and place in bottom of a large glass trifle dish or bowl. Pour sherry over cubes. Top with pears, fruit cocktail, and peaches.

CUSTARD

1 In a medium saucepan, heat milk and vanilla over medium-high heat and bring to a boil. In a large bowl, whisk egg yolks, cornstarch, flour, and granulated sugar until combined. Once milk comes to a boil, pour over egg mixture and whisk vigorously until combined. Transfer mixture back to saucepan over medium heat and cook another 1 minute or until mixture thickens slightly, whisking continuously.

2 Transfer custard to a shallow tray to cool about 10 minutes. Custard will thicken up more as it cools. Once cool, spoon on top of fruit and let set 30 minutes.

TOPPING

In a medium bowl, beat cream until stiff peaks form. Spoon whipped cream over top of Trifle and sprinkle with chocolate. Serve immediately, or refrigerate up to 4 days.

Bread and Butter Pudding

What a great way to use up any leftover gluten-free bread! This old-fashioned English Bread and Butter Pudding is a classic comforting dessert layered with raisins, cinnamon, and nutmeg. Serve warm or cold.

12 slices gluten-free bread, crusts removed

¼ cup (55g) vegan buttery spread

½ cup (70g) raisins

1 teaspoon ground cinnamon

½ teaspoon ground nutmeg

1¼ cups (300ml) unsweetened almond or other dairy-free milk

¼ cup (60ml) dairy-free soy cream

2 large eggs

¼ cup plus 1 tablespoon (65g) granulated sugar, divided

1 teaspoon vanilla extract

1 Preheat oven to 350°F (180°C) and grease an 8" × 8" baking dish with buttery spread.

2 Generously butter each slice of bread with buttery spread. Cut each slice into 2 triangles and cover bottom of prepared dish with overlapping triangles. Sprinkle half of raisins, half of cinnamon, and half of nutmeg over bread, then layer remaining bread, followed by remaining raisins, cinnamon, and nutmeg.

3 In a small saucepan, heat milk and soy cream over medium heat until mixture starts to simmer (don't let it boil), about 2–3 minutes. Set aside.

4 In a medium bowl, beat eggs, ¼ cup sugar, and vanilla with an electric mixer on medium speed until pale. Pour warm milk mixture into egg mixture and continue to whisk until combined.

5 Pour egg mixture over bread and sprinkle with remaining 1 tablespoon sugar. Let soak 30 minutes.

6 Bake 40 minutes until golden brown. Serve warm straight from the oven.

SERVES 6

Per Serving:

Calories	385
Fat	16g
Sodium	417mg
Carbohydrates	56g
Fiber	1g
Sugar	20g
Protein	7g

GLUTEN-FREE BREAD

This recipe requires twelve slices of gluten-free bread; however, if your bread runs on the smaller side, you can add a few more slices.

Peach Cobbler

SERVES 6

Per Serving:

Calories	368
Fat	11g
Sodium	294mg
Carbohydrates	68g
Fiber	5g
Sugar	49g
Protein	4g

This old-fashioned Peach Cobbler recipe is made using fresh ripe peaches but can be easily made with canned peaches. A simple dish that is perfect served with a scoop of dairy-free ice cream.

FILLING

6 medium-sized ripe peaches, peeled, cored, and sliced

1 teaspoon vanilla extract

1 teaspoon ground cinnamon

1 tablespoon lemon juice

¼ cup (55g) granulated sugar

COBBLER

¼ cup plus 1 tablespoon (75g) vegan buttery sticks

1 cup (160g) gluten-free all-purpose flour

¾ cup plus 1 tablespoon (160g) superfine sugar

¼ teaspoon salt

1 teaspoon baking powder

¾ cup (180ml) unsweetened almond or other dairy-free milk

FILLING

1 Preheat oven to 350°F (180°C).
2 In a small saucepan, heat peaches, vanilla, cinnamon, lemon juice, and granulated sugar over medium heat about 3 minutes, stirring continuously, until sugar is dissolved. Set aside.

COBBLER

1 In an 8" × 8" baking dish, add buttery sticks and place in oven to melt while you prepare batter.
2 In a large bowl, mix flour, superfine sugar, salt, and baking powder. Slowly add milk to form a thin batter and pour into prepared baking dish over buttery sticks. Smooth with a knife and top with peach mixture.
3 Bake 40 minutes and serve warm.

Rhubarb Crumble

This classic Rhubarb Crumble is a great way to make the most of seasonal rhubarb. Serve with dairy-free ice cream or custard.

1 pound (500g) chopped rhubarb

1 cup (200g) granulated sugar, divided

1 teaspoon ground cinnamon

1¼ cups (200g) gluten-free all-purpose flour

½ cup plus 3 tablespoons (150g) vegan buttery sticks

½ cup (50g) gluten-free rolled oats

1   Preheat oven to 350°F (180°C) and grease an 8" × 8" baking dish with buttery spread.

2   In baking dish, add rhubarb. Sprinkle with ¼ cup sugar and cinnamon and mix well.

3   In a large bowl, add flour and buttery sticks and rub mixture together with your fingertips until it resembles bread crumbs. Stir in remaining ¾ cup sugar and oats. Sprinkle on top of rhubarb.

4   Bake 35 minutes. Serve warm or store in refrigerator for up to 2 days and reheat before eating.

SERVES 6

Per Serving:

Calories	454
Fat	21g
Sodium	200mg
Carbohydrates	64g
Fiber	6g
Sugar	34g
Protein	5g

No-Churn Coconut Vanilla Ice Cream

Make your own dairy-free no-churn ice cream with this simple four-ingredient recipe. The best part is how easily adaptable it is: You can add your favorite flavors and fillings!

2 cans (14-ounce or 400ml) full-fat chilled coconut milk

7 ounces (200g) vegan sweetened condensed coconut milk

¼ teaspoon salt

1 teaspoon vanilla extract

1   Remove full-fat coconut milk from refrigerator and scoop solid cream layer that has formed at top of can into a large bowl (discard coconut water or save for later use). Beat coconut cream with an electric mixer on medium speed to form stiff peaks. Add condensed coconut milk, salt, and vanilla and beat until combined.

2   Pour mixture into a medium container and freeze at least 6 hours before eating. Store in the freezer for up to 3 weeks.

SERVES 10

Per Serving:

Calories	217
Fat	18g
Sodium	85mg
Carbohydrates	12g
Fiber	0g
Sugar	10g
Protein	2g

Rocky Road

Who doesn't love rocky road?! This recipe is so simple to make, combining marshmallows, cherries, raisins, and biscuits in melted chocolate. You can adapt the recipe to your taste by adding dried fruit, nuts, or cookies of your choice. Digestive biscuits are the traditional choice among Brits, but gluten-free graham crackers are just as good!

SERVES 9

Per Serving:

Calories	322
Fat	17g
Sodium	125mg
Carbohydrates	42g
Fiber	2g
Sugar	29g
Protein	2g

3½ ounces (100g) dairy-free dark chocolate

3½ ounces (100g) dairy-free milk chocolate

¼ cup plus 2 tablespoons (80g) vegan buttery spread

3 tablespoons light corn (golden) syrup

7 gluten-free graham crackers (or gluten-free digestive biscuits)

¼ cup (50g) mini marshmallows

¼ cup plus 1 tablespoon (50g) raisins

¼ cup (50g) candied cherries

1. Line a 9" × 9" baking dish with parchment paper.
2. In a large saucepan, combine dark chocolate, milk chocolate, buttery spread, and corn syrup over low heat. Stir until melted and combined, about 3 minutes. Remove from heat.
3. Place crackers in a large zip-top plastic bag and crush into chunky crumbs using a rolling pin or heavy saucepan. Add crumbs to chocolate mixture along with marshmallows, raisins, and cherries.
4. Transfer mixture to prepared pan. Press mixture into pan using your fingers or an offset spatula. Smooth top. Refrigerate at least 3 hours before slicing. Store in an airtight container at room temperature for up to 4 days.

Syrup Sponge Pudding

This ultimate winter dessert can be made in a matter of minutes. It's delicious served with dairy-free ice cream.

SERVES 6

Per Serving:

Calories	727
Fat	34g
Sodium	639mg
Carbohydrates	103g
Fiber	1g
Sugar	71g
Protein	5g

¾ cup (250g) corn (golden) syrup

Zest and juice of ½ medium lemon

1 cup plus 1 tablespoon (240g) vegan buttery sticks

1 cup plus 3 tablespoons (240g) packed light brown sugar

3 large eggs

1½ cups (240g) gluten-free self-rising flour

¼ teaspoon xanthan gum (omit if flour blend already contains this)

¼ teaspoon salt

5 tablespoons unsweetened almond or other dairy-free milk

1 Preheat oven to 350°F (180°C) and grease an 8" × 8" baking dish with buttery spread.
2 In a small bowl, mix corn syrup with lemon zest and juice and pour into bottom of prepared baking dish so that entire bottom is covered.
3 In a large bowl, beat buttery sticks and sugar until creamy. Add eggs one at a time and continue to beat until combined. Fold in flour, xanthan gum, and salt. Whisk in milk. Pour mixture into baking dish on top of syrup. Bake 40 minutes and serve warm.

Chocolate and Almond Nectarines

These Italian-style baked nectarines are filled with the delicious flavors of chocolate and almonds. Serve with dairy-free ice cream.

SERVES 4

Per Serving:

Calories	349
Fat	21g
Sodium	122mg
Carbohydrates	36g
Fiber	5g
Sugar	28g
Protein	6g

MAKE IT BOOZY

To make this more of an adult dessert, add two tablespoons of sherry or Madeira wine to the orange juice before you pour it over the nectarines.

4 medium nectarines, halved and pitted

¼ cup (55g) vegan buttery sticks

½ cup plus 1 tablespoon (50g) ground almonds

¼ cup (50g) superfine sugar

1 large egg, beaten

3 tablespoons (35g) roughly chopped dairy-free dark chocolate

Zest of 2 large oranges, divided

1 Preheat oven to 350°F (180°C).
2 Scoop out a little flesh from each nectarine half and chop into fine pieces. Transfer nectarines, cut-side up, to an 8" × 8" baking dish and set aside.
3 In a large bowl, beat buttery sticks and almonds until combined, then add sugar and beat until combined. Stir in chopped nectarine, egg, chocolate, and half of orange zest to form a creamy consistency.
4 Spoon mixture into each nectarine half. Pour juice from oranges over mixture and sprinkle remaining half of zest on top.
5 Bake 30 minutes until golden brown. Serve warm.

Peanut Butter Cups

These three-ingredient Peanut Butter Cups are extremely easy to make and are a great snack idea for any peanut butter lover.

1 cup (175g) dairy-free dark chocolate chips, divided

6 tablespoons smooth peanut butter

¼ teaspoon sea salt

1 Line six cups of a twelve-cup muffin tin with cupcake liners.

2 In a small microwave-safe bowl, melt ½ cup chocolate chips in microwave on high in 30-second intervals, stirring between each cook time, until melted. Add 1 tablespoon to each cupcake liner. Place in freezer 30 minutes until firm.

3 Spoon 1 tablespoon peanut butter on top of each chocolate cup and place back in freezer 30 minutes.

4 In the same small bowl, melt remaining ½ cup chocolate chips in microwave on high in 30-second intervals, stirring between each cook time, until melted. Spoon on top of peanut butter. Add salt and freeze 1 hour.

5 Store in refrigerator in an airtight container for up to 2 weeks.

MAKES 6

Per Serving (1 peanut butter cup):

Calories	256
Fat	17g
Sodium	74mg
Carbohydrates	21g
Fiber	3g
Sugar	15g
Protein	5g

USE A DIFFERENT NUT BUTTER

These Peanut Butter Cups are really adaptable and work great with other nut butters such as almond or cashew.

Oatmeal Energy Balls

Enjoy these Oatmeal Energy Balls for breakfast or as a tasty snack. They only take a matter of minutes to make, and you can easily substitute your favorite nut butter.

1 cup (90g) gluten-free rolled oats

½ cup plus 1 tablespoon (120g) smooth peanut butter

2 tablespoons amber honey

2 tablespoons ground flaxseed

½ cup plus 1 tablespoon (100g) dairy-free milk chocolate chips

¼ teaspoon salt

1 In a large bowl, add all ingredients. Mix well until fully combined and roll into eight balls.

2 Place on a baking sheet lined with parchment paper and set in refrigerator 2 hours to set. Store in refrigerator in an airtight container for up to 7 days.

MAKES 8

Per Serving (1 ball):

Calories	221
Fat	13g
Sodium	75mg
Carbohydrates	23g
Fiber	3g
Sugar	12g
Protein	6g

Cashew and Ginger Energy Balls

MAKES 10

Per Serving (1 ball):

Calories	143
Fat	5g
Sodium	11mg
Carbohydrates	23g
Fiber	2g
Sugar	12g
Protein	3g

For a delicious and healthy snack, try these simple no-bake energy balls. They are filled with dates, cashews, oats, and ginger, but you can substitute just about any other ingredients you like.

1 cup (175g) pitted and roughly chopped Medjool dates

⅔ cup (100g) cashews

1 cup (90g) gluten-free rolled oats

2 teaspoons ground ginger

¹⁄16 teaspoon sea salt

½ teaspoon vanilla extract

In a food processor, pulse all ingredients until combined to form a sticky dough. Roll into ten equal-sized balls and place in refrigerator on a baking sheet lined with parchment paper 1 hour before serving. Store in refrigerator for up to 2 weeks.

Coconut Chocolate Bars

MAKES 10

Per Serving (1 bar):

Calories	313
Fat	24g
Sodium	16mg
Carbohydrates	20g
Fiber	4g
Sugar	13g
Protein	3g

These five-ingredient chocolate bars have a tasty coconut-flavored center with a dark chocolate shell.

1 (14-ounce or 400ml) can full-fat chilled coconut milk

2½ cups plus 1 tablespoon (180g) desiccated coconut

1 teaspoon vanilla extract

3 tablespoons pure maple syrup

1 cup (180g) dairy-free dark chocolate chips

1 Open can of full-fat coconut milk and scoop solid cream layer into a food processor (discard coconut water or save for later use).
2 In processor, pulse desiccated coconut, vanilla, and maple syrup until combined.
3 Shape mixture into small bars and arrange on a baking sheet lined with parchment paper. Refrigerate 1 hour to set.
4 In a small microwave-safe bowl, heat chocolate chips in microwave on high in 30-second intervals, stirring between each cook time, until melted. Dip bars into chocolate to coat.
5 Place back in refrigerator 1 hour to set. Store in an airtight container in refrigerator for up to 7 days.

No-Bake White Chocolate and Raspberry Cheesecake

With a graham cracker base and creamy white chocolate and raspberry filling, this No-Bake White Chocolate and Raspberry Cheesecake tastes just like the real thing. You certainly won't know it's gluten- and dairy-free!

BASE

3¼ cups (320g) gluten-free graham crackers (or gluten-free digestive biscuits), crushed to fine crumbs

½ cup plus 3 tablespoons (150g) vegan buttery spread, melted

FILLING

1¾ cups (400g) dairy-free cream cheese

¾ cup plus 1 tablespoon (120g) confectioners' sugar

1 teaspoon vanilla extract

1 cup plus 1 tablespoon (250ml) dairy-free heavy cream

1 cup plus 2 tablespoons (200g) dairy-free white chocolate, melted and cooled

1½ cups (200g) fresh raspberries

SERVES 12

Per Serving:

Calories	531
Fat	37g
Sodium	453mg
Carbohydrates	47g
Fiber	2g
Sugar	27g
Protein	3g

DAIRY-FREE CREAM

This recipe requires a dairy-free cream that can be whipped, such as heavy cream, as the thickened cream helps the cheesecake hold its shape.

BASE

In a medium bowl, mix cracker crumbs with melted buttery spread and press into base of a 9" deep round springform cake pan greased with buttery spread.

FILLING

1 In a large bowl, add cream cheese, sugar, and vanilla. Whisk using an electric mixer on medium speed until combined.

2 In a medium bowl, whisk heavy cream until thickened. Add thickened cream to cream cheese mixture and whisk until just combined. Stir in melted chocolate and fold in raspberries.

3 Spoon Filling onto Base and smooth top with a knife. Refrigerate at least 4 hours up to overnight. Store in refrigerator for up to 2 days.

Peanut Butter Puffed Rice Bars

MAKES 9

Per Serving (1 bar):

Calories	312
Fat	19g
Sodium	126mg
Carbohydrates	36g
Fiber	2g
Sugar	22g
Protein	6g

These no-bake Peanut Butter Puffed Rice Bars are topped with a layer of chocolate and can be made in a matter of minutes with just six ingredients.

½ cup plus 3 tablespoons (150g) smooth peanut butter

¼ cup plus 1 tablespoon (100g) amber honey

2 tablespoons coconut oil

¼ teaspoon salt

4 cups (100g) gluten-free puffed rice cereal

1 cup plus 2 tablespoons (200g) dairy-free milk chocolate chips

1 Preheat oven to 350°F (180°C) and line a 9" square springform cake pan with parchment paper.

2 In a large saucepan, combine peanut butter, honey, oil, and salt. Heat over low heat until melted. Stir in puffed rice and mix until fully coated.

3 Pour puffed rice mixture into prepared pan, ensuring it's pressed in firmly. Refrigerate 1 hour.

4 In a small microwave-safe bowl, heat chocolate chips in microwave on high in 30-second intervals, stirring between each cook time, until melted. Pour over puffed rice mixture. Refrigerate another 2 hours until fully set. Cut into squares and store in an airtight container in refrigerator for up to 4 days.

No-Bake Cookies and Cream Cheesecake

The ultimate rich and delicious no-bake cheesecake filled with tasty cookies and cream cookies, this dessert is so easy to make—you don't even have to turn on the oven!

BASE

3¼ cups (320g) crushed gluten-free cookies and cream cookies

¼ cup plus 2 tablespoons (80g) vegan buttery spread, melted

FILLING

1¾ cups (400g) dairy-free cream cheese

¾ cup plus 1 tablespoon (120g) confectioners' sugar

2 teaspoons vanilla extract

1 cup plus 1 tablespoon (250ml) dairy-free heavy cream

1½ cups (160g) finely chopped gluten-free cookies and cream cookies

SERVES 12

Per Serving:

Calories	438
Fat	28g
Sodium	409mg
Carbohydrates	46g
Fiber	0g
Sugar	29g
Protein	1g

BASE

In a small bowl, mix cookie crumbs with buttery spread and press into base of a greased 9" deep round springform cake pan greased with buttery spread.

FILLING

1 In a large bowl, add cream cheese, sugar, and vanilla. Whisk using an electric mixer on medium speed until combined.

2 In a medium bowl, whisk heavy cream until thickened. Add thickened cream to cream cheese mixture and whisk until just combined. Stir in chopped cookies.

3 Spoon Filling onto Base and smooth top with a knife. Refrigerate at least 4 hours up to overnight. Store in the refrigerator for up to 3 days.

No-Bake Vanilla Cheesecake with Strawberry Sauce

SERVES 12

This No-Bake Vanilla Cheesecake has a gluten-free graham cracker base, creamy vanilla filling, and strawberry sauce topping. It's a delicious dessert that everyone will enjoy!

3¼ cups (320g) crushed gluten-free graham crackers (or gluten-free digestive biscuits)

½ cup plus 3 tablespoons (150g) vegan buttery spread, melted

1¾ cups (400g) dairy-free cream cheese

¾ cup plus 1 tablespoon (120g) confectioners' sugar

3 teaspoons vanilla extract, divided

1 cup plus 1 tablespoon (250ml) dairy-free heavy cream

1½ cups (300g) frozen sliced strawberries

¼ cup (55g) granulated sugar

1 teaspoon cornstarch

Per Serving:	
Calories	462
Fat	32g
Sodium	438mg
Carbohydrates	42g
Fiber	1g
Sugar	22g
Protein	2g

1 Grease a deep 9" round springform cake pan with buttery spread.

2 In a large zip-top plastic bag, place crackers and crush into fine crumbs using a rolling pin or heavy saucepan (you should have about 3 cups of crumbs). Transfer to a large bowl and stir in melted buttery spread. Press mixture into bottom of prepared pan. Set aside.

3 In a large bowl, add cream cheese, confectioners' sugar, and 2 teaspoons vanilla. Beat using an electric mixer at medium speed until smooth.

4 In a medium bowl, beat cream until soft peaks form. Add to cream cheese mixture and stir until just combined.

5 Spoon filling over cracker base and smooth top with a knife or offset spatula. Refrigerate at least 4 hours or overnight.

6 In a medium saucepan, add strawberries, granulated sugar, and remaining 1 teaspoon vanilla. Mix well and bring to a simmer over medium heat. Continue to cook and stir until strawberries soften and collapse, about 10 minutes. Stir in cornstarch and simmer 1 minute. Pour sauce over cheesecake or serve alongside. Store in refrigerator for up to 2 days.

Five-Ingredient Vegan Truffles

MAKES 10

Per Serving (1 truffle):

Calories	198
Fat	14g
Sodium	1mg
Carbohydrates	16g
Fiber	4g
Sugar	9g
Protein	2g

ADAPTING THE RECIPE

These chocolate truffles are easily adaptable depending on your flavor preferences. Add orange extract or almond extract, or roll them in chopped hazelnuts. Add more or less maple syrup depending on how sweet you like your truffles.

These easy-to-make vegan truffles can be switched up with your favorite flavors, fillings, and toppings. They are the perfect edible gift for a friend or family member—or yourself!

7 ounces (200g) dairy-free dark chocolate (70% cocoa content or higher), broken into pieces

¼ cup plus 3 tablespoons (100ml) dairy-free heavy cream

1 teaspoon vanilla extract

2½ tablespoons pure maple syrup

¼ cup plus 3 tablespoons (50g) cocoa powder

1 In a large heatproof bowl, add chocolate.

2 In a medium saucepan, heat cream, vanilla, and maple syrup over low heat until mixture starts to simmer (don't let it boil). Pour cream over chocolate and stir until chocolate is melted and mixture is smooth. Refrigerate about 4 hours until solid.

3 Remove chocolate mixture from refrigerator and add cocoa powder to a small plate. Scoop out 1 tablespoon chocolate mixture, roll into a ball, then roll in cocoa powder. Place on a baking sheet lined with parchment paper. Repeat with remaining chocolate mixture and refrigerate 1 hour before eating. Store in refrigerator for up to 2 weeks.

CHAPTER 12

Make It Vegan

Vegan Cookies and Cream Brownies

MAKES 9

Per Serving (1 brownie):

Calories	405
Fat	19g
Sodium	270mg
Carbohydrates	63g
Fiber	5g
Sugar	43g
Protein	4g

These fudgy and gooey chocolate brownies are topped with cookies. You won't believe that vegan brownies can taste this great!

½ cup (115g) vegan buttery spread

1 cup plus 3 tablespoons (250g) granulated sugar

¼ cup plus 1 tablespoon (80ml) soy milk

2 teaspoons vanilla extract

¾ cup (120g) gluten-free all-purpose flour

¼ teaspoon xanthan gum (omit if flour blend already contains this)

1 teaspoon baking powder

½ cup plus 3 tablespoons (75g) cocoa powder

¼ teaspoon salt

½ cup plus 1 tablespoon (100g) dairy-free milk chocolate chips

12 gluten-free and vegan chocolate sandwich cookies

1 Preheat oven to 375°F (190°C) and line a 9" × 9" baking dish with parchment paper.

2 In a medium saucepan, melt buttery spread over medium heat. Remove from heat and add sugar. Whisk until combined. Add milk and vanilla and whisk until combined.

3 In a medium bowl, combine flour, xanthan gum, baking powder, cocoa powder, and salt. Add to sugar mixture and mix well. Fold in chocolate chips.

4 Pour batter into prepared pan. Press cookies into top of batter and bake 25–30 minutes or until a skewer inserted in center comes out clean.

5 Cool in pan at least 45 minutes, then refrigerate 2 hours before cutting into squares. Store in an airtight container at room temperature for up to 4 days.

Vegan Victoria Sponge Cupcakes

Treat yourself to a light and fluffy vanilla cupcake with a jammy center and generous dairy-free buttercream topping. These cupcakes are made without eggs, so they are suitable for vegans.

CUPCAKES

¾ cup plus 1 tablespoon (200ml) soy milk

1 teaspoon apple cider vinegar

¼ cup plus 1 tablespoon (75ml) vegetable oil

1 teaspoon vanilla extract

1¼ cups plus 2 tablespoons (220g) gluten-free self-rising flour

¼ teaspoon xanthan gum (omit if flour blend already contains this)

1½ teaspoons baking powder

½ teaspoon baking soda

¼ teaspoon salt

¾ cup plus 2 tablespoons (180g) superfine sugar

10 teaspoons strawberry jam

BUTTERCREAM

½ cup plus 3 tablespoons (150g) vegan buttery sticks

2 cups plus 1 tablespoon (300g) confectioners' sugar

ASSEMBLY

10 hulled fresh strawberries

CUPCAKES

1 Preheat oven to 350°F (180°C) and line a twelve-cup muffin tin with ten cupcake liners.

2 In a large bowl, whisk milk, vinegar, oil, and vanilla. In a separate large bowl, mix flour, xanthan gum, baking powder, baking soda, salt, and superfine sugar. Mix wet ingredients into dry ingredients.

3 Divide mixture between ten muffin cups and bake 25 minutes or until a skewer inserted in center comes out clean. Let cool on a wire rack for 1 hour.

4 Once cool, cut a small hole in top of each Cupcake with a serrated knife. Spoon 1 teaspoon jam into each hole.

BUTTERCREAM

In a medium bowl, beat buttery sticks with an electric mixer on medium speed until soft. Gradually add confectioners' sugar, continuing to beat up to 5 minutes until combined and creamy.

ASSEMBLY

Scoop Buttercream into a piping bag. Pipe onto Cupcakes and top each with 1 strawberry. Store in an airtight container at room temperature for up to 3 days.

Vegan Chocolate Chip and Walnut Banana Bread

This recipe is perfect for using up leftover bananas! Made with staple vegan ingredients, the result is a bread that is fluffy, moist, and packed full of chocolate chips and walnuts.

3 large ripe bananas, peeled and mashed

½ cup (105g) packed light brown sugar

¼ cup plus 1 tablespoon (80ml) vegetable oil

1 teaspoon vanilla extract

1½ cups (240g) gluten-free self-rising flour

¼ teaspoon xanthan gum (omit if flour blend already contains this)

1 teaspoon baking powder

2 teaspoons ground cinnamon

½ cup plus 1 tablespoon (100g) dairy-free milk chocolate chips

1 cup (100g) chopped walnuts

1 Preheat oven to 350°F (180°C) and line a 2-pound loaf pan with parchment paper.

2 In a large mixing bowl, add banana, sugar, oil, and vanilla. Mix well.

3 Add flour, xanthan gum, baking powder, and cinnamon. Mix until fully combined. Stir in chocolate chips and walnuts.

4 Transfer mixture to prepared pan and bake 40 minutes until golden brown and a skewer inserted in center comes out clean. You may need to cover top with aluminum foil for last 10 minutes to prevent cake from browning too much.

5 Remove from oven and let cool before slicing. Store in an airtight container at room temperature for up to 3 days.

SERVES 12

Per Serving:

Calories	280
Fat	14g
Sodium	123mg
Carbohydrates	38g
Fiber	3g
Sugar	17g
Protein	3g

RIPE BANANAS

For this recipe the riper the banana, the better! It's a great way to use up black bananas you would usually throw away.

Vegan Dark Chocolate and Cranberry Cookies

If you're after a vegan cookie recipe, the search is over! These cookies have crispy edges and a chewy middle, filled with chocolate chips and dried cranberries. Deliciously decadent!

MAKES 12

Per Serving (1 cookie):

Calories	243
Fat	11g
Sodium	201mg
Carbohydrates	36g
Fiber	3g
Sugar	22g
Protein	2g

¼ cup plus 1 tablespoon (70g) granulated sugar

½ cup (100g) packed light brown sugar

¼ cup plus 3 tablespoons (100ml) vegetable oil

3 tablespoons unsweetened almond or other dairy-free milk

1 teaspoon vanilla extract

1¼ cups plus 3 tablespoons (230g) gluten-free all-purpose flour

¼ teaspoon xanthan gum (omit if flour blend already contains this)

1 teaspoon baking powder

1 teaspoon baking soda

¼ teaspoon salt

½ cup (90g) dairy-free dark chocolate chips

½ cup (70g) dried cranberries

1 In a large bowl, whisk granulated sugar, brown sugar, oil, milk, and vanilla.

2 Add flour, xanthan gum, baking powder, baking soda, and salt. Mix well to combine. Stir in chocolate chips and cranberries. Roll into twelve balls and spread out on two baking sheets lined with parchment paper, pressing down slightly to flatten. Refrigerate 1 hour.

3 Preheat oven to 350°F (180°C).

4 Bake cookies about 12 minutes until soft. Cool on a wire rack for 1 hour and store in an airtight container at room temperature for up to 3 days.

Vegan Chocolate Cupcakes

Enjoy these Vegan Chocolate Cupcakes that taste just like the real thing, topped with a dairy-free chocolate buttercream.

CUPCAKES

¾ cup plus 1 tablespoon (200ml) soy milk

1 tablespoon apple cider vinegar

¼ cup plus 1 tablespoon (75ml) vegetable oil

1 teaspoon vanilla extract

1¼ cups (200g) gluten-free all-purpose flour

¾ cup plus 2 tablespoons (180g) superfine sugar

1½ teaspoons baking powder

1 teaspoon baking soda

¼ teaspoon xanthan gum (omit if flour blend already contains this)

¼ cup (30g) cocoa powder

¼ teaspoon salt

BUTTERCREAM

¾ cup plus 2 tablespoons (200g) vegan buttery sticks

2¼ cups plus 2 tablespoons (350g) confectioners' sugar

¼ cup plus 3 tablespoons (50g) cocoa powder

MAKES 10

Per Serving (1 cupcake):

Calories	494
Fat	24g
Sodium	417mg
Carbohydrates	71g
Fiber	5g
Sugar	53g
Protein	4g

CUPCAKES

1 Preheat oven to 350°F (180°C) and line a twelve-cup muffin tin with ten cupcake liners.

2 In a large bowl, whisk milk, vinegar, oil, and vanilla. In a separate large bowl, mix flour, superfine sugar, baking powder, baking soda, xanthan gum, cocoa powder, and salt. Mix wet ingredients into dry ingredients.

3 Divide mixture between ten cupcake liners and bake 25 minutes or until a skewer inserted in center comes out clean. Let cool on a wire rack while making Buttercream.

BUTTERCREAM

1 In a medium bowl, beat buttery sticks with an electric mixer on medium speed until soft. Gradually add confectioners' sugar and cocoa powder, continuing to beat up to 5 minutes until combined and creamy.

2 Scoop Buttercream into a piping bag and pipe onto Cupcakes. Store in an airtight container at room temperature for up to 3 days.

Vegan Carrot Cake Cupcakes

This is the perfect vegan carrot cake: moist, fluffy, deliciously spiced with raisins and walnuts, and topped with a dairy-free buttercream frosting.

¼ cup plus 3 tablespoons (100ml) vegetable oil

¾ cup (150g) packed light brown sugar

2 teaspoons vanilla extract, divided

1 cup plus 1 tablespoon (250ml) soy milk

1¾ cups plus 2 tablespoons (300g) gluten-free all-purpose flour

¼ teaspoon xanthan gum (omit if flour blend already contains this)

1½ teaspoons baking powder

1 teaspoon baking soda

2 teaspoons ground cinnamon

½ teaspoon ground nutmeg

1 teaspoon ground ginger

¼ teaspoon salt

3 medium carrots, peeled and grated

½ cup (50g) chopped walnuts

¼ cup plus 1 tablespoon (50g) raisins

¾ cup (160g) vegan buttery sticks

2 cups plus 3 tablespoons (320g) confectioners' sugar

16 walnut halves

MAKES 16

Per Serving (1 cupcake):

Calories	351
Fat	18g
Sodium	253mg
Carbohydrates	47g
Fiber	3g
Sugar	32g
Protein	3g

1 Preheat oven to 350°F (180°C) and line a sixteen-cup muffin tin with cupcake liners.

2 In a large bowl, whisk oil, brown sugar, 1 teaspoon vanilla, and milk. In a medium bowl, combine flour, xanthan gum, baking powder, baking soda, cinnamon, nutmeg, ginger, and salt. Add flour mixture to sugar mixture and beat until combined. Fold in carrots, walnuts, and raisins.

3 Divide mixture between sixteen muffin cups and bake 20–25 minutes or until a skewer inserted in center comes out clean. Cool in muffin tin 5 minutes, then transfer cupcakes to a wire rack. Cool completely, about 30 minutes.

4 In a large bowl, beat buttery sticks with an electric mixer at medium speed until soft and fluffy. Gradually add confectioners' sugar, continuing to beat up to 5 minutes until creamy. Add remaining 1 teaspoon vanilla and beat until combined.

5 Frost cupcakes and top each with a walnut half. Store in an airtight container at room temperature for up to 3 days.

Vegan Blueberry Muffins

These light, fluffy, and moist muffins are filled with bursts of blueberries.

MAKES 10

Per Serving (1 muffin):

Calories	193
Fat	8g
Sodium	202mg
Carbohydrates	31g
Fiber	2g
Sugar	17g
Protein	2g

¾ cup plus 1 tablespoon (200ml) soy milk

1 teaspoon apple cider vinegar

¼ cup plus 1 tablespoon (75ml) vegetable oil

1 teaspoon vanilla extract

1¼ cups (200g) gluten-free all-purpose flour

1½ teaspoons baking powder

½ teaspoon baking soda

¼ teaspoon salt

¼ teaspoon xanthan gum (omit if flour blend already contains this)

¾ cup (150g) superfine sugar plus 1 tablespoon for dusting

¾ cup (150g) fresh blueberries

1 Preheat oven to 350°F (180°C) and line a twelve-cup muffin tin with ten cupcake liners.

2 In a large bowl, whisk milk, vinegar, oil, and vanilla. In a separate large bowl, mix flour, baking powder, baking soda, salt, xanthan gum, and sugar. Mix wet ingredients into dry ingredients and fold in blueberries.

3 Divide mixture between ten muffin cups and bake 25 minutes or until a skewer inserted in center comes out clean. Sprinkle with remaining sugar.

Vegan Meringue Kisses

This recipe uses aquafaba, which is the water from canned chickpeas, for a crisp meringue that tastes just like the real thing.

MAKES 24

Per Serving (1 kiss):

Calories	21
Fat	0g
Sodium	0mg
Carbohydrates	6g
Fiber	0g
Sugar	6g
Protein	0g

¼ cup fresh raspberries

¼ cup plus 3 tablespoons (100ml) aquafaba

¼ teaspoon cream of tartar

½ cup plus 2 tablespoons (130g) superfine sugar

1 teaspoon vanilla extract

1 Preheat oven to 230°F (110°C) and line two baking sheets with parchment paper.

2 In a small bowl, add raspberries and use a spoon to press down to form a purée. Press through a sieve, discard seeds, and set aside.

3 In a large bowl, beat aquafaba and cream of tartar until mixture starts to foam. Increase speed to medium and beat to form stiff peaks. Add sugar 1 teaspoon at a time. Add vanilla and beat until thick and glossy.

4 Spoon raspberry juice into a piping bag. Swirl bag so juice covers entire inside of bag. Spoon meringue into bag. Pipe meringue kisses onto prepared baking sheets and bake 1 hour and 15 minutes until crisp on outside. Turn oven off; leave kisses in oven with door open 1 hour.

WHIPPING AQUAFABA

Patience is key when it comes to whipping aquafaba: This part of the process can take up to 10 minutes to reach the stiff peak stage.

Vegan Chocolate Fudge Cake

This vegan version of a classic chocolate fudge cake is made without eggs, but you won't know! Heat a slice in the microwave on high for 30 seconds before eating for the ultimate fudgy treat.

CAKE

1 cup plus 2 tablespoons (185g) gluten-free self-rising flour

1 teaspoon baking powder

¼ teaspoon xanthan gum (omit if flour blend already contains this)

½ teaspoon salt

¾ cup (150g) superfine sugar

¼ cup plus 3 tablespoons (90g) packed light brown sugar

¾ cup plus 1 tablespoon (90g) cocoa powder

1½ cups plus 3 tablespoons (400ml) unsweetened almond or other dairy-free milk

1 teaspoon vanilla extract

¼ cup (65ml) vegetable oil

2 teaspoons apple cider vinegar

BUTTERCREAM

½ cup plus 3 tablespoons (150g) vegan buttery sticks

1¾ cups (260g) confectioners' sugar

¼ cup plus 2 tablespoons (40g) cocoa powder

SERVES 12

Per Serving:

Calories	372
Fat	16g
Sodium	323mg
Carbohydrates	60g
Fiber	4g
Sugar	41g
Protein	3g

CAKE

1 Preheat oven to 350°F (180°C) and line an 8" deep round springform cake pan with parchment paper.

2 In a large bowl, combine flour, baking powder, xanthan gum, salt, superfine sugar, brown sugar, and cocoa powder. Set aside.

3 In a small saucepan, heat milk over medium heat until it starts to simmer. Remove from heat and stir in vanilla, oil, and vinegar.

4 Gradually whisk wet ingredients into dry ingredients until mixture is smooth. Pour mixture into prepared pan and bake in center of oven about 50 minutes or until a skewer inserted in center comes out clean. Let cool completely, about 1 hour, in pan.

BUTTERCREAM

1 In a medium bowl, beat buttery sticks with an electric mixer on medium speed until soft. Gradually add confectioners' sugar and cocoa powder, continuing to beat up to 5 minutes until combined and creamy.

2 Spread Buttercream generously on top and sides of Cake and smooth with a knife. Store in an airtight container at room temperature for up to 4 days.

Vegan Lemon Traybake

Enjoy this tasty Vegan Lemon Traybake topped with a crunchy sugar topping and a zesty lemon icing.

CAKE

1 cup (220g) vegan buttery sticks

1 cup plus 1 tablespoon (220g) superfine sugar

¾ cup (180ml) soy milk

1¼ cups plus 2 tablespoons (220g) gluten-free all-purpose flour

2 teaspoons baking powder

½ teaspoon baking soda

¼ teaspoon salt

¼ teaspoon xanthan gum (omit if flour blend already contains this)

½ cup plus 1 tablespoon (50g) ground almonds

Zest of 2 medium lemons

2 tablespoons lemon juice

2 tablespoons granulated sugar

ICING

¾ cup plus 1 tablespoon (120g) confectioners' sugar

2½ tablespoons lemon juice

CAKE

1   Preheat oven to 350°F (180°C) and line a 9" square springform cake pan with parchment paper.

2   In a large bowl, beat buttery sticks and superfine sugar until creamy. Add milk and beat until combined. Add flour, baking powder, baking soda, salt, xanthan gum, almonds, and lemon zest. Mix until fully combined.

3   Transfer mixture to prepared pan and bake 35–40 minutes or until a skewer inserted in center comes out clean.

4   In a small bowl, mix lemon juice and granulated sugar. Prick top of cake with a skewer and drizzle juice mixture over top. Let cool completely, about 1 hour, in pan.

ICING

1   In a small bowl, mix confectioners' sugar with lemon juice until icing reaches desired runny consistency.

2   Pour Icing over Cake and let set 1 hour. Store in an airtight container at room temperature for up to 2 days.

Index